THE NUCLEAR CRISIS READER

THE NUCLEAR CRISIS READER

Edited by
Gwyn Prins

VINTAGE BOOKS
A DIVISION OF RANDOM HOUSE
NEW YORK

A Vintage Original, September 1984
First Edition

Published in the United States by Random House, Inc., New York. Published in Great Britain by Chatto & Windus Ltd.

Library of Congress Cataloging in Publication Data
Main entry under title:
The Nuclear crisis reader.
Includes bibliographical references.
1. Atomic warfare—Addresses, essays, lectures.
2. Atomic weapons—Addresses, essays, lectures.
3. Deterrence (Strategy)—Addresses, essays, lectures.
4. Strategy—Addresses, essays, lectures.
5. Military policy—Addresses, essays, lectures.
6. Atomic weapons and disarmament—Addresses, essays, lectures.
I. Prins, Gwyn.
U263.N75 1984 355'.0217 84-48003
ISBN 0-394-72768-1

Manufactured in the United States of America

CONTENTS

PREFACE

In January 1983 a group of British scholars at the University of Cambridge published *Defended to Death: A Study of the Nuclear Arms Race*. This work sought to provide the public with an accessible and fully documented history of the nuclear arms race, as well as information on some of its effects, and it included a chapter that offered an outline of what a proper (i.e., non-nuclear) defense policy for Britain and for NATO might look like.

It became clear to some of us later that year that the further exploration of these detailed policy questions with the help of military colleagues might be a valuable step to take, and accordingly a small, private *ad hoc* seminar was convened at Emmanuel College in September 1983 to consider alternative strategies for NATO in the immediate future. Some but not all of the contributors to the present book came to Cambridge, as did several people whose writings are not included in this volume. Participants in the seminar were:

Rt. Rev. Dr. John Baker, Bishop of Salisbury
General Sir Hugh Beach
Admiral E. J. Carroll
Dr. Julian Cooper
General Sir Anthony Farrar-Hockley
Professor W. B. Gallie
Admiral Noel Gayler
Chaplain (Major General) K. D. Johnson
John Keegan
General Jochen Löser
Professor Robert Neild
Dr. Gwyn Prins (Convenor)
Dr. Paul Rogers
Dr. Hew Strachan
Lady Sugden

Much of the seminar was taken up with detailed discussion of operational aspects of military reform. But as the seminar proceeded, and as we began to consider collectively the shape of the book which would arise from it, it became apparent that the main emphasis should lie in the questions which have logical priority over matters of technical and tactical reform. These questions now compose this work.

It was originally intended to include here also some of the detailed essays which address the substance of the military reform plans. But the gratifying degree to which the preparation of such schemes has now advanced means that these questions are too complex and too important to be easily condensed without risk of misrepresentation. Therefore they are reserved for a future, comprehensive treatment of their own.

The Cambridge seminar was made possible by generous support, which is gratefully acknowledged, from the Joseph Rowntree Social Service Trust and the Joseph Rowntree Charitable Trust. Additional funding came from the Cambridge Defence and Disarmament Research Fund, established with earnings from the earlier book. Earnings from this present book will also be placed in the Fund to facilitate future work. The generosity of the contributors in forgoing royalty makes this possible.

The seminar was given practical assistance by Emmanuel College and the University Extra-Mural Board and the hospitality of the late Sir Morris Sugden and Lady Sugden of Trinity Hall. Marian Sugden was instrumental in arranging the seminar. The Editor's debt to her is, as ever, very great. Richard Kamm efficiently tape recorded and transcribed the proceedings.

The Editor is also grateful to Jeremy Lewis of Chatto & Windus for his support and advice during a hectic autumn of editing and to James Ryan for his expertise in bringing this book into its final shape, to the Governing Body of Emmanuel College for sabbatical leave to facilitate the preparation of the book, to Chris and Mellany Batten for the loan of their Cornish home in which to do it, to his long-suffering family for putting up with it and to the contributors for tolerantly succeeding in meeting unreasonable deadlines.

GWYN PRINS

INTRODUCTION
THE PARADOX OF SECURITY
Gwyn Prins

There was once a time when the debate about defense and disarmament appeared to the public to be simple. On the one side were governments and generals. They were seen to favor nuclear weapons as an essential contribution toward a strong defense. On the other were assorted clerics, teachers and malcontent critics. They were seen to oppose nuclear weapons and by extension to display an emotional rejection of war of any kind or for any purpose. The governments called their critics naive idealists or attributed more treasonable motives to them. The critics called the presidents, prime ministers and soldiers warmongers and suspected them of disreputable and conspiratorial motives. Both groups talked past each other, no dialogue occurred and the nuclear arms race went on.

That has all now changed. In 1984 no reasonable person can still believe such crude stereotypes because the whole vital debate about international security is plainly happening at a better informed and more mature level. There are distinguished new voices to be heard, especially those of men who have held the highest military and diplomatic offices, saying things which are totally unexpected to those who have not yet understood how great has been the sea-change of the last five years.

For the first time, and in an important way, this book brings these voices together and shows the extent to which the forty years' consensus within the Western strategic community has been broken.

Therefore, this volume is intended to introduce people to the terms of the new debate about defense and security. It appears at this particular moment because only now are these formidable critics free in their retirement to make their opinions known to the public (although all the military contributors did speak of and act upon their views while on active service). The combination of their judgments is important because, unlike other critics, it is impossible to regard these men as prophets in the wilderness. They were recently at the center of power, and they remain close to it.

The breaking of the consensus within our strategic community over the last five years has been one of the most important departures of the nuclear age. This is not to suggest that the intelligent and dedicated people who over the years have devoted great effort to the search for security in the presence of nuclear weapons have all been fools. What has happened is that people with senior military or diplomatic responsibility have found that alarming trends in the nuclear field demand different answers to those they formerly gave. The questions have not changed. The questions are those which their duties to their respective nations require them to ask. They are practical and, in the military sphere, often technical as well. They are questions shaped by the objective of protecting national or Alliance security. What has changed dramatically (although not without warning from the history of the nuclear age) has been the sharp, downward trajectory both of the superpower relationship, now gripped in the frozen hostility of a new Cold War, and of nuclear strategy, now frighteningly entwined with operational concepts—and missiles—designed for fighting wars. The two developments are not unrelated.

In order to build anew and on strong foundations, it is first necessary to demolish the unsafe and decrepit building that is to be replaced. This work is undertaken in the first part of the book. In the first three chapters, from the perspective of high command and in one case of the highest command, three American officers offer different but converging analyses which together undermine and remove from future serious debate a number of illusions about the military usefulness of nuclear weapons. Admiral Carroll explains how a generation of ill-conceived thinking about nuclear deterrence permitted the perversion of strategy from which arose the current and exceedingly dangerous view that the credibility of defense is enhanced by a nuclear war-fighting posture. The theme of the perverse failure to face up to the true nature of the revolution in warfare brought about by the nuclear weapon is taken up by a former Commander-in-Chief, Admiral Gayler. Echoing judgments, made shortly before his assassination, by one of Britain's most distinguished military leaders, Admiral of the Fleet Earl Mountbatten of Burma, Admiral Gayler amplifies their shared view that there are no sensible military uses for nuclear weapons and that until this is understood and accepted in our military and political establishments, our actions intended to increase national security will inexorably continue to erode it. General Collins makes this plain in another way, by revealing in some detail why, in a straightforward military analysis, the current NATO strategy of "flexible response," with plans for controlled escalation in the use of nuclear weapons, makes absolutely no sense.

But the utility of nuclear weapons is often claimed to be mainly political, and it is clear that in so far as they *are* useful, that must be true. But how useful are they? This crucial question has not received sufficient historical analysis. In Chapter 4, Professor McGeorge Bundy, who served through the Cuban Missile Crisis in President Kennedy's cabinet, gives it that attention. His conclusion is striking: attempts to use atomic blackmail for specific ends have almost always failed. This has implications for those, for example in France and Britain, who see in the threat of nuclear blackmail a justification for independent national nuclear weapons. Yet if this threat is less serious than some fear, Professor Polanyi shows in Chapter 5 that the threat of a new and vicious upward spiral of the nuclear arms race extended into space is real, frightening and imminent. This looming possibility is a classic example of the failure of imagination and understanding which has created a world already shared with 50,000 nuclear weapons.

How did we get into this mess? Was it just a failure to understand the proper place for nuclear weapons? In the second part of the book a deeper current is explored. Professor MccGwire argues that the problems are in no sense a result of stupidity. Were it so, our plight would be more easily remedied. Rather it has been the use of deterrence as the prism through which to view the world that has distorted our perceptions. Nuclear weapons have interacted with and strengthened that habit, but they alone are not the problem. Thus our escape from the nuclear threat will not be assured without a transformation of the way in which we view our neighbors, and especially the Soviet Union. This second part of the book thus pivots around two entangled and vexed problems: what should we think of deterrence and how should we regard the Soviet Union?

In Chapter 7, Professor Garthoff homes in upon the linking device: the worst-case assumption. He argues that a consequence of the elevation of a military strategy—deterrence—into a pillar of the world order has been the hoisting of the worst-case assumption out of its proper environment of tactical planning into the sphere of diplomatic assessment. The effect has been damaging, for the illegitimate and promiscuous use of worst-case assumptions in assessing Soviet intentions upon the evidence of their capabilities has steadily reinforced the most negative, hostile and threatening perceptions of them.

What are Soviet intentions in fact? In the last two chapters of Part II, two Sovietologists turn directly to this question. Dr. Holloway offers a clear historical interpretation of recent Soviet behavior, especially in relation to the arms race; and in Chapter 9 one of the united States' most distinguished diplomats, Professor George Kennan, argues eloquently for the urgent need to achieve the great shift in mutual perceptions which Professor McGwire also concluded was the basic need.

In the third part, the book turns to investigate three significant issues of principle, which can be roughly characterized as ethical, legal and philosophical. They serve to give perspectives of time and of moral standard to an issue which is often considered as one of pure pragmatism and yet which subverts much of what we most cherish in our civilization. Chaplain (Major General) Johnson pursues in Chapter 10 the nagging doubts about the moral status of nuclear deterrence which have been present throughout the nuclear age. He argues that the theologians have so far failed to face the conclusion of their logic—that, in a spirit of repentance, the Christian churches must forthwith remove all moral sanction from the strategy of nuclear deterrence. From his dual perspective as soldier and minister he argues this case with unique authority.

Equally, if we value the rule of law we must be prepared to submit nuclear strategies, as any other, to its scrutiny. In fact one consequence of the last forty years has been the steady erosion of the status of international law, honored mostly in the breach by nation-states living in a state of nature overshadowed by the Bomb. Yet Professor Griffith properly insists in Chapter 11 that so long as we claim to remain civilized peoples and to respect law, we should attend to its verdict. He finds that the verdict upon nuclear deterrence is overwhelmingly negative, and that the arguments for its legality advanced by government lawyers are open to grave objection. So we should understand the size of the cloud under which, in terms of civilized values, the nuclear strategic world order lives.

The nuclear problem is not one of overwhelming intellectual difficulty, argues Professor Gallie in Chapter 12, yet among all others it is peculiarly oppressive to us. Why? The answer he offers is set in the sweep of a bold consideration of European history since the Enlightenment. It is because, if true, the criticisms of the first half of this book threaten not only contemporary policy, but also deep and common assumptions about the role of force and the primacy of the state. Professor Gallie investigates the roots and the reflexes of that possibility.

In Part IV attention turns toward the steps that will lead away from the edge of the nuclear abyss. Professor Galbraith explores the nature of the power which gives military establishments such a tenacious grip upon policy, for without an appreciation of this, reform will be difficult. Professor Neild ties down prescriptively a major thread which has run through the book when he explains how the primacy of political signals in the shaping of force structure may have tangible consequences. What those consequences may be in terms of economic choices and different alternative non-nuclear strategies is indicated in Chapter 15 by the defense economist Malcolm Chalmers, who provides some detailed pointers for a systematic and precise military reform of NATO. And in the final chapter Admiral Gayler spells out the way in which a proper understanding of the relationship between nuclear weapons and security can give us a realistic, swift and effective prospect of actually beginning to dismantle the world's nuclear stockpile.

Central to this book is an argument about the true nature of security and the effect of nuclear weapons upon it. Here the case is made that the relationship is one of immovable hostility: the nuclear weapon is the enemy of security. Yet what precisely does the word "security" mean? One disorienting effect of the nuclear age is upon meanings, and so the concept deserves special attention.

In the West, no concept and no word has suffered more in this strange metamorphosis than "security." (In the East, it has been "peace" that has been suffocated in too close an embrace by rigid and authoritarian regimes.) Commonsense tells us what security is. It is a state of mind, not an order of battle. In a troubled world of unruly nation-states, military force (which is, by definition, non-nuclear) may have a necessary part to play in protecting security, but military force is not a sufficient guarantor of security. Nor is security to be equated with military force and its attendant supports. Security is produced by general social well-being. Social well-being is the sum of individual fulfillment, which depends upon the civilized arbitration of conflicts of interest in society, which in turn depends upon a just provision of goods, services and opportunities for all. Security is thus intimately bound up with another important concept that has been badly abused: freedom. Freedom from want, freedom of thought, freedom from fear: life, liberty and the pursuit of happiness. These are the minimum requirements of security. They are goals not easily fulfilled. So security is a state of mind which also contains future hope. For that, it is a necessary precondition that there be an unquestioned assumption that there will *be* a future. This assurance the nuclear strategic prescription for peace in our time cannot give. And so here the fixed antagonism between nuclear weapons and security is most basically to be seen.

But how has the opposite idea, that the nuclear weapon upholds and preserves security, gained such currency? There are three reasons, two of which are obvious: one, that it would be hard for normal minds to live undisturbed by the latent horror of nuclear weapons if they could not believe in a countervailing positive view of them; the other, that once emptied of its commonsense meaning, flattened and mutated, the concept of security no longer has the internal fiber to resist the fallacy. The third reason arises from the shadowy ramifications which oppress us, and which Professor Gallie explores. It is central to the paradox of security.

In Chinese pharmacology, the different amounts of active principle contained by different preparations are described as qualities—the soldierly quality, the magisterial quality and the princely quality. The great student of Chinese science, Sir Joseph Needham, once asked a mainly medical audience to vote upon which term described drugs with the largest quantity of active principle. Overwhelmingly they chose the princely quality, and were entirely wrong. For in Chinese thought, the highest quality of power is that which obtains the desired effect with the *least* force, or in pharmacological terms, with the *smallest* quantity of active principle, which is diametrically the opposite of our cultural expectation.

The medical students revealed in a simple way an important fact about European civilization: it is obsessed with visible power. Language is a powerful guide to values, and the frequency of idioms of conquest is revealing: the conquest of the oceans in the age of overseas expansion, the conquest of science, and so on. Nor is it idiom only, because world history for hundreds of years has been most immediately the history of the European conquest of other peoples. And the two principal agents in that conquest have been two features of European life of which we are especially proud: our technological prowess and the political device of the nation-state. From the combination of these two has come a powerful and deeply embedded assumption. Security is assumed to subsist in the commonwealth of the state, and the way that a state is best protected is by amassing to itself the most destructive weapons that science can devise in order to deter would-be aggressor states. This visible, usable physical power is the mark of a European prince.

It is this truism which is challenged by the nuclear revolution in warfare and, as Professor Gallie observes, if the challenge is upheld, what then can stand of our old working assumptions? The challenge may be conveniently condensed into three slogans, companions to those from George Orwell's famous novel *1984*:

POWER DOES NOT EQUAL SECURITY
POLITICAL POWER DOES NOT EQUAL MILITARY POWER
MILITARY POWER DOES NOT EQUAL NUCLEAR WEAPONS

The first runs counter to all our cultural expectations; the second rejects the numbing paralysis engendered by the militarization of diplomatic thought and practice; the third recalls the role of nuclear weapons in promoting that dangerous process, and at the same time the great misunderstanding which has thrown military forces and the nuclear weapon out of perspective by lumping them together.

The paradox of security is not only that in the nuclear world those habits of mind and expressions of power to which we are accustomed are no longer consistent with security, even in its restricted form of defense. Were it merely so, the situation would be only unfortunate rather than grave, and it would be stable. The paradox is bitter because the relationship between nuclear weapons and security is volatile and corrosive. It is an inverse relationship: the more that people and states seek to increase their own security by the old methods, but with the new atomic power, the less security they have; and the more that heightened insecurity is sensed, the faster the arms race becomes, the heavier its economic burden, and the more hateful, aggressive, expansionist and devious the enemy appears. In this way the spiralling accelerates viciously and hope of escape recedes as the nuclear presence spreads over the whole political landscape.

There was only ever one hope. Professor MccGwire addresses it in his chapter. It was that the rhetoric about the positive attributes of the nuclear bargain would be overwhelmed by contrary evidence, and that contact would be re-established between the professionals and ordinary people. Once this began to happen, it would become possible to make a comprehensive reappraisal and suggest authoritative, concrete alternatives. This book is part of a growing volume of evidence which suggests that this is, indeed, taking place—in ways which are not usefully described in the conventional political categories of "left" and "right." The unifying theme is that, when both are properly understood, the nuclear weapon and security are seen to belong in different worlds. And while there may be different views about the nature and sequence of the steps to be taken, there is unanimity in perceiving that a choice must now be made.

What will be the consequences of acknowledging the antagonism between nuclear weapons and security? The first is appreciating, as

Admiral Carroll puts it, that no one is secure unless all are secure. This means that the interdependence of the nations of the world will become the primary factor in formulating national policy. A second consequence follows. The nuclear weapon has until now overwhelmed consideration of the other elements that together compose security. Once its shadow is removed, they can be given their proper significance.

Once movement, along with civility, proper diplomacy and restrained language, return to the conduct of East–West affairs, two further developments become possible. We can look clear-sightedly at the Soviets and see them as they are, not as we fear they are or wish to compel them to be. For this, as is shown especially in Part II of this book, a distinction must be made between one's personal view of the Soviet system and the assessment of its foreign-policy intentions. We may then also make possible by persuasion, trade, example and the relaxation of tension the changes in the Soviet system which we and many in the East desire, and which we can never accomplish by intimidation and abuse. For the Soviet Union, exactly the same is true.

As a balance is restored between the political, economic and military spheres of state, two obvious and important practical questions arise. What is the prudent view to take of the role of nuclear weapons as we begin to move away from the precarious present, given that they cannot and will not be abolished overnight? And once our armed forces are liberated from the invasion of their structures by nuclear weapons, how may they be best designed to promote general security?

All the contributors in this volume agree that what now passes for "deterrence" is not a modest, evolutionary modernization of the concepts of the 1950s to meet new circumstances, but a serious perversion of them; nor will present and proposed developments of strategy or of hardware do anything but make a bad situation worse. All of them also agree that, leaving aside questions of ethics or legality and from a purely pragmatic point of view, the only logically coherent nuclear strategy is one in which each superpower (and only each superpower) holds an invulnerable nuclear capability sufficient to devastate the other, and no more than that minimum, solely to deter nuclear attack by the other.

Of course this means disposing of illusions such as "nuclear umbrellas." It also means making alliances that claim to be military fulfill their objectives by military, not nuclear, means. (This need not be, by the way, a prescription for a "conventional" arms race.) Such a minimum, invulnerable nuclear force would be congruent with what McGeorge

Bundy has called "existential deterrence." Some contributors see such a nuclear posture as a sufficient end in itself, others view it as a transitional stage in a longer process. But achieving it would be so great an improvement on our present state that such differences of opinion are academic. All would welcome it as an urgent and clear medium-term goal. Measures to achieve it are spelled out in the final chapter.

But it must be said that the investigation of ways of getting NATO back to doing what the North Atlantic Treaty said that it should do, instead of absent-mindedly threatening with incineration the countries that it is supposed to be defending, is not just a technical discussion of the military sciences. In conducting an examination of alternative courses of action, the simple formulation of the arguments shows that these questions, which were for so long locked away from serious public scrutiny, are matters of real choice. The act of analysis removes the spurious image of stability and balance, and with it also that sense of dull inevitability which hangs over the nuclear issue and which inhibits or freezes thought. Choice brings the realization that there really are different ways of seeing the world. A central purpose of this book is to demonstrate plainly the range, urgency, substance and answers to some of the basic questions of our time, which have until recently been silenced by the overwhelming intrusion into international affairs of the nuclear weapon.

It would be wrong to presume that this book aims to close the debate. In some areas it is certainly true that clear and strong conclusions can be seen, but in others not. In this and in other senses, the book is a sign of the times, for it represents a combination of forces that would not have meshed in this way a decade ago, and it enters a public forum better attuned to the tensions in the defense debate and better informed to consider them than ever before. It is therefore the hope of the authors that at the end of the arguments put in the following pages the next stage of the confrontation with the dilemmas of our nuclear world can begin.

Robert Oppenheimer, the scientific director of the Manhattan Project which created the atomic bomb, remarked in later life that in time, this nuclear age would be seen as a phase in human history that was transitory, dangerous and degrading. Either it would be understood in this way or there would be no one there to make the judgment. Now is the time when we are challenged to take sides. Shall we prefer to prolong the nuclear gamble against lengthening odds, or shall we prefer security?

PART I *How useful are nuclear weapons?*

1 NUCLEAR WEAPONS AND DETERRENCE *Eugene J. Carroll*

Rear Admiral Eugene J. Carroll Jr., US Navy (ret.), saw duty in both the Korean and Vietnam Wars, and also served several assignments in the Atlantic Fleet. He was promoted to the rank of Rear Admiral in 1972. From 1977 to 1979 Admiral Carroll served on General Alexander Haig's staff in Europe. As director of military operations of all US forces in Europe and the Middle East, he was closely involved in NATO policy formation. His last assignment on active duty was in the Pentagon as Assistant Deputy Chief of Naval Operations for Plans, Policy and Operations. In this capacity he was engaged in US naval planning for conventional and nuclear war. He is now Deputy Director of the Center for Defense Information, Washinton, DC.

Not long before he was sacked for being soft on arms control, Mr. Eugene Rostow, then Director of the United States Arms Control and Disarmament Agency, stressed the crowning importance of nuclear deterrence. US foreign policy, he said, "turns ultimately on the deterrent power of the American nuclear umbrella—the rock on which the renaissance of the West since 1945 was built and the foundation for its security."[1] This pronouncement implies the existence of a threatening horde poised and ready to overwhelm us all at the first hint that we are not prepared to obliterate them with nuclear weapons; nothing else stays their evil ways. The quality of this hyperbole may be judged by noting that Mr. Rostow also declared that the defense of NATO was a "permanent and immutable geopolitical interest of the United States." An immutable geopolitical interest is as hard to imagine as the rock of nuclear deterrence!

It is probably true that the existence of nuclear arsenals on both sides has produced an increased element of caution in superpower relations. As Professor Bundy will explain in Chapter 4 of this book, however, it would be unwise to jump directly to a causal link in our explanation of contemporary history. True, there has been no open war in Europe for thirty-eight years, and fear of nuclear war may have helped to propel world leaders to some worthwhile efforts during the last decade to control the arms race and seek political accommodations to lessen East – West tension. But it does not follow that war has been deterred solely by the nuclear threat. There are many, many other practical military, political and economic factors which weigh against superpower conflict far more effectively than the incredible abstraction of nuclear deterrence.

In fact, if nuclear deterrence had any part of the significance that conventional wisdom ascribes to the concept, ours would be a far different world. Ours is not a world at peace. Today there are about forty armed conflicts in progress.[2] Only five of these are classic cross-border wars, but eight involve foreign troops, either as combatants or peacekeepers. Many others are sustained by superpower support, with the US serving as the major supplier to twenty combatants and the USSR supplying thirteen. In some instances the adversaries are fighting proxy East – West wars which create the obvious risk of involving the principals. If nuclear deterrence truly inhibits military conflict, it is not evident in the growing pattern of armed violence around the world.

Nevertheless, the true believers cite these regional, low-level wars as proof that deterrence is real. After all, they say, the nuclear powers have avoided direct confrontation despite the obvious, active conflicts of interest in many of these situations. Of course, there can never be any direct and final proof of this assertion, one way or the other. Therefore we must turn to indirect, circumstantial evidence and judge on the balance of that. The nuclear enthusiasts make a perverse analysis of war since 1945 and, in their conclusion drawn from that record, again ignore all the other factors which shape the international order. Theirs is a classic example of faulty *post hoc* logic: The nuclear powers have not fought a war because their weapons deter each other; therefore, they will not fight a war in the future.

The flawed quality of this logic is made evident by examining the fundamental assumptions upon which the concept of deterrence rests. First, the potential aggressor must always conclude that the adversary has adequate survivable nuclear forces to inflict an unacceptable level of damage on the aggressor if attacked directly or provoked by action against third parties. Second, the potential aggressor must be convinced that the adversary has the will to use nuclear weapons. The potential aggressor decides whether deterrence exists. These decisions can never be predicted with complete confidence by the adversaries. This lack of certainty plays an important part in driving the nuclear spiral inexorably upward. There can never be enough weapons, ever more destructive as they are, to satisfy either side as they both strive for complete confidence in their nuclear deterrent.

In this process, both sides fail to give any weight to three other essential requirements for sustained deterrence. Both sides rely on the implicit assumption that the following three conditions exist today, and will continue without failure in the future.

First, *all nuclear forces will be controlled by rational leaders* who comprehend that nothing can be gained by the use of nuclear weapons; that, in fact, such use may well be suicidal. Rational leaders will surely be aware of the many warnings to this effect, none more stark than those of Lord Mountbatten: "In the event of a nuclear war there will be no chances, there will be no survivors—all will be obliterated."[3] But madmen cannot be deterred. Driven by fear, hatred or ambition which transcends reason, all warnings may be ignored and deterrence will fail.

Second, *no aggressor will miscalculate the vital interests of a nuclear power* and precipitate an unintended conflict. Even rational leaders pursuing critical objectives can undertake high-risk initiatives based on faulty information or misjudgments. Rational leaders under political pressure can also declare the existence of vital interests which virtually commit their nation to military action in very unfavorable circumstances, as President Jimmy Carter did: "An attempt by any outside force to gain control of the Persian Gulf region will be regarded as an assault on the vital interests of the United States of America, and such an assault will be repelled by any means necessary, including military force."[4] It is arguable that such pronouncements serve more to increase the probability of confrontation and miscalculation than they serve to establish credible military commitments.

Third, *there will be no accidental nuclear events or command, control, communication or sensor malfunctions* which trigger a nuclear response by the threatened or injured nation. History, human fallibility and the laws of probability all guarantee that there will be accidents and there will be human failures and equipment malfunctions in the future just as in the past. The changing nature of nuclear weapons systems and nuclear strategy strongly suggest that these events will become more frequent, more threatening and more immediate in the coming years.

A brisk review of how the theory of nuclear deterrence has developed will allow us to assess just how likely it is that these three conditions will continue to hold.

Nuclear strategy: From "massive retaliation" to nuclear war-fighting

According to the original theory, in the age of "massive retaliation," nuclear weapons were viewed as the ultimate sanction *against* war. An aggressor was supposed to be deterred by fear of total annihilation if he crossed the line from acceptable to criminal behavior. It is doubtful whether this concept ever had any validity. If it did, then it was only immediately following the destruction of Hiroshima and Nagasaki while the United States still possessed a monopoly of nuclear technology and the demonstrated will to employ nuclear weapons in war. But once the idea was lodged in the minds of the strategists, the concept persisted in US strategic doctrine and dictated heavy military reliance on large, mass destruction systems believed to raise the greatest fears in our adversaries. Nuclear weapons were not to be used to win a war, they were to prevent war.

Perhaps the clearest expression of this doctrine emerged in the words of then Vice-President Richard Nixon in 1954:

"Rather than let the Communists nibble us to death all over the world in little wars we would rely in the future primarily on our massive retaliatory power which we could use in our discretion against the major source of aggression at times and places that we choose.

We adjusted our armed strength to meet the requirements of this new concept and, what was just as important, we let the world and we let the Communists know what we intended to do."[5]

Two years later, profiting from the example set by the Anglo-French Suez invasion, Soviet troops crushed the Hungarian uprising with great force and consequent bloodshed. The USA was impotent in the face of this, and the episode demonstrated at once the danger of relying on US promises of support for "counterrevolutionary" movements at the same time that it destroyed forever the credibility of the threat of massive retaliation when attached to specific incidents. It is particularly significant that the US still enjoyed a pronounced level of superiority in nuclear weapon delivery systems over the Soviet Union when they invaded Hungary.

Despite the clear and permanent demise of deterrence as a coercive threat based on massive retaliation, there was very little movement toward any coherent new concept of deterrence. One evolutionary way station was the "second strike force." This was first formally identified in the Secretary of Defense Annual Report to the Congress in 1963. Although the language began to hint at flexibility in nuclear warfare, the second strike force was still clearly intended to deter war, not fight and win one.

The doctrine of "flexible response" was first clearly expressed by Secretary of Defense Schlesinger in his report to the Congress in 1974:

> "What we need is a series of measured responses to aggression which bear some relation to the provocation, have prospects of terminating hostilities before general nuclear war breaks out, and leave some possibility for restoring deterrence."[6]

The words are ambiguous, probably intentionally, and it is not clear whether the "measured responses" would include tactical nuclear responses to conventional attacks. Other language in the report referred to the need for a "flexible response" in the event deterrence failed and implied that we were still seeking forces to deter general nuclear war. The declared goal fell far short of winning a nuclear war.

As late as 1980 President Carter's Presidential Decision 59 emphasized the need for a flexible nuclear response as a deterrent, not as a war-winning strategy. Secretary of Defense Harold Brown stressed this point in testimony to the Senate Foreign Relations Committee:

> "PD-59 does not assume that we can 'win' a limited nuclear war, nor does it intend or pretend to enable us to do so. It does seek both to prevent the Soviets from being able to win such a war and to convince them that they could not. I do not believe that either side could 'win' a limited nuclear war. I want to ensure as best we can that the Soviets do not believe so either."[7]

This clear, repeated doctrinal emphasis on deterring nuclear war, not winning one, was consistent with the past and was reflected in US arms control policies which sought to create finite limits on nuclear arsenals. It was also evident in a number of decisions during the Carter Administration to cancel or defer the production of new nuclear weapons systems judged to be in excess of those needed for deterrence, even under the flexible response doctrine.

Of course, there had always been a group of nuclear policy-makers who had sought a nuclear war-fighting capability. The most notable of these was General Curtis LeMay, whose thinking was reflected in the shape of the Strategic Air Command, which he had a major role in creating. But what is new today is that implemented plans to build nuclear war-fighting capabilities have been matched by declared policy.

For the first time we see nuclear war-fighting dominant in declared policy.[8]

The process of change began under President Carter, who saw the need to bolster his image on defense in order to be re-elected. This was the well-known and dangerous phenomenon of the "liberal hawk." In various degrees he was reacting to the Iranian hostage crisis, the Soviet invasion of Afghanistan and candidate Ronald Reagan. In his last two years in office, President Carter submitted defense budgets for $182 billion and $212 billion, up $70 billion over those two years.

This pattern was continued under President Reagan, whose 1984 defense request was for $313 billion. But, more ominously, the formal goal had been changed. In his first budget request the new goal was stated succinctly: "US defense policies ensure our preparedness to respond to and, if necessary, successfully fight either conventional or nuclear war."[9] For the first time, conventional and nuclear war were equated and both could have a successful outcome.

The literature now abounds with formal statements which define the new US policy of deterrence based upon nuclear war-fighting forces capable of prevailing over the Soviet Union. The clearest exposition of the new doctrine was contained in Secretary of Defense Weinberger's Department of Defense *Fiscal 1984–1988 Defense Guidance*. This document was leaked to the press in June 1982, and has been widely quoted since. It represents the considered thought of very senior members of the Administration.

> "United States nuclear capabilities must prevail even under the condition of a prolonged war . . . Should deterrence fail and strategic nuclear war with the USSR occur, the United States must prevail and be able to force the Soviet Union to seek earliest termination of hostilities on terms favorable to the United States . . . US strategic nuclear forces and their command and communications links should be capable of supporting controlled nuclear counterattacks over a protracted period while maintaining a reserve of nuclear forces sufficient for trans- and post-attack protection and coercion."

Secretary Weinberger made it clear that this ability to fight and prevail was not just at the strategic level: we must be ready to respond "*across the full range of plausible nuclear war-fighting scenarios* with the Soviet Union."[10]

Thus was constructed a complete justification for the production and deployment of every new type of nuclear weapon and weapon delivery system which modern technology can provide. And, to be certain that the enemy is deterred at every plausible level of nuclear war-fighting, we must add numbers of weapons as well as new systems.

Based on this rationale, US nuclear war-fighting programs require the production of more than 17,000 new nuclear weapons by 1992. These include new families of battlefield weapons to support a "first use" doctrine; enhanced intermediate range theater systems to intensify threat levels against the adversary's territory; and major additions to intercontinental systems with "time urgent, hard target kill" capabilities, otherwise known as "first strike" weapons.[11]

What will all of these new weapons and delivery capabilities do for deterrence? Superficially it would seem that a potential adversary would be ever more fearful of annihilation by the growing American arsenal and thus be deterred more effectively. Certainly the fact that the United States will spend more than $400 billion to produce nuclear forces capable of prevailing in nuclear war should convince any adversary that we will use those forces. US rhetoric also strengthens that conclusion: "We don't want to fight a nuclear war, or a conventional one either, but we must be prepared to do so if such a battle is to be deterred, as we must also be prepared to carry the battles to our adversary's homeland. We must not fear war."[12] And that means nuclear war.

The superficial conclusion that development of the US nuclear war-fighting force will enhance deterrence has one major defect. The adversary will not passively suffer subjection to an increasing threat. There will be comparable preparations for nuclear war involving more weapons and new delivery systems on both sides. There may well be efforts to increase defensive capabilities as well as offensive threats, and the resulting nuclear balance will be more threatening and less stable. No one can say whether either side will end up more deterred or, on the contrary, more determined to rely on a first strike strategy, the absolute antithesis of what is intended.

Growing threats to deterrence

Given the unpredictable effects of preparing to prevail in nuclear war, what are the prospects for maintaining the three basic requirements for sustained deterrence which were mentioned earlier?

The first requirement, *rational leadership and decision-making*, is clearly imperilled. As arsenals grow, potential destruction increases, reaction times shorten and the offensive–defensive equation becomes unclear: governments will be driven by intense fear in time of crisis.

Imagine a replay of the Cuban missile crisis of 1962 in 1992. One perceives at once that a calamitous outcome would be a far stronger possibility. Even in the absence of major changes now planned in the nuclear forces of both the US and the USSR by 1992, it is certain that each side would be fearful that the other was contemplating a preemptive strike, and, unlike 1962, would be sure that it could happen. Fear does not support rational thought and considered decisions. The slightest misunderstood action in time of crisis could well produce a first strike with the very weapons we are building in the name of deterrence.

Yet another way in which the continued nuclear build-up increases the probability of irrational leadership is through nuclear proliferation. As long as the nuclear superpowers race ahead, the drive in the Third World to possess nuclear weapons will proceed largely unchecked. At least ten new nuclear powers will emerge in the short term and as many as twenty nations will join the nuclear club in this century. One need only note that Libya, Iran, Pakistan and Argentina are among the leaders in efforts to acquire nuclear weapons. There is absolutely no assurance of rational decisions in any one of those nations but there is great danger that irrational use, particularly in the Middle East, could rapidly involve the superpowers.[13]

Secondly, there is the question of *miscalculation*. Development and expansion of nuclear war-fighting forces do nothing to reduce opportunities for serious miscalculations by either side. To the extent that equipping, training and deploying nuclear war-fighting forces look more like preparations for war than measures to avert war, they will serve to confuse our adversary and lead to mistaken estimates of our capabilities and intentions. Such miscalculations are made more likely by the rhetoric that accompanies the arms build-up. All of the official declarations about prevailing in nuclear war make statements such as President Reagan's to the British Parliament in June 1982 even more threatening: "What I am describing now is a plan and a hope . . . which will leave Marxism–Leninism on the ash heap of history."[14]

The nature of modern battlefield systems also makes miscalculation more likely. These systems would be physically threatened almost immediately in any conventional conflict, forcing early decisions about enemy intentions and capabilities. "Use them or lose them" decisions may be precipitated before adequate information is available to prevent critical miscalculations.

In another sense, however, the dangers of miscalculation are not directly related to nuclear weapons. One only has to look back to the

Falklands tragedy to observe the classic war of miscalculation. Under intense domestic political pressure and provided with inaccurate information concerning British intentions and capabilities, General Galtieri embarked on a desperate adventure. From their side, the British had given every indication that this remnant of Empire would not be defended. For example, Parliament was in the process of enacting legislation which would have removed citizenship from the Falkland Islanders; the British had also withdrawn the ice patrol ship *Endurance*. Misreading these signals, Galtieri invaded despite the fact that he was attacking the territory and citizens of a nuclear power. By this one action he demonstrated that nuclear superiority does not deter war and that fear of nuclear annihilation does not prevent fatal miscalculation. Now we must wait for history to reveal how close his miscalculation came to provoking a nuclear response, but if both Argentina and the UK had possessed nuclear capabilities in 1982 is it not almost certain that one side or the other would have resorted to their nuclear weapons before accepting defeat?

Turning to the third requirement for a stable and effective deterrent, we can recognize that the chance of a significant nuclear *accident* is increased substantially by an expansion of nuclear arsenals. The growing danger arises from a number of factors. Foremost is the increased threat each side poses to the retaliatory forces of the other. Both sides must move to a high level of force readiness in any period of tension, even adopting such dangerous doctrines as "launch on warning." Sensor or computer malfunctions, common in the past and inevitable in the future, will become more significant and require faster responses, allowing less time for careful appraisal and conservative human judgment.

Proliferation will have the same, or a worse, effect on deterrence with respect to accidents than it will have in terms of miscalculation. The new nuclear powers will have dangerous problems in learning the safety rules and sense of responsibility which (in large measure) guide the present major powers. It is impossible to conclude that nuclear weapon accidents capable of injuring or threatening the major powers will not be more likely when many of today's nuclear aspirants have nuclear arsenals and delivery systems.

Not every accident would create a risk of nuclear war, but accidents, or incidents, generated by terrorist activity would have a special potential to create ambiguous situations in which superpower involvement could be serious. Another specific problem will increase also as more nations develop submarine-launched missile systems: a missile climbing from the open sea is truly stateless. Whether launched by accident or by design, it would create an acute risk of response by the injured power against the presumed aggressor.

Every essential requirement for successful deterrence is therefore weakened by a continuing escalation of the arms race. If the process continues unabated, the question will be when, not whether, a nuclear war will break out.

What is to be done if this danger is to be reduced? No one can answer this question in detail with authority or confidence, because no one can forecast the feasibility or ultimate effectiveness of any single approach to the problem. But it is possible to set out certain basic principles and suggest certain measures consistent with those principles which offer promise for the future.

Five principles which point in a new direction

The first point to grasp is that *nuclear weapons serve no useful military purpose*. In Chapters 2 and 3 below, Admiral Gayler and Lieutenant General Collins describe their lack of military utility, just as Lord Mountbatten did before them:

> "As a military man with half a century of active service I say in all sincerity that the nuclear arms race has no military purpose. Wars cannot be fought with nuclear weapons. Their existence only adds to our perils because of the illusions which they have generated."[15]

The United States fought a costly, destructive and prolonged war in Southeast Asia and ultimately surrendered without ever finding any justifiable use for any of its 30,000 nuclear weapons.

A second principle follows. On the evidence of the nuclear age so far, reviewed by Professor Bundy in Chapter 4, *the dangers arising from nuclear weapons far outweigh their very limited political utility*. Nuclear threats are inherently incredible to sane people, and they have no coercive potential in international relations. Former US Secretary of State Henry Kissinger once asked himself the relevant question:

> "What in the name of God is strategic superiority? What is the significance of it, politically, militarily, operationally, at these levels of numbers? What do you do with it?"[16]

A third principle is that *nuclear proliferation must be prevented*. It is an urgent, mortal threat to any hope of getting the arms race under control.

And in the 1980s we must remember that we stand on the verge of substantial proliferation unless we act decisively and soon.

A fourth and more general principle is that *we have reached the age of mutual security. No one is secure unless all are secure.* The destructive power of 50,000 nuclear weapons threatens the survival of mankind on this planet. Thus, all nations share a common need to reduce the risk of nuclear war. No nation can escape the risk or make itself safer by increasing the risk to another nation or nations. For thirty-eight years the dangers of total destruction have been increasing because nations have sought their own security at the cost of others. We must abandon this destructive approach and adopt the concept of mutual security. In Chapter 5 Professor Polanyi spells out this lesson in connexion with the escalating arms race in space.

If this principle is accepted, the fallacy of seeking to increase deterrence by increasing the level of nuclear threat is immediately obvious. Only by reducing the threat against others can we induce them to reduce their threat against us.

A fifth and final principle is also general, but has particular relevance in Europe. *People are deterred from war by many factors, of which military power is only one.* Nuclear weapons do have a place in the equation of power today. Invulnerable US and Soviet submarine missiles, for example, do serve as a deterrent against nuclear war. But the issue of nuclear superiority is irrelevant in the security equation. In the final analysis, war will come, or will be averted, entirely without respect to any consideration of nuclear "superiority." The normal, traditional issues and interests which govern international relations and political decisions will be dominant. Our preoccupation with, and justifiable fear of, nuclear annihilation obscures the fundamental factors which move us toward or away from war. Mr. Rostow's hyperbole which opened this chapter is a classic example of the way that the nuclear enthusiasts blind themselves to this, and thereby carry us all with them into mortal danger in search of perfect deterrence embodied in nuclear war-fighting forces.

There are no easy, risk-free solutions to the problem of averting nuclear war. If there were, wise men would have found them during the thirty-eight years of growing danger. But one fact appears more clearly every day. Nuclear deterrence based upon the development of nuclear war-fighting forces is a failed doctrine. There is no safety, no survival, if both sides continue to build and deploy war-fighting forces designed to prevail in nuclear conflict. Safety lies ultimately in changing our way of thinking about the role of military power in the nuclear age. Armed with new insights, rather than new weapons, we then may be able to reduce or eliminate the basic causes of conflict in a vulnerable, interdependent world.

2 A COMMANDER-IN-CHIEF'S PERSPECTIVE ON NUCLEAR WEAPONS *Noel Gayler*

Admiral Noel Gayler, US Navy (ret.), was commissioned in 1935 and served during World War II as a carrier fighter pilot. His subsequent sea commands included fighter and experimental squadrons, and carriers. After the war he worked in the Office of Naval Research and at the Bureau of Aeronautics, and was Assistant Chief of Naval Operations (Development). He has been a member of the Defense Science Board, and he has acted as consultant to the Rand Corporation, the National Security Agency, the Los Alamos Scientific Laboratory and the National Academy of Science. He has served as Naval Aide and Military Assistant to the Secretary of the Navy, and was US Naval Attaché in London. From 1967 to 1969 he was Deputy Director of the Joint Strategic Target Planning Staff, the body which designs the Single Integrated Operational Plan (SIOP). From there he became Director of the National Security Agency, and from 1972 until his retirement in 1976 as a four-star admiral he was Commander-in-Chief of all US forces in the Pacific. He is currently working with the American Committee on East–West Accord.

Ben Franklin said, "If you're going to be hanged tomorrow it sharpens your mind remarkably." In the same way, when you become a Commander-in-Chief, an obligation to get down to cases is extremely effective in sharpening your mind about the things that you might have to accomplish. Military means, their political implications, logistic requirements and other ramifications in the theater become your responsibility. In my case my responsibility was to be the Pacific Command—all the branches of the armed forces of the United States. This is geographically a very large and complicated theater, and quite unlike the Central Front in Germany, except with respect to the Korean border.

In this chapter I shall discuss the military employment of nuclear weapons from the functional standpoint, and selected tasks for which you imagine they might be useful within the Pacific theater. I shall even have the temerity to write about the European theater, although the

2 A COMMANDER-IN-CHIEF'S PERSPECTIVE ON NUCLEAR WEAPONS *Noel Gayler*

Admiral Noel Gayler, US Navy (ret.), was commissioned in 1935 and served during World War II as a carrier fighter pilot. His subsequent sea commands included fighter and experimental squadrons, and carriers. After the war he worked in the Office of Naval Research and at the Bureau of Aeronautics, and was Assistant Chief of Naval Operations (Development). He has been a member of the Defense Science Board, and he has acted as consultant to the Rand Corporation, the National Security Agency, the Los Alamos Scientific Laboratory and the National Academy of Science. He has served as Naval Aide and Military Assistant to the Secretary of the Navy, and was US Naval Attaché in London. From 1967 to 1969 he was Deputy Director of the Joint Strategic Target Planning Staff, the body which designs the Single Integrated Operational Plan (SIOP). From there he became Director of the National Security Agency, and from 1972 until his retirement in 1976 as a four-star admiral he was Commander-in-Chief of all US forces in the Pacific. He is currently working with the American Committee on East–West Accord.

Ben Franklin said, "If you're going to be hanged tomorrow it sharpens your mind remarkably." In the same way, when you become a Commander-in-Chief, an obligation to get down to cases is extremely effective in sharpening your mind about the things that you might have to accomplish. Military means, their political implications, logistic requirements and other ramifications in the theater become your responsibility. In my case my responsibility was to be the Pacific Command—all the branches of the armed forces of the United States. This is geographically a very large and complicated theater, and quite unlike the Central Front in Germany, except with respect to the Korean border.

In this chapter I shall discuss the military employment of nuclear weapons from the functional standpoint, and selected tasks for which you imagine they might be useful within the Pacific theater. I shall even have the temerity to write about the European theater, although the closest I have been to responsibility there was as a subordinate Flag Officer in the Sixth Fleet in the Mediterranean.

Let me begin by stating my main proposition plainly, so that there may be no misunderstandings. It is my view that there is no sensible military use for nuclear weapons, whether "strategic" weapons, "tactical" weapons, "theater" weapons, weapons at sea or weapons in space. I hope to make that case in this essay. I hope also to evaluate something of the politics and its relationship to reasonable objectives, the history of the development of nuclear weapons and its relationship to our security situation. Sometimes I shall write from a purely American and sometimes from a NATO perspective. I will try to keep these clear and in both cases to say something about real security, as opposed to the kind of "security" thought to arise from the possession of, and threat to use, nuclear weapons.

Taking the Pacific first, when I was Commander-in-Chief (Pacific) I could not find, in scrutinizing the whole of the Pacific command, any area where it would conceivably have made sense to explode nuclear weapons in order to carry our military objectives. Clearly our experience in the Vietnam War suggests that we would not do such a thing. We did not do even "conventional" things which were well within our capability because of understandable political and humane constraints.

Nor could I see a case for nuclear weapons anywhere else on the Asian continent. For example, the Korean Demilitarized Zone is one flashpoint that comes immediately to mind. My evaluation, together with that of the senior generals, both Korean and American, responsible for the defense of the Demilitarized Zone and of the city of Seoul and its approach and environs, was that it simply was not necessary to contemplate a nuclear strategy. The potential channels of attack on Seoul are highly concentrated, the defenses are well in place, and Seoul itself is protected by a river in front of it. It is a great city. As we know, great cities eat up armor pretty fast if they are well defended. In addition to that, history suggests that even if Seoul were taken in a quick punch, which we thought most unlikely, military recovery would still be possible, as indeed the US demonstrated when we landed at Inchon once before.

Furthermore, with respect to the Asian continent as a whole, we have to face the fact that there is a political consideration of overwhelming importance. The only use of nuclear weapons has been against an Asiatic people. I know, from conversations over the *sake*, that they remember that. There are many who ask whether, in the context of the closing phase of World War II, nuclear weapons would have been used in the same way against a non-Asiatic people. I think that question is asked widely throughout Asia. For that reason, it is my belief that the use of a nuclear weapon against any Asian people, for any purpose whatsoever, would polarize Asia against us. It would clearly not be worth the candle. For all these reasons I saw no need for nuclear weapons in the Pacific theater, and I so stated.

Another potential theater, of course, is maritime Russia: the Soviet naval forces dispersed through the Pacific area, their bases, lines of transit, choke points. All I would say about that is that, while it is an important place, it is less important than the entire problem that would be involved if you were actually to fight Russia. But I have one caveat. I get very concerned about US and NATO planning for major redeployments of our forces from the Pacific in the event of war with Russia, because I observe that the USSR has two ends. The Soviets have a vast amount of military force out there, and it is inconceivable that they would stand passive on that front while war was fought out to a conclusion in Europe. I think that is of particular importance when you consider such things as shipping and military airlift—things which are conceivably deployable to the other theater. Redeployment in the first critical weeks of war is not practicable anyway.

In the Middle East, there have been various scenarios proposed, including the initiative use of nuclear weapons to block certain passes down into Iran and so forth. Pacific Command did a considerable study of that potentiality and came to the conclusion that we were so outgunned by the Soviets in nuclear delivery capabilities and in respect of the small number of highly critical targets we owned, compared with the very large number of less critical targets that they had, that it was not something that we should open up, on strictly military grounds.

These are some of the considerations in the Pacific theater. I am now going to turn, with not too much humility, to NATO. I have seen some pretty persuasive studies which support my own conclusion that we could not possibly gain an advantage by the initiative use (first use) of nuclear weapons to defend Europe against a conventional attack.

The first consideration is that, were we to use them except as a demonstration, we would have to use them in the number of tens and low hundreds. Attack on this scale would be required to stop, say, four nominal tank breakthroughs (a common assumption). The number of noncombatants killed would be very high. I have seen competent estimates which suggest that a median number killed might be a million people. It is difficult to believe that that kind of slaughter of civilians could take place without creating serious strain within the Alliance between Germany, whose citizens would be killed, and the rest of the Alliance. It is my view that the single most important component of Alliance strength is the unity of the Alliance, and therefore anything that threatens that unity is a very dangerous thing for us all. No more unnecessary and pointless danger to the unity of the Alliance than Euromissile deployment can be imagined. Whatever its purported European origin, it is a major cause of disunity now. It was always possible to secure a major reduction in Soviet weapons by foregoing our deployment—to the great advantage of all hands.

The danger of escalation after the first use of nuclear weapons I regard as being extremely high. From authoritative pronouncements at the Ustinov/Ogarkov (Minister of Defense/Chief of Staff) level and a lot of other sources, it seems clear that the USSR does not recognize the notion of a limited nuclear war. It is a little hard to tell what their doctrine really is because it is somewhat contradictory, but it seems to be, "We get hit and we are going to hit back, full bore." There are some other writings which suggest that maybe they will hit back with only ten times as much. But the question of whether you escalate in one jump or two does not seem to be of great interest, if the probability of escalating is very high, as it is.

Finally it does not appear that relative advantage would accrue to NATO from a nuclear first use, because of the fact that we have a far more vulnerable target system, smaller numbers of highly critical targets like harbors, depots and airfields, and that the Soviets have a capability to attack those sorts of targets with nuclear weapons at least comparable to ours. The technical advantage of accuracy, which at present the West has, strikes me as being one of those fleeting things. If the Soviets want the accuracy to destroy hard targets, they can surely get it, as they have already done with intercontinental ballistic missiles (ICBMs). I think it is misleading to believe that we are going to get a permanent technical advantage here.

The problem of authorizing use is very severe. I personally do not believe that a President of the United States would be likely to release tactical nuclear weapons to stop a conventional attack. I think he would see, and his advisers would tell him, that the risk of the total destruction of Europe and the total destruction of the United States would be too high. So no commander could count on these weapons when push came to shove. We are told that this conclusion results in great political strains in the Alliance because it seems to detach the United States from its pledged support of NATO. I prefer to turn that around. What is the credible commitment of the United States to Europe that you can count on in any and every circumstance? To me, the credible commitment is that our troops, supported by our air force and, indirectly, by our navy, will fight in any and all circumstances. That can be counted on. What cannot be counted on, in my judgment, is that America would initiate a nuclear war. I rather doubt that we would, in circumstances that I understand.

But there is a further justification offered for the possession of tactical nuclear weapons. As a matter of fact it was so justified to me by former Supreme Allied Commanders (Europe) in this way. It is that while they believe that in the end the authority to release nuclear weapons would probably not come from the President, it was very important to keep the Soviets guessing. If that is a serious doctrine, as it clearly seems to be, I find it to be very dangerous indeed. To bluff someone successfully you need to know him pretty well. For nations to bluff each other successfully they need to know each other pretty well. And the US and USSR do not, in my opinion, know each other at all well.

In my fairly good contact with that part of Russian official society that specializes in the examination of the United States, I am struck by how very little they fundamentally understand of us, the West in general and the United States in particular. They have intimate familiarity with statistics, geography and all of those innumerable things, but they seem to believe that, behind the façade of President, Congress, public opinion and press there is a tight and secret cabal which runs the United States, and that the rest is all window-dressing. That they think this is not unreasonable, because that is the way that they run their own country: the Politburo and the Central Committee decide everything and the rest is just window-dressing. Nonetheless it illustrates that, in some very fundamental ways, they do not understand us. They do, I believe, suspect us of hoping, wishing, waiting for the opportunity to overturn their form of government by extreme pressure or even by force of arms. I really believe they think that is what we are up to. We know—at least, I hope that we know—that we would never do anything like this, but clearly they do not.

On the other hand, I suspect that there are major shortcomings in our (I am speaking of Americans now) general understanding of the nature of Soviet society. I tend toward the view and advice of the George Kennans and Averell Harrimans of this world rather than of those who believe that the Russians are the focus of all evil. The Soviets are the focus of some evil, to be sure, but "all evil" is a bit of an overstatement. I think we know clearly that they are a pragmatic people as well as ideologues.

Unfortunately, this view is not as clear in the minds of some of our statesmen as I believe that it should be. Instead we hear too much blood-curdling rhetoric, too much of Soviets as twelve-foot-high demons. In consequence, we witness extremely unsettling new departures proposed in weapons technology.

I want to dwell a little upon this relationship between the strident content and tone of this view of the Soviets and the sort of weapons development that people who believe that menacing picture seem to favor. I shall illustrate this from two main areas with which I am professionally familiar. I think it is worthwhile to look briefly at space, especially because of the President's call for the development of defensive space measures. My remarks here complement the analysis in Professor Polanyi's chapter later in the book.

We can put aside the nuclear offensive potential of space pretty quickly. It turns out that because of orbital mechanics, you cannot put nuclear weapons in space, even if they are not prohibited by treaty, in such a way that you can summon them down onto a target in any reasonable time. They are likely to be over the Antipodes when you want them down over the target and that seems to be an insuperable problem.

So far as the defensive aspects are concerned, the "Star Wars" scenario of energy beams based in space has technical difficulties that I think you can characterize as without precedent: just enormous. It has operational difficulties of the same kind; it has a standard of demand which is very close to perfect, which has never been attained by any defense under any circumstances and particularly not on the first attempt with a very complex system; it has problems about pointing, tracking, target acquisition and data handling that will not stop. The bases from which these beams are generated, pointed and so forth are themselves extremely vulnerable, whether in space or on earth. It is apparent that the effort mounted to stop a missile or warhead is disproportionately greater than the effort required to provide that missile. But they particularly suffer from the "fallacy of the last move" (that is, the notion that we can construct these systems and there will be no countermeasures by the opposition). It turns out that countermeasures are simple, practical and cheap. You can readily interfere with the pointing, or you can reflect the energy (if you can use a mirror to reflect a laser beam you can make the target missile a mirror also), or you can harden or conceal the target, and so forth. So far as energy beams are concerned, of course, nobody has yet produced a neutral beam of anything like the requisite power and you cannot use charged beams because of deflection by the earth's magnetic field. Finally, the Soviets have the option of conducting all their missile launch acceleration in the atmosphere, in which case no electron beam can put the missile under attack, because the atmosphere will shield it. All they may need to do is just about to double their present acceleration. It turns out, on some rough calculations, that the energy required is not significantly greater than the way they do it now. You just spend it twice as fast; you get the acceleration in the atmosphere, and only the warheads travel through space.

Now the political argument for these notions is an interesting one. On the one hand it depends upon an unreal and scary view of the Soviets; on the other, it evokes science as a god. It says, "If you get the right people, work at it long enough and spend enough money on it, surely science will find a way." They cite in support some of the wrong prophecies that were made by very eminent scientists in the past about being unable to do this, that or the other. But the difficulty is that it is not that kind of problem. It is not the kind of problem that a scientific breakthrough, whatever that is, will solve. It is a problem not amenable to single-point solutions but more like crime in the streets or the drug problem. In military terms, it is a problem very much like antisubmarine warfare (ASW).

I have been in and around ASW for forty years, and there have been some very good scientists and a huge amount of money spent working on this problem. Over all of these years, I would guess that we are somewhat worse off with respect to the attack submarine. The submarines have improved faster than the antisubmarine weapons. So would the countermeasures to "space defense." Just to invoke science in a general way as an infallible god and to base strategy on that assumption is an illusion.

Then there are ideas about insulated nuclear war. There was a special idea, of great interest to me as a naval officer, which was often discussed about ten years ago. It was that somehow or other you could have an insulated nuclear war at sea—a nuclear war in which the only people to get hurt would be sailors. I think that that kind of insulation is highly unlikely. War would surely spill over to land, as would war in space. But a more concrete objection is that any such initiative use of nuclear weapons at sea would be very much to the disadvantage of the Allies, because we are the outfit with the big ships and we are the outfit largely dependent on surface ships to keep the seas open. The differential advantage we might get from going after a submarine with a nuclear depth bomb is just not worth it. In addition it has the interesting characteristic that if you blow one beneath the surface of the sea, you will ring the ocean acoustically for several hours and lose the capability to track anybody. As a tactic that is soft-headed, deeply obnoxious—and militarily futile.

But space, or nuclear antisubmarine warfare, are not the only areas where the misuse of science leads us into danger. The point about ASW bears extension to the main theme of this chapter, the military employment of strategic and theater nuclear weapons in general. I lump strategic and theater weapons together. I do not see any difference between them, observing that it really does not make any difference where the weapon starts from: it only makes a difference where it lands, with what yield and what accuracy. So the difference, if any, is only political. Also, things we are accustomed to call strategic weapons, for example submarine weapons, are in fact just as easily classified as theater weapons: if you send the missile over the Barents Sea or from the Western Approaches into central Europe, in either case you are certainly in the theater of operations. So I think we are justified in treating these two things together. Not at all incidentally, it would greatly clarify and facilitate arms control negotiations were we to drop these meaningless distinctions.

In respect to the "strategic exchange," I think that as time goes on we see increasingly how very little we comprehend what those innocuous words mean. Take the synergistic effects upon the biosphere. A lot of work has been done on this in recent years. In the United States a high-level scientific group has announced that the ecological effects of a major nuclear exchange may be so devastating that we might lose all of the people, not just a lot of them (not to mention the animals, plants and other living things on our blue earth). Something like that is not provable, of course, but Professor Sagan and his associates are extremely competent. The calculations, as far as the layman can tell, are reasonable. The assumptions are reasonable. Nor are they alone; other scientific research tends to converge on this prognosis. So the probability of a total end to mammalian life through the "nuclear winter" cannot be dismissed.

For me, even more than before, this really puts in perspective the question of whether there is any military use which is worth the possibility, let alone the high probability, of that indescribable catastrophe taking place. The usefulness of a strategic nuclear capability is that of deterrence. And that is not military usefulness. The consequence of that conclusion is that you should design your nuclear forces to constitute the minimum credible deterrent, which, to me, is the minimum totally survivable deterrent against nuclear attack. Having achieved that, you do not want to do anything more that raises the probability of nuclear war. In particular, you want to give up counterforce doctrines. The idea that you can minimize damage to yourself by attacking nuclear forces, for example missile silos, does not bear examination. If you put missile silos or command centers at risk you then create an incentive to shoot first, shoot on warning. Nothing could be more unstable or dangerous.

With respect to the question of nuclear doctrine, a good deal has been made, in the past, of the purportedly different character of civil defense in the United States and the USSR. I think that all one needs to say about that is that civil defense against nuclear attack in the USSR is no more effective than it is in the United States. The yield and accuracy of nuclear weapons now are such that you can successfully attack any point target whose location you know. The general effects are so widespread that the ordinary civil defense measures, which usually amount to fallout shelters, are inadequate—even, perhaps, counterproductive. In attempts to relocate populations of cities, to create expedient fallout shelters, imagine digging in the ground around Moscow or Minneapolis in the middle of winter to make a hole in which to live with your family for three weeks underneath three feet of earth. What do you do about food? What do you do about heat? What do you do about water? What do you do about waste disposal? What do you do about plain survival? Civil defense in the Soviet Union is, like many other things in that country, "*pokuzuka*." That is a Russian word meaning "show without substance." Like pronouncements about "winning the battle of the grain" and "carrying out the mandates of the Twenty-Sixth Congress," it does not bear any relationship to the real world. Soviets regard these pronouncements much as Americans regard TV advertisements—not to be confused with fact.

Given the enormous risks, given the lack of reasonable military objectives or of political purposes commensurate with those risks, I think we can say that neither strategic nor theater nuclear weapons have usefulness except insofar as they deter—not conventional attack, but nuclear attack, and they should be designed for that purpose alone. If they were so designed, they would be very different from the forces we now have.

This, by the way, is not a statement that we must be either red or dead. I think that there is a third possibility and it is one that I, personally, am most eager to engage. It is not at all clear to me why NATO Europe, plus the United States, plus in all probability Japan, and certainly Australasian countries and other allies of the kind that were mobilized in World War II, why this enormous preponderance in men, industrial and technological capacity cannot be harnessed to an effective "conventional" defense. To attempt to do that, whether or not it costs more money (and it is not clear that it would) is the right way to go in defense policy—in the correct sense of the term—rather than to talk about demonstrative use of nuclear weapons, initiative use of nuclear weapons, limited use of nuclear weapons or anything else of that kind, which carries inevitably the risks that I have described.

How did we get to this sorry pass in which we find ourselves? Let me recall the historical path we have followed. The history of the development of nuclear weapons by the Allies, and particularly by the United States, has been a consistent story of shooting ourselves in the foot. When we built the atomic weapon, we built the one thing that could put the United States at risk. Before that, here we were, with the world's greatest navy, oceans on both sides, the world's most effective air force (not disparaging the RAF—we were just bigger) with weak, friendly neighbors north and south and with a very capable army. Who on earth could have come against us? Then we invented the one thing that made it possible for Qaddafi and Khomeini and some unknown terrorist to threaten us, were they to get hold of one. We had a lot of hubris at that time. We thought that after our extraordinary brilliance and our enormous industrial effort during the World War, nobody else would be able to build one of these things; that our only problem was to use our nuclear monopoly wisely in the interests of peace, freedom, and whatnot in the world. When the Soviets exploded "Joe I"—their first atomic bomb—four years later, it was a horrid shock. As you know, we reacted to it very quickly, although not without a lot of dissent among the scientific community. We raised the ante by a factor of a thousand, and invented the hydrogen bomb. In consequence, defense, which had been made extraordinarily difficult by the arrival of the atomic bomb, now became impossible with the advent of the H-bomb, and so it remains. So what did we do next?

In order to put Russia at risk, we invented the intercontinental bomber. That was in two steps: B-47s and B-52s, with a little aberration with B-58s in the middle. After a pause, the Soviets responded principally with ICBMs, which was the only major instance in which they were ahead of us (by about a year). So then the warning time went down from many hours, with bombers, to a few minutes with missiles. Each of us fooled around with anti-ballistic missile systems until we both became convinced of the impracticability of building an effective ABM to protect populations. We build submarine-launched ballistic missiles (SLBMs), and this was a step toward stability because they were very nearly invulnerable then, and they still are now. Not being threatened, they offer no incentive to shoot in a hurry. Then we turned right around again and in a fit of technological push and absence of vision with respect to the operational consequences, we invented the multiple independent re-entry vehicle (MIRV). Thus we build the one thing that could put all of our land-based forces at risk and we are now living with the consequences of the predictable Russian response to that—to raise the ante again. Today, we are in the process of getting big in the cruise missile business and that will make effective verification of some nuclear systems virtually impossible. We are talking about getting into space—again, with the same notion that, somehow, we are going to get a technological edge or, in the case of Europe, defense on the cheap. We should have learned better by now. Let this be plain: from my experience of many years service in the technical field, including a spell in intelligence, I assert that there is no prospect of getting a significant permanent technological edge in nuclear weapons over the USSR.

There are some illusions which muddy the water. One is the illusion of the necessity for a nuclear "balance," as it is called, at every level, in every type of nuclear system. What does that mean? Take the strategic level. What are the results when you do the grim necessary business of calculating as best you can how many people are going to get killed on each side in a general nuclear exchange? I used to do this professionally as Deputy Director of the Joint Strategic Planning Staff and I do not think the situation has changed much, except for the worse, since then. It turns out that the results are quite insensitive to force levels. At our present levels a difference of 1,000 missiles or so makes little difference. This is remarkable. It flies in the face of previous military theories, Lanchester's Square Law in particular. It is counter-intuitive, but it is undoubtedly true; and it means you have to change your way of military thinking. It may make a difference what your targeting policy is: whether you target cities or not. It certainly makes a difference what your fusing policy is: whether you fuse to create fallout or not. It makes a difference in these calculations which way the wind is blowing the fallout. But you can hardly find a use for more than 1,000 weapons, more or less, on either side.

The illusion of technical superiority I have touched on. There really is no difference in the capability to destroy a distributed target between a very old system, such as a tired old Bear bomber, and a maneuvering hypersonic re-entry vehicle. Both can destroy New York just as well. There is one exception: the single instance of trying to destroy hard targets. That of course is the counterforce problem I have already mentioned, and to put those targets at threat has a negative value—it makes you less secure, not more.

But there is a lot of fear around that if we move away from the illusion of nuclear "balance" to the only sensible strategy of minimum invulnerable deterrence, the Soviets will somehow find a way to cheat us and to gain some sort of advantage over us. Two more illusions must be dismantled here. The first illusion is that verification in the smallest of all fine details of everything is important. It simply is not; which leads to the second and larger concern. This is the illusion that there is a significant capability for a clandestine build-up which then can be unveiled suddenly, so that one day the Premier of the Soviet Union can say to the President, "Ah! Gotcha!" That is illusion too, because if the clandestine build-up is big enough to be important then it has to be very big; and if it is that big it is almost certainly detectable. It is also true that you have to look at the whole intelligence problem (of which verification is a part) not only from our standpoint, of wanting assurance that we know, but from their standpoint, wanting assurance that we do not know. Intelligence work is a probabilistic sort of thing. There is a one percent chance that we have a "mole" in the Kremlin and we know everything they do. There is a ninety-nine and forty-four hundreths percent chance that if they build a replica of the Pentagon along the banks of the Moscow river, we will get pictures of it. The whole intelligence exercise operates along a continuum like that.

But their problem is to be reasonably sure that we do not know. To say it again, that is very different from our problem, to be reasonably sure that we do know. In the verification area, which occupies us very much politically, I think we have to recognize that what we need to know is really not juridical departures from treaties, but departures which make a difference. Having been deeply involved in the verification issue, and buttressed by other people who have been also at a very senior level, I think we can say with a great deal of confidence that any attempt to build a sufficient clandestine capability to make a difference would certainly be detected. We cannot be sure of detecting all minor violations. We can be sure that if they are technical or interpretive violations we will have arguments forever. But we can also be sure that if there are violations big enough to make a difference, then we will see them.

I have given some of the reasons why I think that the military usefulness of nuclear weapons is not only zero, but is actually negative. Among other things, it diverts attention, at least in the United States and, I think, in Britain also, away from those military requirements which are real. Such capabilities are the ability to keep open the seas and the air routes which link together the Alliance. I do not think any of my successors in the Pacific or any of the Commanders in the Atlantic think that we are capable of pushing cargoes across those oceans in the face of the Soviet submarine and air threat, except under very favorable assumptions (mostly of getting big tactical edges which we may or may not get). That is an important military deficiency. In contrast, I cannot believe that not having an MX missile, say, is an important military deficiency. The ability to hold ground in places of one's choosing (and, of course, Europe is the prime one, but not the only one) is another major military requirement. These are major, important, strategic requirements. There is no way that nuclear weapons or nuclear weapons expenditure can help to fulfill them, and they are neglected because command attention is so focused upon nuclear weapons and because the necessary funds are diverted to nuclear weapons.

I am not advocating a conventional arms race. I do not trifle with the thought of war—I have seen too much of it to do that. Nor do I ignore the real threats that exist in the real world. These we must resolutely counter. But as a military man who has served for almost half a century, I am appalled and angered by the way that military virtues have been subverted by the nuclear weapon, that security has been steadily eroded by the build-up in the stockpiles, never faster than today, and that the future of us all now stands in jeopardy because of the grotesque failure of imagination and reason from which has grown the dangerous nuclear doctrine now in vogue.

In the last and greatest speech of his long and distinguished career, a speech in which he addressed many of the same issues that have been my concern in this chapter, Admiral Mountbatten said:

> "There are powerful voices around the world who still give credence to the old Roman precept—if you desire peace, prepare the war. This is absolute nuclear nonsense . . ."

How right he was, and how tragic that five years later I find the situation much as he saw it, only worse. We are actually speeding up our march toward that final abyss of which he spoke.

In the final chapter of this book, I shall outline a number of straightforward, simple, practical ways in which we and the Soviets can move swiftly to end the nuclear peril. Nothing in our lifetimes will be more important than to engage ourselves to this end. Nothing in the long history of humanity will be more important; for without success there will be no more history.

3 CURRENT NATO STRATEGY: A RECIPE FOR DISASTER *A. S. Collins*

Lieutenant General A. S. Collins, US Army (ret.), served throughout World War II as an infantry commander in the Pacific. His subsequent service took him to the Department of the Army General Staff, to the United States Military Academy, to field command in Europe and to the Faculty of the Army War College. He acted as an adviser to the Korean Army before becoming Assistant Deputy Chief of Staff for Operations on the Army General Staff. He left in 1965 to command the Fourth Infantry Division, and he took the division to Vietnam the following year. In 1967 he returned to the Army General Staff as Deputy Chief of Staff for Force Development, but was re-assigned to Vietnam in 1970 to command the First Field Force. From 1971 until his retirement in 1974 he was Deputy Commander-in-Chief of the US Army in Europe. General Collins died in January 1984 while this book was in production.

Today our military strategy no longer conforms to reality: it threatens national survival, and does little to enhance the long-term security interests of the United States or the Western Alliance as a whole.

Preventing nuclear war should not be the goal only of peace demonstrators or activists who question any use of US power. It should be an imperative for every American concerned with the security of our nation. The power of nuclear weapons is simply awesome. Having fought in two wars, I still have not seen anything comparable to what I saw in Hiroshima in October, 1945. I spent a day looking around the city over which the first, small, primitive atomic bomb had been exploded two months earlier. It was hard to believe that one bomb could devastate such a large area, or that it could kill so many people and create such a variety of casualties. I tried to relate it to other battle areas I had seen and other towns which troops had fought through and liberated. There was no correlation. Since then, as a soldier, I have never considered nuclear war to be a rational form of warfare or a rational instrument of policy. This excerpt from a recent study explains why:

"A-bomb damage . . . is so complex and extensive that it cannot be reduced to any single characteristic or problem. It must be seen overall, as an interrelated array—massive physical and human loss, social disintegration, and psychological and spiritual shock—that affects all life and society. Only then can one grasp the seriousness of its total impact . . . The essence of atomic destruction lies in the totality of its impact on man and society and on all the systems that affect their mutual continuation."[1]

This does not mean that the United States should unilaterally disband its nuclear forces. That would be sheer folly when other nations retain such an awesome capability. Nuclear systems, however, should be limited to what is essential to deter hostile nuclear powers from making nuclear attacks: a minimum assured deterrent.

Any reasonable person who is suggesting a change in strategic policy must approach the subject with considerable humility and a keen awareness how little is actually known about highly classified and complex nuclear plans. Those who work on highly classified material, however, often operate in tight compartments and do not have an opportunity to address the wider perspectives. Many create their own blinkers and neglect those aspects that cannot be quantified—such as morale or panic, attitude and stability of the people under attack, and how the society will function during and after a nuclear war. Furthermore, while much has been written in academic and military journals on the subject, the fact remains that these treatises are speculative because a two-sided nuclear war has never been fought. What could result from a major nuclear exchange is probably beyond the grasp of human comprehension.

Nuclear strategists often describe nuclear attacks, in which millions would be killed and wounded, as though they were great chess games with cities, aircraft carriers, great industrial areas, and other sources of national power as the pieces. As each one is destroyed, that piece is removed from the board and the match goes on as usual. Control and restraint are automatically assumed. Such a visualization may intrigue those who have never seen a war first hand, but when families, homes and factories are involved, and the weapons are exploding and contamination is spreading over the land, people will not react rationally. Nor will there be restraint, for control and belief in restraint will have broken down and the pressures to respond massively to limit further destruction will be unstoppable in this chaotic and emotional environment.

Furthermore, if a decision in favor of a minimum assured deterrent is not made, distortions of sound strategic planning will result in additions to the US strategic arsenal that could increase the risk of nuclear war and thus threaten the survival of the United States. Distortions, in fact, creep into both strategic and tactical warfare planning. In each case, the distortion derives from a persistent policy of developing and deploying additional nuclear capabilities. These systems may not be necessary to assure the deterrence which has so far prevailed; further, they may destabilize the nuclear relationships between the United States and the Soviet Union.

The curtailment and inadequate support of US conventional forces in the 1950s resulted from the belief that conventional forces would not be needed because of US nuclear superiority. In the 1960s and 1970s US analysts also believed that tactical nuclear weapons would compensate for our enemies' more powerful conventional forces. This is a dangerous myth, and because it is so widely accepted, the merits of a nuclear strategy must be addressed at the tactical as well as the strategic level. Strategic and tactical nuclear war are different in scope and objective, but the difference becomes academic to the inhabitants of the geographic area in which the more limited tactical nuclear war is to be fought. Tactical nuclear war would quickly become strategic or total war for small nations and the local populations over whose fields and cities nuclear weapons are exploding. Hiroshima, after all, was destroyed by what is considered to be one small tactical nuclear weapon in today's arsenal.

I do not believe that a tactical nuclear war could be fought in areas like Western Europe for more than a few days, or even a few hours, without getting out of control. It is possible that a series of limited nuclear exchanges could take place at sea, or possibly in the air over deserts or polar ice caps. The visibility in these environments is excellent, and communications capabilities on ships and planes are greatly superior to those available to commanders engaged in land warfare. So it might be possible to control a limited number of nuclear attacks where there are few people and the lifelines of a civilized society are not at risk. Admirals might trade destroyers, cruisers, or even an aircraft carrier for similar enemy warships. It is difficult, however, to visualize more than two or three of these limited exchanges before some commander loses patience and tries to destroy an enemy flotilla with several higher-yield weapons. Then the enemy commander would surely assert that the battle was no longer tactical and request authority to respond with strategic weapons before all was lost.

Because tactical nuclear weapons will have devastating effects on both civilians and fighting troops, any strategy oriented toward the eventual use of nuclear weapons requires close scrutiny and critical challenge.

Nuclear planners should begin by relating known occurrences on conventional battlefields to possible similar happenings on the nuclear battlefield. They should also apply the same honesty and realism in recognizing what enemy nuclear weapons can do to Allied forces as they do in proclaiming what US weapons will do to enemy forces.

In combat the major concern of a commander is the number of casualties his unit will take in accomplishing its mission. The smaller the unit, the more personal the commander's concern gets. It is instructive to look at the conventional battlefield through the eyes of the infantry, which in World War I, World War II, Korea and Vietnam sustained 80–85 percent of the casualties. If a 150-man company has 10–15 men killed on any one day, the unit had a bad day. A well-trained and disciplined unit, however, will adjust to the losses and get ready to move out on the next mission, figuring that such losses will not occur again for a long time, at least not to their unit. Suppose there were 50–100 dead with a proportional share of wounded? Suppose this was a frequent occurrence?

How will troops react to casualties anticipated on the nuclear battlefield where "a single nuclear burst in one battle can produce enough losses to make whole units ineffective"?[2] There will be burns, blindness, radiation sickness and blast-associated wounds. Thousands of civilians will suffer these casualties, too. How will all these casualties be cared for? What medical support system will be adequate? Who will bury the dead? What is the military judgment on how these operational, human and logistic problems will be handled?

Comparisons can be made to the fire-bombings of Tokyo and Hamburg, and to natural disasters. In these situations others could come to the rescue of the shocked populace, but in a nuclear conflict would they be able to do so? The speed at which things happen is of great significance. During World War II, over a period of approximately twenty-eight months the Third Infantry Division had 4,992 men killed in action, and the Fourth Infantry Division lost 4,097. What happens when that many men can be killed in only a few minutes with a few well-aimed tactical nuclear weapons? What are the replacement capabilities? The psychological factors will exceed any known battle stress by a wide margin.

On the battlefield the front-line soldier is always tired. He does not get much sleep, he learns to snatch a few winks whenever he gets the chance.

Nights are a mental and physical strain on his system; he is often cold and wet. Just maintaining basic personal sanitation is a chore. The combat soldier needs some stability, to get a chance to rest and restore his strength and spirit. But how much stability will there be on the nuclear battlefield?

Articles and field manuals prescribe almost constant movement as the way to avoid nuclear attack, but in combat, movement attracts enemy attention, and enemy attention invites hostile fire. The tanks and mechanized vehicles which provide mobility require tons of spare parts, fuel, and constant maintenance. When and how will the spare parts and fuel be acquired? When will the mechanics have time to do the maintenance? When will that soldier who is on the move every night get any rest? When will he have a chance to prepare those alternative positions and protective shelters which are essential to survival? These are hard and time-consuming tasks, leaving little, if any, time for rest.

Consider known weapon effects and try to visualize the number of dead and wounded, craters and blowdown, flash blindness, contamination, fallout, heat intense enough to melt rubber, fuse communications gear and ignite fuel supplies. Are extended operations feasible in that environment? My prediction is that operations on both sides would come to a sudden halt within a few days. At this point the futility of resorting to tactical nuclear war would become all too obvious.

Another major concern in battle is the uncertainty of information and the quality of a commander's intelligence. Writers often refer to the "fog of war;" this is an apt phrase. A combat commander seldom knows what really is on the other side of the battleline. Military planners should pay more attention to the reality of uncertainty in combat and what that might portend in the nuclear combat environment. This is a problem for all the armed services, but an even more serious one in a land battle where the forests and hills provide concealment for forces and cover from scanning radar. The following examples from sea and air actions in the past fifteen years will attest to this point.

In 1967, the Israelis claim they mistook a US communications ship, the *USS Liberty*, for a hostile vessel and bombed it. In the invasion of Cyprus the Turkish Air Force sank a "Greek" destroyer that turned out to be one of their own. Did anyone really know what was happening in the Tonkin Gulf at the time of the incident? How good was the intelligence in the Mayaguez incident? These are examples of what happens under combat conditions offering better visibility and considerably less confusion than in any land combat situation. Consider a pilot's difficulty in identifying the target while giving close support to ground troops in combat.

Proponents of tactical nuclear warfare handle all this with the magic word "control." But the smaller weapons proposed or already in the inventory are intended for use in an environment in which an Army field manual says, "Once nuclear weapons are released, employment of these weapons should be authorized to the lowest tactical commander possible."[3] Another paragraph on tactical nuclear warfare implications says, "The need for greater dispersion under conditions of tactical warfare will lead to greater reliance on timely and independent actions by small-unit commanders. Communications may be severely disrupted, troop formations will become more susceptible to infiltration, and units may become isolated for extended periods . . ."[4]

That gives a good picture of how operations might be on a nuclear battlefield. But which controls will work? I do not know of any land combat conditions more certain to create confusion, guarantee mistakes and cause casualties to both civilians and NATO forces than the ones described. It is in the area of control and release of authority that so much of the theory on the use of tactical nuclear weapons falls apart. How does one control the yield of weapons? The number of weapons? Target systems? More to the point, once tactical nuclear weapons are employed, they will destroy or disrupt the command, communications and control capabilities which are essential in keeping a nuclear war limited.

That there are two sides to any fight is often overlooked when civilians and both political and military leaders discuss what we will do in a nuclear war. People talk about keeping a nuclear war limited as if all this violence, movement, and dying will take place in some antiseptic laboratory where precise measurements of results and predictions of enemy reactions can be anticipated and noted. It is just possible that our rules and limitations may be unacceptable or misinterpreted by the opponent—or vice versa. A major part of the uncertainty in battle pertains to the unpredictability of the human mind. For some obscure reason, too many Americans tend to believe that in a nuclear war the enemy will recognize our action for what we intend it to be. Yet this does not happen in our daily lives where the stakes are not nearly as great. There is no excuse for assuming that mutual understanding is going to be more commonplace in war where fear, fatigue and the pressure of time are constant factors.

What will the reply be to the first use of these weapons? Historically, US forces cannot claim any awards for restraint in the use of firepower;

we really pour it on. Once the nuclear barrier is broken, it is hard to believe that commanders, steeped in the US military tradition of concern for the lives of their troops, will respond with moderation, especially if their units have suffered severe losses in the first attack. Soviet doctrine leaves no room for doubt: their nuclear response will be massive and overwhelming.[5]

Defense planners and military commanders must stop deluding themselves on tactical nuclear operations. In land warfare there is nothing limited about tactical nuclear warfare if enemy forces have the capability to respond in kind. This brings me to the use of tactical nuclear weapons in the defense of NATO and a distortion of strategy in the tactical nuclear field.

NATO provides the best place to examine the rationale for a tactical nuclear war and a strategic distortion that flows from it. The defense of Western Europe is a top military priority in supporting the national security objectives of the United States, and the tactical nuclear option has been consistently studied and extensively war-gamed in NATO maneuvers and exercises.

In the early 1970s Senator Mike Mansfield persistently stated that more tactical nuclear weapons and fewer men could provide the US contribution to NATO's defense at less cost. To strengthen NATO support for a tactical nuclear defense of NATO, several Secretaries of Defense have emphasized the need for smaller, more accurate nuclear weapons, especially the enhanced radiation weapon which is a missile warhead.

The case made for the enhanced radiation weapon is that it would be very effective against Soviet massed armor attacks and less destructive than other small tactical nuclear weapons already stockpiled in Western Europe. The Department of Defense believes this weapon will help correct the dangerous imbalance in conventional forces, particularly armor, between the Warsaw Pact forces and NATO. Some believe the neutron weapon will reduce the probability of nuclear war, while others have hoped that the new weapon would make tactical nuclear war more palatable to NATO nations.

Despite all these hopes, the new weapon will at best add little to NATO's defense, and at worst could lead it to disaster. Aspects of military operations pertaining to asymmetries between US and Soviet nuclear weapons systems and operational doctrine will indicate why.

From my own study, Soviet nuclear doctrine appears to be more comprehensive, consistent and realistic than similar US doctrine. The difference between Soviet and US tactical nuclear doctrines, and the difference in yield and range between US and Soviet tactical nuclear weapons, guarantee that US scenarios and theories of controlling tactical nuclear war would lead to NATO's defeat. These points are especially significant:

"Yields of Soviet tactical nuclear weapons, most of which are missiles, range from several kilotons to several megatons, and thus on balance are distinctly more destructive than US weapons; Soviet delivery systems are demonstrably less accurate than NATO's; and Soviet doctrine does not recognize the potential graduations of tactical nuclear warfare that are such a feature of flexible response."[6]

The nuclear doctrine of Soviet forces is clear and explicit on this last point. An attack on Soviet forces with a few, small nuclear weapons constitutes a nuclear attack, and Soviet doctrine provides for a mass employment of tactical nuclear weapons in response. Any fuzzy thinking on that point would prove disastrous.

The asymmetry between Soviet nuclear weapons and the enhanced radiation weapon would be so great that the larger and less accurate Soviet weapons would be devastating to NATO forces using smaller neutron weapons. Many war games and studies have shown that where the first use of nuclear weapons is careful and discrete, the side initiating the nuclear attack would be overwhelmed by a sudden and massive enemy nuclear response. When asked what he would do if his units were hit by a few small nuclear weapons, any US commander would call urgently for all the nuclear firepower he could get. Are the Soviets likely to be more restrained in similar circumstances?

A major power stands to gain nothing by breaking the nuclear barrier in land warfare in its own territory. Developed nations have densely populated areas and major industrial and transportation systems. The developed nation that breaks the nuclear barrier invites the destruction of these sources of national power. Nonetheless, the highly developed countries of Western Europe do plan for a nuclear defense in the NATO homelands, and the United States as the major nuclear power is fostering the strategy and pushing it to the limit with the enhanced radiation weapon (the neutron bomb).

The neutron bomb would replace weapons already in place which so far have provided adequate deterrence. Although the new weapon is more effective against tanks and less destructive than other nuclear weapons, this does not make nuclear war more acceptable.

Those who support nuclear warfare are prone to stress weapons' effects on the enemy. They have not been nearly as thorough in describing what might happen if the enemy responds with tactical nuclear weapons, and have ignored the effects a two-sided nuclear exchange will have on people, industry and society.

That is why the doctrine for tactical, or limited, nuclear war is not persuasive when subjected to critical review. It may also be why the West is unwilling to make the personal sacrifices to provide the additional personnel and resources for a more credible conventional defense. The people should know what the nuclear bill will be as compared to the commitment that might prevent a nuclear war. While tactical nuclear weapons may help budget problems, they give only the semblance of solving security and survival problems. It is time to stop shielding the people from the knowledge of the full range of effects of nuclear weapons, and time to be more realistic about the price nations will have to pay in a mutual tactical nuclear war on their territory.

Distortions of sound strategic planning derive from overemphasis on nuclear weapons by US political and military leaders. The MX missile is an Air Force example; the enhanced radiation weapon is an Army example. The Navy has them too.

The United States, with its geographic advantage, could well fight a conventional war for thirty years without suffering the casualties and devastation that would result from a few hours of strategic nuclear war, or a few weeks of tactical nuclear war. Several days of tactical nuclear war would be catastrophic for our NATO allies in Western Europe.

In his *Foreign Affairs* article, "The forgotten dimensions of strategy," Michael Howard made this trenchant criticism of Western nuclear strategy:

> "Works about nuclear war and deterrence normally treat their topic as an activity taking place almost entirely in the technological dimension. From their writings not only the socio-political but the operational elements have quite disappeared. The technological capabilities of nuclear arsenals are treated as being decisive in themselves, involving a calculation of outcome so complete and discrete that neither the political motivation for the conflict nor the social factors involved in its conduct—nor indeed the military activity of fighting—are taken into account at all."[7]

This is a valid criticism of the US approach to both strategic and tactical nuclear war. Howard goes on to say that the Western position on nuclear war appears to be both "paradoxical" and "indefensible" and that while we ignore the societal implications of nuclear war altogether, "our adversaries, very wisely, show no indication of doing so." Howard's observations provide a serious indictment of US nuclear strategy.

In my judgment, continued US security depends upon our ability to deter strategic nuclear attacks against the US homeland and to diminish the likelihood of tactical nuclear war in Western Europe. An assured destruction strategy is the best way to achieve the first of these two objectives. Some people place little trust in an assured destruction strategy. They believe the USSR is not as concerned about casualties as the United States is. They fear that the Soviets might chance a first strike and risk US retaliation because their active and passive defenses will limit casualties to 10–20 million deaths, a number no greater than those killed by the Nazis in World War II. Richard Pipes, who makes this argument, also criticizes the reactive nature of the US strategic doctrine.[8] He fails to consider, however, the importance of geography as it pertains to the Soviet Union and her neighbors, and the magnification of the effects of millions of casualties in the span of a few days.

Various estimates of Soviet casualties resulting from a US assured destruction retaliatory attack indicate that as many as 80–100 million Soviets would be killed under several attack scenarios because of serious inadequacies in the Soviet civil defense program. Furthermore, there are numerous methods the United States can use to overcome Soviet defensive efforts.[9]

Even if "only" 20 million Russians were killed in a retaliatory attack, the deaths would occur from within seconds to 96 hours rather than over a period of four years. With so many people killed so suddenly, millions more would die from wounds, disease and starvation. The order of magnitude of problems generated by the compression of time, physical destruction and contamination would be cataclysmic and threaten the very existence of the Soviet Union.

More than most people, the Soviets understand the relationship between geography and national interest. They are very sensitive to the existence of their 4,000-mile border with the People's Republic of China, a country which condemns the Soviet ideological interpretation and claims as its own a portion of Soviet territory. The ability to fight the Chinese and maintain territorial integrity would become a vital consideration to the Soviets after an assured destruction response by the United States. The Soviets know who will take over vast areas of their homeland under such conditions—this is not a matter of playing what the Soviet news agency TASS has referred to as "the China Card," but involves geographic reality. They also are aware that in the chaos following such an attack the Poles, Hungarians, other Warsaw Pact powers, and ethnic minorities in the Soviet Union might decide to revolt. Thanks to its geographical isolation the United States has no comparable disadvantage. Although the United States would suffer severely from a strategic nuclear exchange, the advantages of geography provide some hope that it will survive as a nation within its current boundaries. Not so the Soviet Union.

As strategists the Soviets are opportunistic, and they can and do move swiftly to take advantage of someone else's crisis. Occasionally they make mistakes. When it comes to "Mother Russia," however, they are deliberate and cautious. Historically they have been consummate strategists in defense of their homeland. The Soviets appreciate a strategy they can understand. As long as they believe the United States possesses the means to inflict unacceptable damage in a retaliatory strike and that the United States is resolved to protect its interests, they will be less likely to waste Soviet resources on maintaining a strategic nuclear superiority that will not do them any good. Under these circumstances future arms reduction talks might be more productive for both nations.[10]

The US strategic deterrent should be based upon the capability required to deter the Soviets, and not on matching them weapon system for weapon system. The Soviets' evaluation of threat, with potential adversaries including the United States and NATO, China, and fervent Moslem nationalism across the Southern border, is much more global and geographically ominous to the Soviet Union than our evaluation of the threat the Politburo sees as it looks out from the Kremlin. It should not be surprising that this evaluation, when coupled with past Soviet experience, results in a prodigious defense establishment.

A US commitment to a minimum assured deterrent should be the pillar of US nuclear strategy. There should be no question about it and an announced national policy with strong bipartisan support in the Senate might eliminate any uncertainty. The commitment should include an announced no first strike policy with no waffling or ambiguities. If deterrence of strategic nuclear war is going to work, a clearly stated policy—along with the capability to carry it out—is the surest way to assure its effectiveness. Too often in international affairs the anticipated US response to some hostile act has surprised both friend and foe. In that all-or-nothing field of strategic nuclear war there must be no room for misunderstanding.

A decision on this one point would allow for a substantial reduction in strategic nuclear weapons. This would allow for some shifting of funds and other resources to make the necessary improvements in the conventional capability in order to reduce the likelihood that a war in Western Europe would turn into a nuclear conflict. Ideas on this are explored later in this book.

Suggestions on a tactical nuclear strategy are much more difficult to develop. The dispersal of tactical nuclear weapons around the world, the marked variation in weapons types and effects, and the attitude of allies who see these weapons as giving them a special relationship with the US will create many political–military problems.

A first step on the long road might be the creation of a joint task force for the employment of tactical nuclear weapons. Nuclear weapons cannot be used without the approval of the President and the head of state of the allied nation where the weapons are to be employed. Approval and release from these levels of government do not permit immediate use, so delay is inevitable. There would be ample time to deploy weapons and systems to the areas in which they are to be used if a crisis indicates the need. Furthermore, these weapons are so destructive that only a few will have to be used before the warring nations either escalate the use of nuclear weapons or find another way to solve their problems.

A joint nuclear task force with elements stationed at national stockpile sites adjacent to major air bases in the United States would solve some of the problems inherent in having these sites dispersed around the world. The conversion of all personnel and funds, saved by the consolidation of dispersed units and storage sites, to conventional capabilities would give impetus to building up conventional forces. Then perhaps NATO nations would be unable to use Uncle Sam as a whipping boy each time an unpopular nuclear issue arises in Western Europe.

The establishment of such a task force might also encourage the NATO nations to find ways to shore up their conventional defenses so that tactical nuclear weapons would not have to be used to defend Western Europe. Soviet forces could be stopped by a conventional defense if NATO nations only made the effort.[11] The NATO alliance has one and a half times the population of the Soviet Union and twice its Gross National Product. It is absurd to say that NATO does not have the capability for a conventional defense of Western Europe. The will may be missing, but not the means.

National leaders must consider the disadvantages as well as advantages of nuclear war. Military leaders have a duty to inform both their political leaders and the people of the Western Alliance of the dangers inherent in nuclear strategies. If military leaders do this, civilian decision-makers will be in a better position to make judgments on the forces required to carry out the military aspects of an overall strategy that will be in the national interest. If different means and greater sacrifice by the people are required to develop strategies that do not threaten national survival, the people should be informed of what the sacrifices are. They should also know what the bill will be for nuclear strategies which mortgage long-term safety for short-term expediency.

Clausewitz emphasized that war cannot be divorced from political life: "Whenever this occurs in our thinking about war, we are left with something pointless and devoid of sense."[12] If the nuclear strategies that US leaders now depend on for national security are ever executed, future generations will recognize how "pointless and devoid of sense" they were—if they are there to see.

There are numerous ways to reduce the probability of a nuclear tragedy for the United States and for our NATO allies. One way is to adopt strategies that are less dependent on large stockpiles of nuclear weapons and place more emphasis on conventional capabilities. Meanwhile national leaders should vigorously pursue limitations on stockpiles and deployments of nuclear systems and weapons. The objective should be to first limit, and eventually to ban, nuclear weapons worldwide. This will not happen in the short term, but it could take place over a period of twenty-five years. Achieving this objective should be the aim of any national leader responsible for national security and concerned about national survival.

4 THE UNIMPRESSIVE RECORD OF ATOMIC DIPLOMACY *McGeorge Bundy*

Professor McGeorge Bundy is Professor of History at New York University. He was previously Professor of Government and Dean of the Faculty of Arts and Sciences at Harvard University. From 1961 to 1966 he was Special Assistant to the President for National Security Affairs, serving under Presidents Kennedy and Johnson. He then became President of the Ford Foundation. He is currently engaged in a major study of diplomacy in the nuclear age.

In addressing the question of the role of nuclear weapons in diplomacy, it is well to begin with an expression of one's own general position on the nuclear problem. My view of these weapons is that for my own country they are a necessary evil. I do not think it acceptable for the United States to renounce the possession of nuclear capabilities while they are maintained in the Soviet Union. In that most basic sense I accept the need for nuclear deterrence and am unimpressed by arguments that neglect this requirement. I wish I could see any early prospect of a reliable abolition of these weapons, but I do not. I see no signs of the sort of transformation of behavior which would allow the two overarmed superpowers to abandon these weapons and be confident of each other's good faith in so doing. I believe that it is not wise to denounce the excesses committed in the name of deterrence without recognizing that unless one thinks it better to accept complete and unilateral nuclear disarmament for the West, there is a present basic need for the United States to maintain nuclear weapons and delivery systems that are sufficient to deny to an opponent the plausible prospect of any acceptable result from nuclear aggression. I do not think this task is as demanding as many American advocates of new weapons have argued, and I think that one way of reducing the hazards of the nuclear age is to understand more clearly the sharp limits on their usefulness for anything but the avoidance of nuclear war. Still I begin by accepting the need of my own country for a sufficient nuclear deterrent.

I also believe that not all the consequences of the nuclear arsenals are bad. The very existence of nuclear stockpiles has created and enforced a considerable caution in the relations among nuclear-weapon states, so that where the interests of those states are clear and their political and military engagement manifest, as with the Soviet Union and the United States in Eastern and Western Europe respectively, there is an intrinsic inhibition on adventure which is none the less real for being essentially independent of doctrines—and even of nuclear deployments—on either side. I have elsewhere called this phenomenon "existential deterrence,"[1] and I think it has more to do with the persisting peace—and division—of Europe than all the particular nuclear doctrines and deployments that have so often bedeviled the European scene. I believe that existential deterrence has been strong in every decade since 1945, and that it would still be strong if the entire plan for new medium-range missiles—ground-launch cruise missiles and Pershing IIs—were unilaterally canceled by NATO tomorrow, or if an American president were simply to decide, as John F. Kennedy did in the earlier case of Jupiter missiles in Turkey, that the Pershing II is a bad system that should be dismantled. To accept a basic requirement for deterrence is not at all to accept all the follies committed in its name.

Indeed the acceptance of nuclear deterrence, for me as for the American Catholic bishops, is "strictly conditioned," not only on a constant readiness to move to agreed arms reductions as drastic as the most skillful and dedicated negotiations permit, but also on a reluctance to depend on nuclear weapons for purposes beyond that of preventing nuclear war. On the historical record since Nagasaki, I think that these weapons have not been of great use to any government for such wider purposes, and I also think a misreading of that record has led to grossly mistaken judgments and to unnecessary, costly, and sometimes dangerous nuclear deployments by both superpowers, and perhaps by others.

Let us begin by considering what good these weapons have done the United States, which was their first and for a short four years their only possessor. I am willing to concede, though it cannot be proven, that in the years of American monopoly, and perhaps for a short time thereafter (in my view, not beyond 1955, at the latest) American nuclear superiority had some military and political value in Europe. We must recognize that fear of what the Russians would otherwise do with what was then an enormous advantage in conventional strength was not limited to Winston Churchill. Niels Bohr too believed that the American atomic bomb was a necessary balancing force, and so did many other highly peaceable men. But the time has long since passed when either side could hope to enjoy either monopoly or overwhelming superiority, so from the standpoint of the present and the future it is not necessary to challenge this particular bit of conventional wisdom. We do not really know that the American monopoly saved Europe in the early postwar years, but we do not know it did not, and we need not decide.

What is more interesting is to examine these years of evident American nuclear advantage from another angle, to try to see what usefulness that advantage may have had in supporting American diplomacy or in restraining specific adventures of others outside Western Europe. Aside from this debatable European case, there is very little evidence that American atomic supremacy was helpful in American diplomacy. Broadly speaking, the years from 1945 to 1949 were a time in which Soviet power and the power of such major Soviet allies as the Chinese Communists was expanding and consolidating itself at a rate not remotely equalled since then, and there is no evidence whatever that fear of the American bomb had any restraining effect on this enormous process. It is true that for a short time in the autumn of 1945 Secretary of State James Byrnes believed that the silent presence of the bomb might constructively affect Soviet behavior at the negotiating table, but in fact it had no such impact, and before the end of the year Byrnes himself had changed his tactics. The importance of this brief and foolish flirtation with atomic diplomacy has been grossly exaggerated by students misreading a marginal and passing state of mind into a calculated effort in which Hiroshima itself is read largely as an effort to impress the Russians.[2] But this misreading is less important than the deeper point that to whatever degree atomic diplomacy may have tempted this or that American leader at this or that moment in those years, it did not work.

The point becomes still more evident when we look at moments which American presidents themselves, in later years, came to see as evidence of the power of the atomic possibility. The two most notable cases are the Soviet withdrawal from Iran in 1946 and the armistice agreement that ended the Korean War in 1953.

In April 1952 President Harry Truman told an astonished press conference that not long after the end of World War II he had given Joseph Stalin "an ultimatum"—to get his troops out of Iran—and "they got out." Truman was referring to events in March 1946, when the Soviet union kept troops in northern Iran after the expiration of an agreed date for British and Russian withdrawal that had been honored by the British. The Soviet stance stirred a vigorous international reaction, and after three weeks of increasing tension there came a Soviet announcement of a decision to withdraw which was executed over the following weeks. Truman never doubted that his messages had been decisive. Out of office, in 1957, he described his action still more vividly: "The Soviet Union persisted in its occupation until I personally saw to it that Stalin was informed that I had given orders to our military chiefs to prepare for the movement of our ground, sea and air forces. Stalin then did what I knew he would do. He moved his troops out." If this statement were accurate, it would be an extraordinary confirmation of the effectiveness of American threats in the age of atomic monopoly, because a troop movement of this sort, in 1946, into an area so near the Soviet Union and so far from the United States could only have been ventured, or feared, because of the nuclear monopoly.[3]

The only trouble with this picture is that no such message ever went to Stalin and no such orders to American officers. What actually happened is wholly different. Stalin did indeed attempt to gain a special position in Iran by keeping his troops beyond the deadline, but what made his effort a failure was not an ultimatum from Truman but primarily the resourceful resistance of the Iranian government, supported indeed by American diplomacy (especially at the United Nations) and still more by a wide and general international reaction. Stalin's was a low-stake venture in an area of persistent Soviet hope. He pulled back when he found the Iranian government firm but not belligerent, his Iranian supporters weak, and the rest of the watching world critical. One of the critics was Harry Truman, and we need not doubt the strength of his feelings. But the messages he actually sent (all now published) were careful and genuinely diplomatic. The United States Government "cannot remain indifferent," and "expresses the earnest hope" of immediate Soviet withdrawal, all "in the spirit of friendly association." There is no deadline and no threat. What we have here is no more than an understandable bit of retrospective braggadocio. As George Kennan later remarked—he had been *chargé d'affaires* in Moscow at the time and was the man who would have had to deliver any ultimatum—Truman "had an unfortunate tendency to exaggerate, in later years, certain aspects of the role that he played" in relations with Stalin.[4]

Regrettably, Truman's retrospective version of events was not harmless. Among stouthearted and uncomplicated anticommunists it became a part of the folklore showing that Harry Truman knew how to stop aggression by toughness, when in fact what he and his colleagues knew, in this case, was something much more important: that their task was to help keep up Iranian courage, but precisely *not* to confront Stalin directly. American diplomacy was adroit but not menacing, and Kennan is right again in describing the result: "It was enough for Stalin to learn that a further effort by the Soviet Union to retain its forces in Persia would create serious international complications. He had enough problems at the moment without that." Truman's messages had certainly helped in this learning process, and not least because they had expressly avoided the kind of threat he later came to believe he made. So his faulty memory led others to learn the wrong lesson.*

Dwight Eisenhower contributed even more than Harry Truman to the folklore of atomic diplomacy. He believed that it was the threat of atomic war that brought an armistice in Korea in 1953. In his memoirs he cited a number of warnings and signals to make his case, and his Secretary of State, John Foster Dulles, told allied statesmen in private a lurid tale of nuclear deployments made known to the Chinese. But here again the historical record raises questions. The decisive shift in the position of the Communists, a shift away from insistence on the forced repatriation of prisoners, occurred before any of these signals was given, shortly after the death of Stalin in March. While Eisenhower certainly intended the whiff of nuclear danger to reach Peking, the records now available make it clear that he in fact held back from any audible threat because of his recognition that it would be as divisive in 1953 as it had been in 1950, when Harry Truman, by a casual press conference response to a question on the possibility of using nuclear weapons, had brought Prime Minister Attlee across the Atlantic to receive assurance that no such step was in prospect. Quite aside from any nuclear threat, there were other and excellent reasons in 1953 for the Communist side to want to end the war: their own heavy losses, the absence of any prospect for further gains, and the continuing high cost of unsuccessful probes of United Nations forces

* The folkloric view of this event is not easy to trace in written works, but I have heard it often from political men who heard it from Truman, and even so careful a student as Stephen Kaplan, quoting Truman's memory as reported above, thinks it was the Truman *démarche*—ultimatum or not—that led to withdrawal: "What made Stalin back off only a few months later was a sudden and strong interest taken by the United States" (Stephen S. Kaplan, *Diplomacy of Power*, Washington, DC, 1981, p.70). I share the judgment of Truman's best biographer that in their satisfaction with their own role the Americans lost sight of the real determinant. "It seems to have gone unnoticed that Iranian tenacity and diplomatic skills had been major factors in that country's deliverance" (Robert J. Donovan, *Conflict and Crisis: The Presidency of Harry S. Truman, 1945–1948*, New York, 1977, p.195).

on the ground. At the most the springtime signals of a nuclear possibility were a reinforcement to Chinese preferences already established before those signals were conveyed.*

Yet Eisenhower clearly did believe that the Korean case showed the value of nuclear threats, and indeed he and Dulles made the threat permanent in the language of a public declaration after the armistice that those who had supported South Korea would respond to any renewed aggression in ways that might not be limited. In two later crises, over the offshore islands of Quemoy and Matsu in 1955 and 1958, Eisenhower used both open references to nuclear weapons and visible deployments of nuclear-armed forces to underline the risks Mao was running. What actually held off the attacking Chinese forces, in both crises, was not these threats but the effective use of local air and naval superiority, but it cannot be denied that the nuclear possibility may have contributed to Chinese unwillingness to raise the stakes. It is also possible that the readiness of the United States to help defend these small and unimportant islands was increased by the fact that against China the United States then held a nuclear monopoly.

In this case too the threat was almost as alarming to friends as to opponents. Fully aware of the fiercely divisive consequences of any actual use of a nuclear weapon, Eisenhower devoted himself in these crises to the energetic and skillful support of the conventional forces and tactics which fended off the Chinese attacks. He was very careful indeed not to lose his control over the nuclear choice, either by any unconditional public threat or by any delegation of authority. The nuclear reply remained a possibility, not a policy. As he told Nixon in 1958, "You should never let the enemy know what you will not do." In the offshore islands affair as in Korea, Eisenhower kept the use of nuclear weapons as something the enemy could not know he would not do, and believed he gained from this stance.[5]

But the President was teaching his Vice President a lesson that was going out of date even as he explained it. The offshore islands crisis of 1958, so far from being a model for the future, turns out to be the last case we have of a crisis between the United States and a nation not the Soviet

* Eisenhower's argument is in his memoirs, *Mandate for Change, 1953–1956* (Garden City, New York), p. 181. The Dulles report is reported in "Memorandum of restricted meeting of Chiefs of Delegation, December 7, 1953" (DDE/Whitman file, Eisenhower papers). Eisenhower's wariness of any visible interest in nuclear weapons is shown in "Discussion at National Security Council meeting on February 11, 1953" (DDE/Whitman file, NSC series, Box 4, Eisenhower Papers). The chronology is worked out in detail in my own work in progress.

Union in which nuclear weapons or threats of their use play any role whatever. Consider the war in Vietnam. Here the president whose inaction proves the point conclusively is the same Richard Nixon who had been Eisenhower's eager student. Nixon came to the White House in 1969 determined to apply to Hanoi the same techniques of credible threat that he thought he had seen used successfully in Korea. If he had continued to believe a nuclear threat would be credible, he would surely have conveyed it. But once he considered the matter carefully he was forced to recognize that there was in reality no way of making a credible nuclear threat because the men in Hanoi knew as well as he did that no American president, by 1969, could in fact have used nuclear weapons in Indochina. To do so would plainly outrage allies and split his own country in half. What you cannot conceivably execute, you cannot plausibly threaten.[6]

The evolution from what Eisenhower believed in 1958 to what Nixon was forced to recognize in 1969 is extraordinarily important, and not all the reasons for it are clear. One of them certainly is the spreading awareness of the danger inherent in the thermonuclear age. The end of the 1950s saw the first large-scale popular reactions to nuclear danger, and the searing experience of the Cuban Missile Crisis gave the threat of nuclear warfare new meaning. More broadly, if less consciously, men had come to believe more and more strongly in the value and importance of respecting the "firebreak" between conventional and nuclear weapons. In September 1964, President Lyndon Johnson had stated the case with characteristic passion and force during his campaign against Barry Goldwater:

"Make no mistake. There is no such thing as a conventional nuclear weapon. For nineteen peril-filled years no nation has loosed the atom against another. To do so now is a political decision of the highest order. And it would lead us down an uncertain path of blows and counterblows whose outcome none may know."[7]

To all these general considerations one must add that by 1969 the morality of the Vietnam War was a profoundly divisive question in the United States. To resort to nuclear weapons in such a war would be to outrage still further the angry opponents of the war and probably to multiply their numbers.

So what Richard Nixon thought he had learned turned out only ten years later not to be so, and by his own wise refusal to present a nuclear threat to Hanoi he reinforced the very tradition whose strength he had not at first understood. If the United States could not threaten the use of nuclear weapons even in such a long and painful contest as Vietnam, in what case was such a threat possible? The answer, today, on all the evidence, is that the only places where a nuclear threat remains remotely plausible are those where it has been present for decades—in Western Europe and in Korea, because of the special historical connections noted above, and much more diffusely and existentially in the general reality that any prospect of direct confrontation between the United States and the Soviet Union presents nuclear risks which enforce caution.

A stronger proposition may be asserted. International support for the maintenance of the nuclear firebreak now operates not only to make nuclear threats largely ineffective, but also to penalize any government that resorts to them. This rule applies as much to the Soviet Union as to the United States. The Soviet government, in the heyday of Nikita Khrushchev, set international records for nuclear bluster. The favorite target was the United Kingdom, not only in the Suez crisis but more generally. Khrushchev clearly believed that his rockets gave him a politically usable superiority and talked accordingly. Yet in fact Soviet threats were not decisive at Suez; they were not even issued until what really was decisive—American opposition to the adventure—had been clear for several days. By 1957 Soviet reminders of British vulnerability, so logical from the point of view of believers in the political value of atomic superiority, were serving only to strengthen the Macmillan government in its determination to maintain and improve its own deterrent. The Soviet triumph in launching Sputnik did indeed help Soviet prestige, but attempts to capitalize on it by crude threats were unproductive.

Still more striking is the failure of Soviet atomic diplomacy in relation to China. Having first made the enormous mistake of helping the Chinese toward nuclear weapons, the Soviets reversed their field at the end of the 1950s and addressed themselves assiduously, but with no success whatever, to an effort to persuade the Chinese that they would be happier without any nuclear weapons of their own. Neither cajolery nor the withdrawal of assistance was effective. Probably nothing could have changed the Chinese purpose, but Soviet unreliability only intensified it, and at no time before the first Chinese explosion in 1964 was the Kremlin prepared to make the matter one of war or peace. By the time that possibility was actively considered, in 1969, the Chinese bomb was a reality requiring caution: in a limited but crucial way the Chinese themselves now had an existential deterrent.

But of course Khrushchev's greatest adventure in atomic diplomacy was also his worst fiasco: the deployment of missiles to Cuba in 1962. It is not clear yet how he hoped to gain from the adventure, but he must have believed that placing these weapons in Cuba would produce advantages of some sort. Whether they were there to be bargained against concessions in Europe, or to demonstrate Soviet will and American impotence, or to establish a less uneven strategic balance, we cannot know. That they were there merely to be traded for a pledge against a US invasion of Cuba we must doubt. Nor need we linger on the fact of the failure.

What deserves attention is rather that in this most important crisis of all we can see clearly three persistent realities: first, it was not what the weapons could actually do but the political impact of the deployment that counted most to both sides; second, both leaders understood that any nuclear exchange would be a personal, political and national catastrophe; third, as a consequence the determinant of the crisis must be in the level of will and ability to act by less than nuclear means. While this set of propositions does not of itself justify President Kennedy's course, it does make clear the folly of Khrushchev's: he left himself open to the use of conventional superiority by an opponent for whom the choice of inaction was politically impossible. I recognize that many students have asserted the commanding importance of US nuclear superiority in the Cuban Missile Crisis, but I am deeply convinced that they are wrong. Along with five other senior members of the Kennedy Administration, including Dean Rusk and Robert McNamara, I am convinced that the missile crisis illustrates "not the significance but the insignificance of nuclear superiority in the face of survivable thermonuclear retaliatory forces."[8]

The missile crisis had powerful and lasting consequences for the notion of atomic diplomacy. It showed the world that both great governments had a profound lack of enthusiasm for nuclear war, and in so doing it reduced the plausibility of nuclear threats of any kind. It also increased the political costs of such posturing. Even before 1962 Khrushchev had learned to try to couch his threats in relatively civil terms—of course I don't want to crush you, but it's only sensible to note that I can.[9] In October 1962, it was precisely nuclear war that both sides plainly chose to stay clear of, and the world took note. Since that time there has been no open nuclear threat by any government. I think it is not too much to say that this particular type of atomic diplomacy has been permanently discredited.

Even the very occasional use of nuclear signals in a crisis has had low importance in recent decades. The most notable case available is the short alert called in President Nixon's name on October 24, 1973, at the height of the Yom Kippur war for the purpose of deterring unilateral Soviet action. This alert, by Henry Kissinger's authoritative account, was intended as a general show of resolution and in no way as a specifically thermonuclear threat. More significantly still, Kissinger's account makes it clear that the alert was unnecessary. The possibility of a unilateral Soviet troop movement to Egypt was effectively blocked by Sadat's overnight decision, before he ever heard of the US alert, to back away from the Soviet proposals.*

In recent years there has been one remarkable revival of the notion of atomic diplomacy, together with an equally remarkable demonstration of its lack of content. The revival occurred among frightened American hawks eager to demonstrate that the Soviet nuclear build-up of the 1970s was conferring on Moscow a level of superiority that would inescapably translate into usable political leverage. In its most dramatic form the argument was that the Russians were getting a superiority in large, accurate ICBMs that would soon allow them to knock out our own ICBMs and defy us to reply for fear of annihilation. This was the famous "window of vulnerability," and the argument was that this kind of strategic superiority, because both sides would be aware of it, would make the Soviet Union's political pressures irresistible around the world. It was all supposed to happen before now—in the early 1980s. The argument was riddled with analytical errors, ranging from the over-simplification of the problems of such an attack through the much too facile assumption that no credible reply could be offered, and on to the quite untested notion that a threat of this kind would have useful results for the threat-maker. It is not at all surprising that history has shown the notion empty. There has been no Soviet action anywhere that can be plausibly attributed to the so-called window of vulnerability, and indeed after riding this wave of fear—and others—into the White House, the Reagan Administration eventually managed to discover that the window did not exist. First, in the spring of 1983, the Scowcroft Commission concluded that the existing capabilities of American forces, taken as a whole, made such a scenario implausible, and in early 1984 Ronald Reagan himself concluded that we are all safer now because "America is back—standing tall," though out there in the real world the strategic balance remains almost exactly the one which led to the foolish fears

* Henry A. Kissinger, *Years of Upheaval* (Boston, 1982), pp. 575–99, especially at pp. 591–2. The fact that the alert proved unnecessary does not make it unwise. The Soviet *démarche* that produced it was a crude effort to change the rules in the Mideast by threat and bluster, and it deserved a firm response.

in the first place. The notion of a new vulnerability to nuclear diplomacy was unreal; perhaps we were dealing instead with a little atomic politics.

A different but equally illuminating episode is that of the seven-year process that has led to the deployment of ground-launched cruise missiles and Pershing II ballistic missiles in Europe. The argument for the new NATO deployments was that without them some part of NATO's credibility would be lost, either because of the new Soviet SS-20s or the new Soviet strategic missiles, or both. (Readers trying to find clarity and internal coherence in the NATO rationale should not assume that failure is their own fault.) It was roundly asserted that without the new deployments Western Europe would be open to nuclear blackmail. Yet in the course of the long and testing debate Moscow has been led to take major steps that plainly *reduce* any prospect of such blackmail. The Kremlin, whatever its private calculation, has become zealous in claiming that it has no nuclear superiority, strategically or in the theater. Such pronouncements do not change the balances that might actually be registered in war, but they dramatically reduce the opportunity for plausible threats. Still more self-limiting is the Soviet declaration of a policy of no first use of nuclear weapons. Again the declaration does not tell us what in fact might happen if war did come, but it makes the use of nuclear threats against neighbors in peacetime a wholly self-defeating enterprise. In the end the battle over the new deployments produced an eye-opening demonstration of the incapacity of Moscow to translate atomic weight into political influence, as Andrei Gromyko crudely attempted to influence the German elections of 1983 and succeeded only in helping those he was trying to hurt.

This episode has other lessons, not so comforting, that relate to a different set of problems. to set them off from the much-overrated notion of atomic diplomacy, let us call them the problems of the diplomacy of deployment—the problems created either within the Alliance or between Moscow and others by new systems of weapons. (Obviously the Cuban crisis could be included under this heading too.) Here the record is less encouraging. It shows that repeatedly, and on both sides, deployments have been executed that have given much more concern to adversaries than comfort to friends. Moreover, because the Western countries are democracies, in which people can readily express any distaste for nuclear warheads as neighbors, there is an imbalance between the two sides, in what is politically manageable, that understandably gives Western planners a sense of grievance—perhaps especially when this imbalance is ignored by anti-nuclear leaders protesting their own evenhandedness but operating effectively only in open societies. Fortunately none of these debated deployments, not even that of the MX missile, has ever concerned a force that was genuinely essential to the maintenance of stable strategic deterrence. I think the right approach to judgment on such deployments should be to include in one's calculations precisely such an element as the political consequences of the deployment. It is not self-evident, to put it very gently, that the "victory" of December 1983, and the safe arrival in Europe of the first ground-launched cruise missiles and Pershing IIs, has left the Alliance stronger and more self-confident than it would have been if it had been decided in 1977 and thereafter that there was nothing in any new Soviet deployment of any sort that required a change in the decision of the 1960s that the right place for American mid-range nuclear weapons supporting NATO was in submarines at sea.

My general moral is a simple one. The more we learn about living with nuclear arsenals, the less we are able to find any good use for them but one—the deterrence of nuclear aggression by others—and the more we are led to the conclusion that this one valid and necessary role is not nearly as demanding as the theorists of countervailing strategy assert. No sane government wants nuclear war, and the men in the Kremlin, brutal and cynical tyrants to be sure, are eminently sane. There are two places still—Western Europe and South Korea—where we Americans do have outstanding undertakings to go first with nuclear weapons if necessary. I believe those commitments are increasingly implausible and ripe for revision.* They may also create pressure for, though they do not in fact require, special and politically neuralgic deployments.

Such deployments are a subset of the competition in weapons systems that is now itself becoming the largest single threat to peace. The systems now coming in sight, especially those that might seem to offer effective prospects for defense, do indeed raise the specter of a world in which at some moment of great tension in the future one side or the other might feel that its only hope was to "preempt"—to go first—to aim at a simultaneous offensive and defensive knockout. That would be another

* The case for moving to a policy of no first use in Europe was put forward afresh by four of us in 1982 and has made considerable progress, though not yet with major Western governments. In essence we believe that Western Europe can be more secure without a first use policy than with one. See McGeorge Bundy, George Kennan, Robert McNamara and Gerard Smith, "Nuclear weapons and the Atlantic Alliance," *Foreign Affairs*, (Spring 1982).

and much nastier world than the one we now have, and it is worth great efforts to see to it that it does not come into being.

Meanwhile what remains remarkable about the enormous arsenals of the superpowers is how little political advantage they have conferred. It is a question for another essay whether other nuclear powers have gained more.

5 WE MUST AVOID AN ARMS RACE IN SPACE *John C. Polanyi*

Professor John C. Polanyi, Sc.D., F.R.S., is Professor of Chemistry at the University of Toronto. He is an honorary member of the American Academy of Arts and Sciences and a Foreign Associate of the American National Academy of Sciences, and he has received many academic honors for his scientific work. He was elected a Fellow of the Royal Society in 1971. Professor Polanyi was the founder of the Canadian Pugwash group (Pugwash is a worldwide forum for scientists from East and West concerned to reduce international tension) and, with F. G. Griffiths, edited The Dangers of Nuclear War.

Among the most threatening examples of conventional thinking in our transformed world is the steady movement toward the acceptance of outer space as a natural extension of the arena for human combat. Even at this early date space technology has achieved enormous importance as an adjunct to military capability. Traditionally whatever has high military utility has represented a target of high importance.

It is particularly tempting in the West to believe that the world's most technologically advanced nations could achieve a decisive military advantage by dominating outer space. Since the weapons planned for space include ballistic missile defenses (BMD) able, in Mr. Reagan's phrase, "to save lives [rather] than to avenge them," it is being claimed that there is also a moral imperative to arm space.

This should not lead us to suppose that the attempt to deploy BMD would appear benign. A movement in this direction by the Soviet Union, designed to "intercept and destroy" incoming US missiles, would be seen as a mortal threat in the West. The Soviets would perceive US deployment of BMD in the same light. A frenzied competition in ballistic missile defense, and counters to BMD, would ensue in response to what would be perceived—rightly—as a move to disarm the opposing side.

Since influential voices in the US urge speedy development of anti-satellite weapons (ASAT) and BMD, it must be that this stems from confidence in the ability to outdistance the Soviet Union. Yet supremacy in space is likely to prove as elusive as in other media. The nature of nuclear weaponry has seen to it that neither side can emerge a winner, in any acceptable sense, from a superpower conflict on earth, sea, or in the air. The advantages offered by successive US technological innovations over the years have been of diminishing significance. In every case they have been matched before long by the USSR.

Will the situation prove different in space? Nuclear explosions (at present banned from space) can also wreak havoc there. Distances are vast, but, as against that, space affords little shelter. In particular the attempt to use outer space to interdict attacks upon targets on earth, i.e. for BMD, will surely fail since nuclear weapons can readily be delivered without passing through outer space. Alternatively those that do pass through outer space can be assisted in penetrating the BMD shield not only by subterfuge (the use of decoys or screens) but also by exploiting the vulnerability of the space systems themselves.

The most probable effect, from an armaments point of view, of a resort to space-based BMD will be the deployment by the opposing side of more numerous strategic weapons to overpower the defenses, more sophisticated strategic weapons to fool the defenses, passively protected strategic weapons to foil the defenses, and actively protected strategic weapons to disable the defenses. As might be expected, plans for BMD research in the US include plans for the early development of these countermeasures.

Such a costly and destabilizing competition in a nuclear-armed world would appear to be an invitation to disaster. The brief chapter that follows does not dwell on the details of that invitation, but stresses the fact that if we move with dispatch and determination we shall find other options open to us. In numerous gestures of arms control the community of nations—the superpowers foremost among them—have warned of the dangers of a slide into an all-out arms race in space. They have united in declaring outer space to be "the province of all mankind," and have until now abided by that declaration. A great number of nations share in the benefits of outer space, and none lay exclusive claim to it.

The introduction of destructive systems into the medium of outer space will not only mark a dangerous new departure in the history of warfare with incalculable consequences for the future, but in addition a signal defeat for the vital notion that increasingly security must be achieved through restraint. National policies in respect of outer space in the coming few years will constitute a test case of the international commitment to responsible behavior.

The militarization of space

It hardly needs to be said that outer space provides a unique new vantage point from which to conduct operations on earth. It is only twenty-five years since the launching of the first crude spacecraft (the Soviet Sputnik—sent into orbit two months after the USSR tested its first intercontinental ballistic missile in August 1957). In the intervening quarter of a century space technology has become intimately interwoven with military technology in general. Four vital military functions—Command, Control, Communications and Intelligence (termed C^3I)—make heavy use, today, of satellite capabilities.

The full catalogue of space devices employed in C^3I is too extensive to be given here. The total military space budget in the USA is currently roughly $10 billion each year. It cannot be very different in the USSR. This money goes to buy four major categories of space system: (i) *Communications* satellites, for relaying messages. It is often said that two-thirds of US military communications are carried by satellite. (ii) A second category of satellite uses infrared detectors to give *early warning* of missile launchings. (iii) Another important category of satellite, equipped with many types of visible, infrared, radar and electronic eavesdroping sensors, collects *intelligence* regarding military capabilities, weapons disposition and readiness of the oppposing nation. (iv) *Navigation* satellites permit a soldier or a vehicle in the air, at sea, or on land, to determine its position with an accuracy of approximately 10 yards in three dimensions, and velocity to 0·4 in/sec. (The numbers cited under this heading look ahead to the full implementation of systems of the level of sophistication represented by the US Global Positioning System, which is to be fully deployed by late 1987.)

This list is incomplete since it makes no mention of some well-established systems such as weather satellites, geodesic satellites, nuclear explosion recognition satellites, and so on. Nor does it mention experimental systems, such as those designed to track shallowly submerged submarines. A special mention should be made of important new types of space vehicles, namely shuttles and manned space stations. Both are likely to be important in improving the sophistication, flexibility and long-term reliability of space-based military activities of the type catalogued above.

It should be stressed that *none* of the activities referred to in this section is banned by any treaty; in fact, some are specifically legitimized by treaty, as will be seen below. Though all are "military" since they support the armed forces, none involves the use of weapons in space or weapons directed against objects in space.

"Militarization" of space is to be distinguished from what has been termed "weaponization" of space. The latter involves the placing of weapons, that is to say destructive systems, in space. Whereas the militarization of space is actual, effective weaponization is still one to four years in the future. Bilateral or multilateral "militarization" arguably increases security and stability by diminishing the danger of accidental or uncontrolled war. It would be difficult to argue that "weaponization" on the part of contending nations contributes to security in the broad and menacing context of strategic weaponry—quite the reverse.

Space weapons

Antisatellite weapons

Development of antisatellite weapons has been under way, off and on, since 1963. During 1963–75 the USA maintained two ASAT bases dependent on ICBM launchers. This early ASAT would have required a nuclear warhead to be effective. It was abandoned, in part, because of the fact that a nuclear explosion in outer space could threaten satellites belonging to the nation launching the attack as well as the nation under attack.

Since 1967 the USSR has been making sporadic tests—approximately twenty in all—of an ICBM-launched interceptor satellite. This ASAT is launched by a ground-based SS-9 rocket into an orbit close to that of the target satellite. It bears a conventional warhead that explodes when the interceptor is roughly 1,000 yards from the target. The device has a record of reliability of only about 50 percent. Tests have been limited so far to low orbits up to a maximum of about 1,000 miles, and have been restricted to a particular inclination to the equator (about 66°).

The US made its first test en route to a lighter, more flexible and versatile ASAT device—a miniature homing vehicle (MHV)—early in 1984. The MHV is designed to intercept by direct ascent, rather than co-orbit, and is being fired from two-stage rockets mounted on an F-15 fighter plane. Direct ascent enables the MHV to reach its target in less than ten minutes, rather than the three-hour flight time prior to interception that is typical of the Soviet device (this slowness of attack on the part of the Soviet design is significant, since it gives the target satellite time to take avoiding action). The movable launch platform will give wider coverage to the US ASAT. The MHV will steer itself toward the target satellite using a heat-seeking sensor, and, if successful, will destroy the target by impact (there is no explosive charge).

Neither the Russian nor the American system is yet operational. Neither nation's system—even if operational—would threaten the high-orbit satellites (at 12,000 miles or more) currently used for missile early warning, for navigation, electronic eavesdropping, nuclear explosion detection, and communications. Nor would they threaten projected deep-space communication and nuclear-weapons-detection satellites located 60,000 miles away from the earth.

The US system could (by adding more stages to the MHV rocket) more readily be developed to the point at which it threatened satellites of this high-altitude type. It is particularly important to forestall this development which would effectively mark the end of the period when space could be regarded as a sanctuary for communication and observation. It was the seriousness of this development coupled with its relative remoteness in time (perhaps ten years hence) that led Prime Minister Trudeau of Canada, in November of 1983, to propose that negotiations begin now on an agreement to ban specifically *high-altitude* ASATs.

The ASAT story has been told in some detail here, since this is currently the space weapon that is closest to being operational.

We noted previously that the militarization of space has, on balance, made the world a less dangerous place by diminishing the hazards of misunderstanding, escalation, and accidental war in general. It is a corollary of this proposition that the deployment of ASATs will make the world more dangerous. Weapons that disable satellites dislocate the central nervous system of the military machine. They favor the attacker, who can prepare for battle before the C^3I blackout occurs. They force the defender to act in haste. Both of these tendencies are destabilizing, and deplorable.

Ballistic missile defense

A second target for space-based weapons systems, of still greater strategic significance than satellites, is an opposing ICBM force. In view of the enormous technical problems inherent in the design of an effective ballistic missile defense, it was thought until recently that discussion of such devices would follow a leisurely and cautious course. Both the technical difficulties and the destabilizing consequences of a competition in BMD (or antiballistic missiles, as they were previously known) have been appreciated since the 1960s. Following extensive national and then international debate, such devices were banned in the ABM Treaty of 1972. However, the debate has now been reopened, in the context of modern space-based technology, largely as a result of President Reagan's "Star Wars" address of March 23, 1983, to which reference was made in the introduction to this chapter.

In response to Mr. Reagan's call for a technological crusade against the ICBM to render "nuclear weapons impotent and obsolete," a commission was founded to examine the feasibility of shielding the United States from attack. The commission, chaired by James Fletcher, former senior administrator of NASA, presented its report to the President in mid October of 1983. According to *Aviation Week* (October 17, 1983) the report stated that "With vigorous technology development programs, the potential for ballistic missile defense can be demonstrated by the early 1990s." The cost of such a demonstration was estimated to be in the region of $25 billion. The cost of deployment of the initial phase by the year 2000 would be in the region of $100 billion.

Since the ICBM is most vulnerable in its boost phase, it must be intercepted at a range of perhaps 1,200 miles with minimal delay. This dictates the use of directed-energy weapons. Directed-energy weapons (DEW) comprise either particle beams (charged or neutral particles) or photon beams. The latter are light beams coming from lasers operating anywhere in the spectrum from infrared to x rays. Since none of these technologies appears viable as a weapons system at the present time, it is difficult to say which is the front runner.

Most research and development work has been directed toward the development of efficient, compact, high-energy lasers in the infrared or visible region, and their associated optics. Recently there has been speculation that laser development for DEW might shift toward x-ray lasers, in view of the efficient absorption of x rays by the target. This property is, however, dearly bought. In order to counter a massive ICBM attack involving 1,000 or more missiles, the x-ray lasers would be required to fire several times per second over a period totalling ten or twenty minutes.

This would require a "machine gun" actuated by nuclear explosions. In view of the extreme vulnerability of orbiting space platforms, and also in view of the fact that one would need so many orbiting platforms in order that a platform would always be within sight of the opponent's missile launching sites, current thinking is that the DEWs would be lofted into space when satellites in high-altitude orbits gave the first warning of a missile firing. This BMD launch would have to be almost instantaneous, precluding elaborate checks of the reality and magnitude of the enemy attack. It would also appear vital, under the circumstances, to keep substantial BMD forces in reserve to counter further waves of attack.

The cost of employing DEWs in space is so high that these weapons systems are not generally regarded as competitive in the ASAT context, where simpler alternatives exist. The context in which DEWs are discussed is that of antiballistic missile defense. Nonetheless, the development of DEWs will be intertwined with the development of ASATs. The testing of DEWs is likely to be against satellite targets. Moreover the fact that DEWs are being developed will stimulate the development of sophisticated ASAT devices in an attempt to frustrate the operation of the BMD components once they are launched into space.

A race to deploy and perfect BMD would be (or would appear to be) a race to deprive the opponent of his ICBM forces. Where the stakes are this high, the quest for a solution to technical problems may be pressed forward in the face of formidable obstacles. The obstacles are indeed formidable, since it will be difficult to deliver (dependably) sufficient energy to numerous small, distant, fast-moving targets, and relatively easy for the attacker to complicate the task of defense.

When confronted with some of the technological problems of the undertaking, proponents of BMD reply that technology has triumphed in problems no less difficult in the past—such as the landing of a man on the moon. The analogy is misleading. It would be more realistic if one were to suppose that inhabitants of the moon possessed of similar technological skills were to devote themselves, over the same period of time, to thwarting the undertaking. The Apollo moon mission, always a high-risk undertaking, would then have been suicidal in its riskiness.

The level of funding for research into space-based BMD has until now remained modest. This is evidence of residual good sense on the part of the two major protagonists, since an arms race in BMD systems will raise fears that will heighten the danger of conflict.

This was recognized in the ABM debate of the 1960s. It is still true today. In the 1960s the ABM systems being proposed were designed for "point defense" of certain military or civilian targets. In the future the lure of such systems will be the possibility of an early defense that nullifies the opponent's attack force. We have stressed the elusiveness of the goal, and we have noted the appalling dangers attendant upon the attempts to achieve it.

Electromagnetic pulse

The electromagnetic pulse (EMP) effect became evident in July 1962 when the US detonated a 1·4 megaton hydrogen bomb at an altitude of 240 miles over the Pacific ocean. About 800 miles away in Hawaii street lights went out, burglar alarms rang and circuit breakers opened in power lines. The diagnosis was that gamma rays had encountered air in the upper atmosphere and ejected Compton electrons. These were accelerated by the earth's magnetic field, and consequently emitted an EMP which, at ground level, exceed 10,000 volts per meter. A single nuclear explosion of this magnitude and altitude in a central location over the US could cause nationwide chaos. In a world committed to the arming of space, this could provide an incentive for placing nuclear weapons in outer space.

The incentive is at present lessened by the fact that the Partial Test Ban Treaty ensures that the EMP weapon is poorly understood, and the Outer Space Treaty bans its emplacement in orbit, or its "stationing" in space. (International law may, however, permit a nuclear weapon to be sent into space by direct ascent, since ICBMs also pass through space and are not banned. Legality would, however, cease to be a prime consideration if nuclear war broke out, since arms control would have failed in its central purpose.)

EMP will also emanate outward into space, and is regarded as a sufficient threat to satellite communication that some (classified) US communications links—such as the Minimum Essential Emergency Communications Network—are likely to include EMP-hardened satellites, now or in the future. (Obviously, a satellite cannot be hardened against a determined nuclear attack.)

EMP is included here as an indication of the complications that can enter and are already entering the strategic picture in space, when space is viewed as a battlefield.

Space treaties

Treaties do two things. They give expression to the fact that in some area the signatories see mutual advantage in regulating their activities. Once in place they take on a limited life of their own, acting as a brake on activities not explicitly contemplated when the agreement was signed. One could add a third benefit, which is that treaties provide a point of departure for further treaties. Much as security based upon weapons provides a basis for planning additional, "modernized" weapons, so also security based on agreements to restrict the competition in weapons can assist in the framing of further agreements.

We should take note, therefore, and even permit ourselves the luxury of some satisfaction, that there exist currently nine agreements which to varying degrees restrict competition in space weapons. If development of ASATs and (particularly) of BMD directed-energy weapons goes forward it will require that treaties be abrogated in favor of the new weapons systems. If instead we forgo these new adventures, we can help signal the fact by strengthening treaties so as to block unambiguously the further development of space weapons.

It will be evident from the list that follows that the nine agreements differ greatly in scope and effectiveness.

(i) The 1963 Limited Test Ban Treaty

This multilateral treaty, often referred to as the Partial Test Ban, binds the parties "not to carry out any nuclear test explosion, or any other nuclear explosion" in the atmosphere or in outer space (or in any environment that could cause the spread of radioactive debris beyond the borders of the state conducting the explosion). Over 100 nations are parties to this treaty.

This treaty did not render the first US ASAT illegal, since it was never tested with its nuclear warhead. However, it made that system still less attractive, since it could not be tested.

(ii) The 1967 Outer Space Treaty

This treaty goes beyond the partial test ban in forbidding the *stationing* in outer space of nuclear weapons, or any other weapons of mass destruction. In addition the treaty bans all military activities on the moon or other celestial bodies.

Neither the 1963 nor the 1967 treaty puts a major obstacle in the way of contemporary space weapons since (with the exception of the x-ray laser) these do not require nuclear explosives. In spirit the Outer Space Treaty militates against deployment of weapons in space, since it was drafted "Recognizing the common interest of all mankind in the progress of the exploration and use of outer space for peaceful purposes . . ." so that outer space would be "the province of all mankind." Such broad generalities have, however, limited value in curbing an arms race in space.

(iii) The International Telecommunications Convention

Over a period of years this expanding body of regulations has attempted to minimize radio-frequency interference with satellite systems. Since such interference could be embodied in ASAT devices, its prior restriction is advantageous. Moreover, it gives evidence of an internationally recognized need to protect satellite links on a global basis.

(iv) The 1971 "Hot Line" Modernization Agreement

This was an update of the 1963 "Hot Line" Agreement. In the updated treaty the US and USSR agreed to cooperate in maintaining two satellite-communications systems, so as to increase the reliability of their direct communications in times of emergency.

(v) The 1971 Agreement to Reduce the Risk of Nuclear War

This agreement, designed to provide safeguards against war through accidental or unauthorized use of nuclear weapons, hinges on the inviolability of ballistic missile early-warning systems—without, however, explicitly guaranteeing that inviolability. "The Parties undertake to notify each other immediately . . . in the event of signs of interference with these systems or with related communications facilities . . ." (Article 3). The treaty serves, at the very least, to acknowledge and to legitimize the mutual dependence of the signatories (US and USSR) on the unimpeded functioning of certain satellite systems.

(vi) The 1972 ABM Treaty

This treaty places impediments in the way of the acquisition of a major category of space weapon: antiballistic missile (ABM) weapons, which we would today term ballistic missile defenses, BMD.

Article V, Item 1, reads, in full: "Each Party undertakes not to develop, test or deploy ABM systems or components which are sea-based, air-based, space-based, or mobile land-based." This would appear to be sufficiently unambiguous. When, therefore, Mr. Reagan committed the US to research into viable space-based ABM systems capable of "nullifying the nuclear threat," he was limiting activity to weapons *research*, since in the same speech he explicitly reaffirmed the US intention of abiding by the 1972 ABM Treaty. Nonetheless, the encouragement of such activities clearly threatens the treaty and provides pressing grounds for wishing to re-examine and strengthen it.

(vii) The 1972 Interim Agreement on Strategic Arms (SALT I)
In common with the ABM treaty and the SALT II treaty, this treaty provides for verification of compliance by "national technical means." It then goes on to bind each party not to interfere with these means of verification. The Soviet Union has not until now explicitly stated that reconnaissance satellites constitute "national technical means." It would be very useful to make this explicit—at long last. Meanwhile this treaty, in the understanding of both parties, represents a landmark in that it precludes not only the shielding of objects subject to treaty from satellite inspection, but also ASAT activity directed against satellites engaged in treaty verification.

(viii) The 1975 Convention on Registration of Objects Launched into Outer Space
According to Article 4, "States launching objects into space should notify the Secretary General of the United Nations of the general function of the space object." Up to the present, statements of function have been so general as to be of little value in providing the reassurance that is needed if an arms race is to be avoided. Even a modest strengthening of this agreement would be a significant step.

(ix) The 1979 Moon Treaty
The treaty outlaws the stationing of weapons of any kind, the testing of weapons of any kind, and the establishment of military bases or fortifications or military maneuvers on the moon or other celestial body (other than the earth). In this restricted domain weapons of *all kinds*—and not just weapons of mass destruction—are outlawed.

This is not a complete list of the conventions governing the use of space. It omits, for example, the Space Liability Convention, and also the Agreement on the Rescue of Astronauts, the Return of Astronauts, and the Return of Space Objects.

It is evident that there exists, for the present, a degree of civilization in space. It is, however, a tenuous fabric, which would be shredded by actions now being contemplated.

Avoiding an arms race in space
In view of the fact that directed-energy BMD systems lie in the future, and ASAT weapons have not yet been developed to the point where they threaten existing satellite systems, it is not too late for an agreement

which would foreclose on an expensive and highly hazardous arms race in space.

There have already been promising discussions on an ASAT ban—the bilateral US–USSR negotiations held in 1978 and 1979. During this period the Soviet Union halted its tests of ASAT weapons. The talks were adjourned following a final meeting in Vienna in June of 1979. At this date Chairman Brezhnev and President Carter signed the SALT II treaty. With SALT II ratification as the most urgent topic on the arms control agenda, considerations of halting a very actual arms race took precedence over measures to halt a potential arms race in space.

A prime condition for arms control is a shared perception that the parties have more to gain from agreeing now, than from continuing their competition in an attempt to achieve military advantage. Given the potential for destruction that already exists on earth, and the disaster that will ensue if through our folly we lose control over these arsenals, it should be evident that space, which houses the most vital control centers, is better left inviolate. When one adds to this the virtual certainty that neither (or none) of the contending parties can achieve an enduring strategic advantage in space, the argument for a prohibition of BMD in space would seem to be as convincing as the argument that led to the successful 1972 ABM Treaty. The move to protect satellites from ASAT activity represents no more than a broadened application of the (already broad) prohibition on interference with "national technical means" embodied in SALT I and II.

A second requirement for successful arms control is a political one: there must be a sufficient desire for a gesture of "conciliation." This condition is met intermittently as we sway between demonstrations of our resolve to defend what we value and acknowledgements of our shared peril.

The Soviet Union has expressed interest in renewed discussions on the prohibition of ASAT activity on several occasions. President Reagan's speech of March 23, 1983, committed the US to abide by the 1972 ABM Treaty, though in spirit his program ran counter to that treaty. Certainly Mr. Reagan's call for a major move to arm space will serve to heighten consciousness of the alternatives and will help force a fundamental re-examination of priorities.

As regards formal proposals for bans on weapons in space, the most recent are the Soviet "draft treaty on the prohibition of the stationing of weapons of any kind in outer space" submitted to the UN in August of 1981, and a further text submitted to the same body in August of

1983. The more recent draft was somewhat more general, prohibiting "the use of force in outer space and from outer space with regard to earth."

These treaties are offered for negotiation. Their precise wording is of less importance than their intent. The stated intention (text of August 1983) is "to prevent an arms race in outer space and thereby reduce the danger of nuclear war threatening humanity . . ." The terms are sufficiently broad to prohibit space-based BMD (banning "any space weapon designed to hit targets on earth, in the air and outer space") and ASATs of any kind (binding the parties "not to destroy, nor damage, nor disturb the normal functioning or modify the trajectory of the flight of space objects of other States"). Verification is to be by "national technical means," each signatory pledging itself not to interfere with the national technical means of the others. Questions regarding compliance (as is the case of existing arms control agreements) should be dealt with promptly by a Standing Consultative Committee, to which the signatories appoint representatives.

There has, at the time of writing, been no official response on the part of the United States government to these proposals. One can readily guess why this may be. In the short run outer space offers opportunities for strategic advantage. The failure to seize these opportunities may mean that costly efforts must be made to protect targets on earth that, prior to the existence of satellite reconnaissance, were secure: the heightened threat to ships at sea from satellite-guided, air-launched cruise missiles is the most prominent example at present. But no fleeting gain in security, no temporary saving in cost, can compare with the long-term loss of security and the vast expenditures stemming from an arms race in space.

So long as there is a lack of interest in a ban on ASAT activity in the US, the technical obstacles to such a ban will be regarded as insurmountable. It is, for example, being asked how one can distinguish any sort of space rendezvous from the testing of an ASAT. The question is a valid one. The answer will be found when there is a desire to find it. It lies in the establishment of agreed "rules of the road" of the type that have made it possible to ascertain in a sufficient fraction of cases whether an automobile is being used for transport or as a weapon.

Fortunately, outer space is very open to inspection. The residue of doubt that may remain will become less important as military doctrine is seen to be free of reliance on satellite destruction. What uncertainty still remains can, moreover, be countered by the incorporation of sufficient redundancy in satellite systems. The cost of this will be less than that of ASAT deployment—followed, inevitably, by anti-ASAT defenses.

The real cost, however, will be paid in another currency, namely the heightened war psychosis in a world in which restraint has once again been overridden and the area of conflict once again extended.

Fostering peaceful and peace-keeping uses of space

It will be evident from an inspection of the agreements listed earlier that the safeguarding of space for peaceful purposes tends to impose barriers to the concurrent arming of space. The greater the commitment to exploiting space for peaceful purposes (including such dual purposes as communication and observation) the greater will be the reluctance to forfeit the security which objects and individuals in space presently enjoy.

The costs of major projects in space are sufficiently high that cooperative activities make financial sense. Politically such activities also make sense, if space is to escape becoming a battlefield. The precedents already exist: the Soviet Union has launched a satellite for India and has included French and Indian cosmonauts in space missions; the United States has made NASA Landsat satellite data widely available, and has launched satellites for Britain, Canada and other NATO countries. The European Space Agency is a going concern, with several joint ventures in the areas of meteorological, communications and earth resources satellites, as well as an organizational structure that provides for the sharing of costs and benefits.

What are needed, however, are conspicuous joint programs involving the US and the USSR in some of the many global tasks that can be accomplished from space. One must look hard for initiatives of this kind in the chill international climate that prevails. One such initiative which deserved wider notice was the offer made by the United States at UNISPACE 82 (the Second United Nations Conference on the Exploration and Peaceful Uses of Outer Space, held in Vienna in August 1982) to embark on, and contribute largely to, a cooperative international study from space of the prospects for "Global Habitability." The study would be aimed at the year 2000 and beyond, and would concern itself with the changing global environment and its implications for the habitability of our planet.

A cooperative project with more profound political implications which could engage the interest of nations currently establishing themselves as independent users of space is the International Satellite Monitoring Organisation (ISMO) or corresponding Agency of the UN (ISMA), discussed for some years past by Pugwash and at the United Nations. The proposal was first placed before the UN by the then President of France, Giscard d'Estaing, in 1978 at the First Special Session of the General Assembly devoted to disarmament. The General Assembly by an overwhelming majority instituted a study of the technical, legal and financial implications of establishing an ISMA, which was to be conducted by a group of governmental experts. The group, drawn *inter alia* from France, Italy, Sweden, India, Romania, Yugoslavia, Austria, Argentina and Egypt, reported at length in August of 1981 (UN document A/AC.206/14). It commended the scheme, and could find no insurmountable technical, legal or financial obstacles. In the immediate future, cost will be the major impediment. Nonetheless, even in the most complete and expensive phase an ISMA would cost the international community each year well under 1 percent of their total annual expenditure on armaments.

An ISMA would probably center on a group of industrially advanced nations (such as those presently involved in the European Space Agency, but with wider political and geographic representation) who, in cooperation, could work toward achieving the earth reconnaissance capability that is currently the monopoly of the superpowers. The very large superpower investment in space reconnaissance in recent decades is evidence of the conviction that there are major gains to national security from such activities. Now that the technology is becoming more accessible, other nations will wish to move in this same direction, for military, political and commercial reasons.

The ISMA concept is intended to provide an organizational framework for these seemingly inevitable developments—a framework that maximizes the contribution of secondary powers' space-based intelligence to the preservation of peace, rather than to the achievement of narrow national goals. The ISMA would stress such functions as the verification of arms control agreements, particularly those which have clear relevance to the security interests of secondary powers (e.g., non-proliferation of nuclear weapons, nuclear-free zones, or regional disengagement). At a somewhat later date the ISMA could involve itself in the technically more demanding activities of crisis monitoring—such as the provision of early warning of hostile preparations—and also the support of UN peace-keeping activities.

The performance of these functions requires the solution not only of technical (reconnaissance) problems, but also of difficult political problems: how much information should be released, in what form, and to whom? These problems will not disappear simply because we choose to postpone addressing them. It would seem preferable that they be addressed today in a far-sighted fashion than taken up a decade from now in a mood of rancor and panic.

The reaction of the superpowers to the proposal for an ISMA has been, to put it mildly, unenthusiastic. They are well aware of the tremendous power of space-based reconnaissance, in both political and military contexts. They have come to trust each other, to a considerable extent, to use this power responsibly. This is a gratifying development. They would be wise, however, to come to terms with the fact that the superpower monopoly of international surveillance by satellite is a technological accident which cannot be sustained. Other nations, fortunately, were willing for a while to acquiesce in the existence of a small club of nuclear powers. The argument for non-proliferation of the instruments of Armageddon was strong. The argument for non-proliferation is going to be a great deal less persuasive where the technology being proliferated provides sovereign nations with a view of the world.

Conclusion

The temptation for the US to exploit its technological ascendancy in order to seize the "high ground" of space, and thereby achieve a decisive military advantage, will be great. The ill-advised Soviet initiative in developing the first tested (albeit extremely limited) antisatellite weapon has provided a ready rationale for a US move to arm space.

This, therefore, is the time to remind Western strategists that a similar fantasy of a secure future through unmatched weapons capability has beckoned repeatedly in the past—with A-bombs, H-bombs, ICBMs and MIRVs. In every case innovation has been followed rapidly by imitation, and the security of monopoly has given way to the familiar fears engendered by an arms race.

In the case of antisatellite weapons this arms race will involve weapons that deafen, blind and disorient military forces—forces possessed of power beyond anything that history has known. In the case of ballistic missile defenses the race will be to disarm the opponent by "rendering [his] nuclear weapons impotent and obsolete." Both of these new avenues for arms racing will arouse fears of the most far-reaching kind—so far-reaching that their contemplation should give us pause. Military capability already depends, and in future is destined to depend, so profoundly on the ability to utilize space for communication, navigation and observation that the argument for maintaining a sanctuary in space should commend itself to a wide constituency.

Nonetheless if we are to succeed in forestalling an arms race in space it will not be purely on the grounds of a military rationale—not, at any rate, a conventional military rationale. It will require thinking which acknowledges that the power of contemporary weapons places a new burden of responsibility on military planners and their civilian masters.

Intellectually such a notion is, by now, a commonplace. Salvation cannot, however, be achieved through the intellect alone; the world awaits an outward and visible sign of conversion to the view that our weapons now threaten to destroy us. A willingness to forgo the lure of outer space as a final arena for global conflict would indeed provide such a sign. Having regard to the appalling dangers of such an arms race, the rejection of space as a battlefield would appear to be not only a possible way of signalling the new perception, but a vital way.

PART II *Deterrence and the real enemy*

6 THE DILEMMAS AND DELUSIONS OF DETERRENCE *Michael MccGwire*

Professor Michael MccGwire is a Senior Fellow in Foreign Policy Studies at the Brookings Institution in Washington, DC, and is currently completing a study of Soviet military objectives. From 1971 to 1979 he was Professor of Maritime and Strategic Studies at Dalhousie University in Canada. Before that he was an officer in the Royal Navy (1942–67), during which time he served as an attaché in Moscow, as a NATO war planner, and as head of the Soviet naval section of Defence Intelligence. He has written extensively on naval matters and has edited and contributed to three books on Soviet naval developments.

In May 1983, the Catholic bishops of America issued their Pastoral Letter "The Challenge of Peace," and the debate surrounding the preparation of that statement helped legitimize a point of view that had been dismissed too casually by the political–military establishments in the West. The letter's central challenge was to the role of nuclear deterrence as the keystone of Western defense policy, and it provided moral authority to the long-standing pragmatic argument that present policies were likely to precipitate the very calamity they were intended to avert.

Perhaps the most significant aspect of the bishops' statement was that it was made in 1983, and not in 1973, 1963 or 1953. Yet the operational dilemmas presented by nuclear weapons and deterrence have been with us now for thirty years or more; so has the ethical dilemma of threatening a greater evil than the one we seek to avert. So why the recent surge in concern? We can be fairly certain that it is not the result of some new moral revelation, and it seems more likely that it reflects a widespread perception that nuclear war is becoming a distinct possibility. And it is this perception that has broken the postwar consensus on the nature of the threat and how best to handle our relations with the Soviet Union.

This collapse of consensus pits the political–military establishments of the Western Alliance against a sizable part of their bodies politic, which now includes a growing number of influential people with extensive experience in senior government and military high command. Except for certain fringe groups, both sides of the argument are equally serious in their concern to avoid war. But they start with very different assumptions about the possibility of nuclear war, and so talk past each other.

The political–military establishments and their supporters argue that nuclear war could only come about as the result of Soviet aggression, therefore the overriding priority is a defense posture which will deter such aggression. The concerned body politic argues that overemphasis on defense and the steady build-up of nuclear weapons makes war more likely, either because of accident or miscalculation or because larger weapon inventories lead to increased tension and tougher political posturing. However, many of these same people favor strengthening NATO's conventional capability.

The political–military establishments argue that investment in defense is not only a sound form of insurance, but it is the only kind where the larger the premium, the less likely the calamity being insured against. The concerned body politic counters with the analogy of the man who is obsessed with the danger of a meteor strike, and steadily increases the thickness of his roof until the house collapses with his family inside.

In many ways it is a dialogue of the deaf. Those who are engaged in the pragmatic policy process of incremental decision-making and implementation are inevitably encased in a perceptual tunnel, where the theoretical analyses determining direction and depth have to be accepted as valid, and assumptions (to the extent they are even recognized) are taken as given. It is just not possible to keep rushing to the surface to check the initial survey, or to see what lies ahead. But what is disturbing about the present situation is that the criticisms of thinking people who did not spend their lives encased in this perceptual tunnel have now been joined by the voices of a significant number of those who did. Coming to the surface on retirement, these senior officers and ex-officials decided to check the survey for themselves, with alarming conclusions of danger ahead.

What made these public servants turn against policies that they had seemed to support in the 1960s and 1970s? More particularly, what happened to deterrence theory, the panacea of the 1950s, and to arms control, the panacea of the 1960s? These concepts were developed by men of great intelligence and goodwill, and provided the basis of Western policy during three decades. Were they inherently flawed, or were their intentions distorted in the application? If we are to escape from our present predicament, we need some understanding of the path we took to get there.

In discussing the evolution of nuclear deterrence and arms control, we must recognize that there was no one theory, doctrine or policy of nuclear deterrence, but a whole series of them which differed between countries and between government departments within countries. Furthermore, there have always been differences between what was said publicly by governments, what was said privately within government, and what was actually done. Nevertheless, there was a central dogma concerning the requirements for deterrence, although much of that dogma was developed as a means of curbing the growth of the US nuclear inventory, rather than to handle the Soviet threat. And there have always been key officials and others who were acutely aware of the inconsistencies and contradictions of the evolving dogma and associated policies, but accepted them as the unavoidable costs of achieving other benefits such as public support and the cohesion of the NATO Alliance.

The purpose of this exposition, therefore, is not to prove others wrong, and we need to keep in mind the circumstances of the early 1950s, when memories of Axis aggression were still raw and grossly exaggerated assessments of Soviet military strength and the Communist drive for world domination were widely accepted as true. Rather, the aim is to describe the evolution of the central dogma, and to identify its inconsistencies and contradictions so that we can assess whether the benefits the theory claims to bring do in fact outweigh the growing costs.

The concept of nuclear deterrence had its roots in the early 1950s, when it was assumed that the Soviets had a great urge to occupy Western Europe, and could only be restrained by the threat of unacceptable punishment. Theoretical interest focused on ways of ensuring that this threat would always be credible, the two elements of the problem being the capability to inflict the punishment and the will to do so. The capability component of credibility required that the means of punishment (originally bombers and later missiles) had to be able to penetrate Soviet defenses, and also be protected against a surprise preventive attack by Soviet forces.

There was nothing very novel about the former requirement, which was just another twist of the offense/defense, action/reaction cycle. But the requirement that the means of punishment be totally secure was new. It gave full rein to a new form of worst-case analysis based on future technical possibilities, as imaginative theorists sought to discover possible chinks in the armor of assured response which a determined opponent might exploit with a bolt-from-the-blue attack at some future date.

The threat perception of Soviet territorial aggression that could only be deterred by nuclear punishment persisted, but meanwhile a new threat emerged which was a byproduct of the Soviet capability to strike directly at the United States. This was the threat of nuclear war itself, brought about by the pressure to preempt. The advantages of getting in the first blow were so great that a prudent leader might decide that he had to launch a nuclear strike even if he only had a suspicion that the other side was contemplating war. This introduced a new concern for the stability of the strategic balance, and the simple requirement to *deter* Soviet aggression came to be qualified by the somewhat contradictory need to *reassure** Russia that the U S would not initiate nuclear war.

There were two main requirements for achieving this strategic stability: a positive one, in the shape of one's own assured second strike capability, which would ensure that it would avail the opponent nothing to strike first, because there would still be enough weapons left to inflict unacceptable punishment; and a negative one, in the form of self-denying ordinances against systems or deployments (offensive or defensive) that might deprive the *opponent* of such a second strike capability. Hence the concept of Mutual Assured Destruction, which was adopted as "doctrine" by the arms control community, although it never became official U S policy.

The assured response requirement for "stability" was similar to one of the two requirements for ensuring "credibility," but much more demanding. For credibility purposes, an assured response implied only that the relevant weapons be protected against surprise by systems designed to launch on warning or under attack. For stability purposes, even launch under attack is not an option, and a sufficient number of the relevant weapons have to be able to survive a deliberate surprise assault in order to be able to inflict the "unacceptable punishment" required for deterrence.

The arms control establishment had its intellectual origins in the recognition of the need for mutual reassurance, but they also accepted the tenets of deterrence theory. As time went by, the divergence between "deterrers" and "reassurers" steadily increased, as the former sought to embellish U S credibility and the latter pursued their search for mutual stability. But the two concepts remained inseparably joined by their

* This is my own term and is not part of the established strategic lexicon.

common requirement for an "assured response," and this symbiotic relationship was reinforced as the deterrers willingly embraced the reassurers' much more demanding definition of what assured response implied. Meanwhile, they both took the Soviet threat as given and, to the extent that there was disagreement between them, it was about what was most likely to prompt a Soviet attack: expansionist urge or reciprocal fear.

The period 1963–75 can be seen as the heyday of arms control, but the underlying theory was never really put to the test. Many of the agreements essentially codified superpower disinterest, as with the sea bed treaty; or budgetary and technological constraints, as with the ABM treaty. The Nuclear Test Ban of 1963 did remove the plague of nuclear contamination of the atmosphere, but it did not effectively restrict nuclear weapons development. The ABM Treaty did seriously constrict deployments, and even some development work that would otherwise probably have occurred. But apart from this, arms control considerations did not cause America to forgo any planned weapons development or deployment during the period, whereas SALT I did cause changes in Soviet programs.

Meanwhile the US military was preoccupied with Vietnam, which diverted its attention from the self-denying ordinances of reassurance theory, such as renouncing greater accuracies or eschewing counterforce systems. Not that reassurance theory inhibited the authorization of the Los Angeles (688) class of nuclear submarine or the development of MIRV, both of which were theoretically destabilizing. Nor did arms control considerations prevent the development of the cruise missile, a process which started in the early seventies.

The most important reasons for the apparent success of arms control were that throughout the 1960s the US continued to enjoy overwhelming strategic superiority, and that by the end of that decade détente had become the catchword for Soviet–American relations. But there is an inherent tension between the concepts of "deterrence" and "reassurance" and between the requirements for "credibility" and "stability." And when push comes to shove, the claims of credibility (which allow the exploitation of new technological opportunities) win out over those of stability (which require their renunciation), and this is what we saw happen as detente began to sour and the Soviets drew abreast of the US strategic capability.

In 1974, when Schlesinger re-emphasized the capability for selected counterforce strikes, it was pointed out that greater targeting flexibility improved credibility by increasing the US capability for proportional response. In 1980, PD-59 (the policy document prepared by the Carter Administration) reasserted this requirement and averred that credibility demanded a US capability to match the Soviet option of being able to wage nuclear war, should it prove inescapable. As soon as detente began to crumble, so did the prospects for arms control. The arms control establishment lost its political constituency, who charged that high theory had resulted in higher force levels and a new arms race. And the arms controllers' own arguments were used by their detractors first to justify continuing arms build-ups, and then to discredit the very concept of arms control.

Given the inherent flaws in the underlying theory, these developments were virtually inevitable. The basic problem was that arms control grew out of deterrence and was not a countervailing theory. It accepted the deterrers' definition of credibility, which assumed a malevolent enemy who would seize any chance, however adverse the odds, to neutralize US deterrent forces by surprise attack. All analyses were US worst case, and never factored in how the Soviets would assess the balance of costs and benefits. Meanwhile, the "reassurance" element of the theory implied that the already high level of capability needed to ensure "credibility" had to be increased yet further to meet the more demanding requirements of "stability" in the shape of an assured second strike capability.

In other words, arms control failed the very first time it was put to the test. But we need to be clear as to the nature of the test. It was *not* whether arms control negotiations were effective in controlling the growth of nuclear inventories. It was whether the results of the negotiations were acceptable to the American political system, in terms of its broader conception of national security. This failure was important in two respects. It tells us something about US security perceptions, a point to which we will return later. And since arms control is an outgrowth of deterrence theory, we would expect the latter to have comparable problems. So, indeed, it does, mainly in Europe, but to some extent within the USA as well.

The problem is one of credibility. Not, I would stress, the credibility of the West's deterrent posture in the Soviet mind. The problem is the credibility of nuclear deterrence *theory* in our *own* minds. In particular, the credibility of the contradictory assumptions that it is the possession of nuclear weapons and the demonstrated ability to use them that matters, but that they will never be used. I suggest that the spreading dissatisfaction with current defense policy reflects the growing suspicion that there are logical inconsistences in existing doctrines and assessments, these fallacies being more often sensed than made explicit.

There was a particular quality to "strategic studies" as it emerged in the 1950s, a sub-discipline that focused almost entirely on the problems of nuclear weapons, deterrence doctrine and, in due course, theories of limited nuclear war. The field was notable for being dominated by theorists from outside disciplines like mathematics, physics and economics, while the military and diplomatic historians who had traditionally covered international relations and strategy were squeezed out, Bernard Brodie and Michael Howard being among the few exceptions. Also involved was a new type of political scientist who focused mainly on American (or perhaps Alliance) defense policy, how it was made and how it could be shaped. To all these people, the Soviet "threat" was a given. The Soviet Union was assumed to be bent on territorial expansion and the concept of monolithic Communist conspiracy was unquestioned. The focus was entirely on Soviet military capabilities and no attention was paid to Soviet interests, to Soviet intentions, or to recent Soviet history.

There were no Sovietologists of standing directly involved in this strategic debate during the 1950s, despite the fact that all theories of limited nuclear war and various types of escalation were based on assumptions about how the Soviets would react in given circumstances. The governing concept of "deterrence" assumed that an almost irresistible urge to seize Europe existed, and of course it was this assumption that provided the basis for all theorizing. There developed a breed of self-styled "tough-minded" strategic analysts, who liked to think through problems abstractly, albeit in a political vacuum. The opponent was not "Soviet man," not even "political man," but an abstraction called "strategic man," who thought in game-theoretical terms. This theorizing provided the intellectual justification for a form of worst-case analysis which was impressive in its quantitative trappings but had only limited relevance to the world as it actually was.

One must not exaggerate the role of academic theories in the practical shaping of policy. But we cannot deny that deterrence theory, and its outgrowth reassurance theory, have largely defined the terms of the strategic debate. Nor can we ignore that, particularly in America, a significant proportion of government officials and consultants in the fields of defense and foreign policy have been drawn from those who have taught or studied these theories at university. It was these theories that defined the agenda and provided the vocabulary of strategic discourse throughout NATO. It was the concepts of reassurance theory that suggested that the solution to our problems lay in arms control, and diverted attention away from the central question of the Soviet–American relationship.

The omission of Soviet man from our strategic theorizing led us to talk in terms of deterring some*one* (the Soviet Union) rather than some *action* (the occupation of Europe). We chose to focus solely on the Soviets' potential capability for military expansion and never addressed the question of whether Soviet interests would be served by such expansion. Yet the underlying purpose of deterrence is to preserve a negative balance in one's opponent's calculation of costs and benefits, and the interests served by the action being deterred are every bit as important as the capability to take that action.

In other words, we did not address the question of "temptation" which is the other half of the deterrence equation. Temptation comprises both the opportunity for successful action *and* the urge to take such action. We chose, instead, to focus exclusively on the factor of opportunity (expressed as relative capabilities) and to neglect the urge factor. It was this kind of reasoning that led to the conclusions embodied in PD-59, and it was these conclusions (when published in 1980) that generated such serious doubts about the theoretical underpinnings of Western defense policy.

At the core of PD-59 was the conclusion that since Soviet doctrine recognized the need to be able to fight a nuclear war, and since the Soviets now had some such capability, the US required a comparable capability in order to maintain the credibility of deterrence across the full range of Soviet options. But did that conclusion necessarily follow? Implicit in the assertion that we needed to increase our deterrent capability was the assumption that Soviet "temptation" had increased. But what were the facts? In the middle 1950s, it was widely perceived that the Soviets had a great urge to military expansion, and we also considered that our defenses in the NATO area were grossly inadequate. In other words, both the urge and the opportunity for action were great, hence Soviet temptation was seen to be high. However, by the middle-to-late 1970s, Western assessments across a broad spectrum of opinion were generally agreed that the Soviet urge to expand their frontiers into Europe was small. And although NATO's theater defenses were still seen as less than fully adequate, relatively capabilities were considerably improved over the 1950s, and the costs they could impose on any Soviet aggression were many times greater.

In other words, the urge for action was small and the opportunity for action had been significantly reduced, hence Soviet temptation was much less than in the 1950s. Yet in the 1980s we concluded that effective deterrence required our existing capability to devastate the Soviet Union with nuclear weapons, *plus* the capability to wage protracted nuclear war. In other words, we acknowledge that enemy temptation has fallen, but nevertheless assert that our deterrent capability must rise. This seems illogical.

A second problem with PD-59 was the argument that since the Soviets believe that to deter Western aggression they must have the capability to absorb an attack and go on and win the subsequent war, *ipso facto* the West needs a similar capability if they are to deter Soviet aggression. In the first place, we should be aware that this misrepresents the Soviet position. The primary Soviet concern is not to deter a premeditated Western attack (a capability they reckoned they had achieved by the latter 1960s, if not much earlier) but with the danger of world war, a danger they see as being inherent in the present international system. They place a very high priority on avoiding such a war (which would be precipitated by the West), but should it prove inescapable, then their objective is to prevail, or at least not to lose. It is this very demanding requirement, and not deterrence, which determines Soviet force posture and operational concepts.

But even if we allow that the characterization in PD-59 is correct, this implies a necessary symmetry between what the Soviets see as being necessary for their own defense, and what is needed to deter possible Soviet aggression, a symmetry that does not exist. It is not hard to think up analogies that demonstrate this fallacy, but perhaps the simplest is to invert the equation. In the mid 1950s, deterring the Soviets from moving into Western Europe was thought to need a capability to destroy about thirty Soviet cities. At this same period the US was talking of "roll-back" and the West would have welcomed the opportunity to "liberate" Eastern Europe if it could have been done at a low enough cost. In other words, the threat we posed to the Soviets was symmetrical to the threat we perceived from them. If we follow the logic of PD-59, this would argue that the West could only have been deterred from trying to liberate Eastern Europe by a Soviet capability to destroy thirty US cities. But in practice, what "cost" was sufficient to deter the West from any such endeavor? Not thirty cities; not even one city, but the probability of conventional conflict with Russia. Indeed, the only times the West has been willing to risk war was when we were on the defensive, as over Berlin in 1948 and 1961.

PD-59 is the product of deterrence theory and demonstrates the perverse results that flow from that abstract style of reasoning. And even now that the Soviets have been brought into the equation, belatedly, only those aspects that support our existing assumptions have been incorporated. Thus we stress the Soviet *operational* emphasis on being able to fight a war if it is forced on them (something that has also been explicit in Western programs, deployments and exercises), but ignore the fact that for twenty years after World War II this was the sole means of deterrence available to the Soviets. We ignore it, because we see no reason for them to have a deterrent. We refuse to contemplate (let alone acknowledge) that Western actions and statements in the 1945–56 period provided ample grounds for concluding that the Marxist prognosis of history was correct, and that the capitalist West was actively planning the downfall of the Soviet state by military and other means.*

We ignore Soviet political–military doctrine about the restricted circumstances that could justify the initiation of conflict (none of which can be met by a premeditated attack), and focus instead on Soviet operational doctrine about how such a war might be fought. We ignore the fact that Marxist–Leninist theory points to war as the seedbed of revolution (a theory that can apply equally to the Soviet Union), and its painful proof in Byelorussia and the Ukraine in World War II. We ignore the cost–benefit equation. We consider Soviet military capabilities without taking into account their requirements, and ignore their history and geostrategic location. And of course we ignore the whole matter of temptation, including the central question of whether Soviet interests would be served by occupying Western Europe even if this could be accomplished without a fight.

This leads directly to a third flaw in current doctrine, the "colonel's fallacy" in threat assessment, so called because the estimate is being

* This assertion is based on a study now in progress entitled *The Threat to Russia: An Estimate of Soviet Military Requirements*. But quite apart from Western rhetoric and specific hostile initiatives, we tend to forget that by 1948, Italy, Japan and West Germany had been brought into the Western fold, and our policies had switched from extracting reparations to rehabilitating their industrial capability. These were not only ex-enemies, but the three founding members of the Anti-Comintern Pact, the three countries whose expansionist ambitions had led to the carnage of World War II, and two of them were long-standing enemies of Russia.

carried out at the wrong level of analysis. At the military–tactical or "colonel" level of threat analysis, the focus is rightly on enemy capabilities, with hostile intentions being taken as given. Worst-case analysis of this kind is wholly appropriate for contingency planning, where the focus has to be on our own vulnerabilities. It is not, however, appropriate at the politico–strategic or "ministerial" level of analysis, which is what concerns us here. At this level we are primarily interested in identifying the most likely course of enemy action, and our concern is as much with our opponent's needs and vulnerabilities as it is about our own.

At the politico–strategic level there are four elements to threat analysis, two of them interlinked. The enemy's "capabilities" are measured against his "requirements" in order to assess whether there is a shortfall or surplus. And the other two elements are "interests" and "intentions." It is hard to determine exactly what is *in* a country's interests (even one's own), but it is much easier to see what is *against* a country's interests. The concept of negative interests is important in avoiding the pitfall of assuming that what is bad for us must be good for our opponents, and a moment's reflection shows that Russia and the West share a broad span of negative interests. Meanwhile, the question of enemy intentions must be addressed directly. If we claim that they should be ignored because they could change overnight, we are in fact imputing worst-case intentions without doing any analysis. Nor are they so volatile. At the national level, intentions are remarkably consistent, and only change radically as the result of fundamental political shifts of a kind that have not taken place in the Soviet Union since the revolution of 1917.

Obviously, this kind of threat assessment is complex, not least the problem of estimating the Soviet Union's minimum essential requirements,* which can range from long-term aspirations that no one expects to fulfill to short-term imperatives in operational contingencies. But we now have a sixty-five years' record of Soviet actions and pronouncements, plus the historical constraints of geography and social inertia. This, combined with our analysis of Soviet interests and the balance of capabilities and requirements, can provide a reasonable basis for estimat-

* See my "Soviet military requirements," in *Soviet Military–Economic Relations: Proceedings of a Workshop on July 7–8 1982*, sponsored by the Joint Economic Committee of Congress and the Congressional Research Service (Government Printing Office, 1983). A longer study is now in progress. The short answer is that the Soviets have enough to cause us justifiable concern, but they do not have "more than they need."

ing their most likely courses of action, particularly in regard to fundamental matters involving war and peace.

This is all rather obvious and we may well ask how it is that we do not carry out our threat assessments along these lines. One reason is the widespread perception that the simple certainties of worst-case analysis demonstrate tough-mindedness. Another reason may be found in the existence of NATO and its large planning staffs. Without in any way detracting from the very real advantages the existence of NATO has brought the West in political as well as military terms, we must recognize that its very success fosters a certain mind set throughout the Alliance. NATO planners are not required to ask "Is there a threat?" but "Where is the threat?", and if it is not on the central front, then it must be on the flanks, and if not there or the Indian Ocean, then what about Finlandization? They are not constrained by the problems which divert national staffs, such as personnel shortages, financial and political demands, but can concentrate full time on planning to fight a war. They are "the keepers of the threat" (I was one myself), and among their more important tasks is to prevent member governments from backsliding.

Most NATO countries use the Standing Group's annual threat assessment as the basis for their force planning. The national defense elites work and talk together across frontiers, and there is a remarkable homogeneity of views, with American ones predominating. But only a tiny proportion of these people work on intelligence problems, and even fewer on the broader questions of Soviet intentions, and intelligence assessments that run counter to established perceptions are not well received by the operational commanders. Although, in strictly military terms, the unity of views achieved by NATO may be counted as one of its greatest successes, unity tends to conformity and thence to tunnel vision.

It is this tendency to conformity and tunnel vision that contributes to the basic disagreement over which is the primary threat: the danger of Soviet aggression, occupation or intimidation; or the danger of nuclear war.

Threat (in this sense) is a function of the scale of the calamity involved (C) and the level of probability (P) that such a calamity will occur. Most of Europe and much of Asia has been occupied at various times in the last fifty years and, unpleasant as the experience may be, most people consider the calamity of nuclear war to be many times greater than that of occupation. Allowing for the sake of argument that the composite value of the two threats is equal, but that the calamity of nuclear war is 100 times greater, this means that the *probability* of occupation must be 100 times greater than that of nuclear war:

$$C_o \times 100\, P_o = 100\, C_n \times P_n$$

Intuition tells us this is unlikely to be true. But the logical consequences of this simple equation are even less plausible. It is generally agreed across a wide spectrum of informed opinion that the Soviet temptation to occupy Western Europe (outside the circumstances of an inescapable general war) is low. If, then, the composite threat of nuclear war is equal to or less than the composite threat of occupation, the equation implies that the probability of nuclear war is at least 100 times *less*. In other words, the threat of nuclear war can be dismissed as negligible. And it is this implication that runs counter to commonsense. The possibility of nuclear war is inherent in the military posture and weapons inventories of the two sides, and this inherent possibility could change to a significant probability in times of tension.

Here lies the root of the disagreement. The concerned body politic accepts this commonsense, whereas the majority of those who argue on the side of the political–military establishment share the silent assumption (often unconsciously) that the probability of nuclear war can be ignored.

But this is not just a disagreement about probabilities. I would argue that this silent assumption is a necessary psychological buffer for most of those who have to think through and apply the practical implications of current defense doctrine.

Disagreement over the *nature* of the threat within the NATO context is only one strand of the debate. Closely intertwined is a disagreement about how best to handle Russia in the world at large, and this disagreement tends to be expressed in terms of the *level* of the threat presented to Western interests by the Soviet Union.

The argument is primarily between the USA and the rest of the Western Alliance, with the European military establishments tending to side with the Americans, and a significant number of US specialists on the Soviet Union siding with the Europeans. The divergence of opinion has emerged over the last decade, and to understand the process we must go back to the first half of the 1960s.

By about 1964, in the wake of the Cuban missile crisis and the signing of the non-proliferation treaty, the West had finally stabilized its perception of the threat from the Soviet Union as a "limited adversary relationship," to use Marshall Shulman's term. Undoubtedly the two blocs were adversaries, but not unlimited ones. The differences, although fundamental, and the conflict of interests, although serious, were not so great as to justify going to war. This was, in fact, very close to the Soviet definition of "peaceful coexistence," which was the policy pronounced by Khrushchev in 1956. In other words, by about 1964 *both* sides had roughly the same understanding of the situation, with both recognizing the inherent constraints on the other's aggressive actions. I suggest that it was because the mutual perceptions of threat were balanced in this way that we were able to move toward some sort of understanding with the Soviets in the sixties, and the process continued until it resulted in the series of treaties of which SALT I and the ABM Treaty are the best known.

Our perception of the Soviet threat which allowed this negotiating process to proceed was about as "realistic" as we are likely to achieve. Imagine a graph of our perception of threat over time, with the threat level on the vertical axis and time along the bottom. We can give this "realistic" level of threat in 1964 a value of 100 on the vertical axis, and between about 1964 through 1969 perceptions of threat remained at about 100 in Western Europe and in America. However, as the SALT negotiating process proceeded, it was found to be politically expedient in America to downgrade the level of threat below this "realistic" level, partly because the attempt to extricate America from the Vietnam War required that the earlier line of a "worldwide Communist conspiracy" be reversed, and partly because it was necessary to oversell the future benefits of détente in order to gain political acceptance for the SALT process. Let us say that the threat was gradually written down to about 80 in America. In Europe the perception of threat remained roughly steady at about 100.

This downward trend in US threat perception was halted and reversed by the 1973 Arab–Israeli war, when, amongst other things, American strategic forces were put on nuclear alert. This halt was welcomed by a range of interests waiting in the wings, people who had never accepted the 100 level of threat as valid, let alone the fall in the public perception of threat below that level. Different groups had different reasons for non-acceptance. There were those who genuinely believed that Russia was not only an adversary, but a highly skilled, malevolent master chess player on the world political scene, who had succeeded in duping the West. Others conceived of Moscow as Antichrist. Some believed that without a very high level of "perceived threat," the American voter would not commit enough resources to defense. There were the people who had never accepted the legitimacy of the Soviet Union and felt that it should be suppressed or destroyed. And then there were those who believed that America's interests (and those of the free world) required it to have superiority over Russia, and were not prepared to accept parity in strategic weapons or in any other respect.

In other words, a wide range of opinions, attitudes and interests were joined to agree that the Soviet threat was, or should be portrayed as, much more than the 100 level. So, from 1973 onward, the value of the American perception of threat steadily rose. The process was accelerated by Angola and was institutionalized by about 1976 with the establishment of various foundations devoted to publicizing this particular perception of the Soviet Union.

The value of American public threat perceptions probably crossed the 100 line in 1975–6 and kept on rising steadily thereafter, fueled by events such as the Soviet involvement in Ethiopia, the Iranian hostage crisis and of course Afghanistan, which was portrayed as an unfavorable tilt in the East–West balance, rather than as a major setback for Soviet foreign policy. With a similar illogic, the developing Polish situation caused the level of perceived threat to rise even further, even though its net effect was to significantly reduce the Soviet Union's military capability. The steady rise in US threat perceptions probably peaked in the spring of 1982, by which time it was clear that the rhetoric about "windows of vulnerability" was not matched by urgent action to change the existing posture, and various groups, including the nuclear freeze movement, had begun to challenge the premises underlying the Administration's policies.

There are understandable reasons for the different perceptions of Russia on the two sides of the Atlantic, not least the differing views of NATO. To Europeans, NATO ties America to the continent and allows them to live with Russia in reasonable security and comfort, and at not too great expense. To Americans, NATO contributes to the balance of power and is an instrument in the global competition with the Soviet Union. But this is only part of the picture, and more important was the broad swing in American public opinion that allowed sectional interests to redefine the Soviet threat during the second half of the 1970s.

To grossly oversimplify, there were a range of factors that actually caused the swing, but the Soviets provided a suitable scapegoat. The most general was America's loss of the unique global predominance which it had enjoyed during the first twenty-five years after World War II. It no longer enjoyed such a large relative advantage in economic and military strength, and rather than seeing this as an inevitable process brought about in large part by America's own enlightened policies, it was seen as a failure. Then there was the deep resentment about the Vietnam War—not that of the antiwar activists, but of the silent and bemused majority who remembered the good intentions with which they had embarked on the enterprise, and yet it all went sour, partly because of the failure of the home front, partly because of the carping of allies, but mainly because America just hadn't been tough enough.

And then came the oil shocks. America no longer enjoyed energy independence and was being held up to ransom by barely developed Arab countries without being able to do anything about it. Next, the Japanese encroached on markets which the US had seen as their natural preserve because of their technological pre-eminence. Then there was all that nonsense of the New International Economic Order, the demands for the transfer of technology, and the endless Law of the Sea negotiations. And as a final straw, there came the Iranian hostage crisis, which America could do little about, but chose to wallow in. Add to all this the downturn in the economy and the insecurity of rising unemployment. The general feeling of American resentment was epitomized by the upsurge of the motto "Don't tread on me."

Meanwhile, Russia had been shaping up nicely as a scapegoat. In the mid 1970s, as provided for by treaty, the Soviet Union began to deploy a new generation of ICBMs to replace the rather inadequate ones it possessed at the time of SALT I. It continued to build up its forces against the Chinese threat, and to restructure its forces facing NATO (including an increased conventional capability) to meet the challenge of flexible response. Overseas, the Angolan civil war erupted in 1975, and here the main difference between the external powers was that the Soviet Union had been supporting its faction since 1962, while the West only moved in after the coup in 1973. The Soviets chose not to leave the field to these newcomers, and when Cuba responded to a South African invading force by flying in troops, the Soviets came to their assistance with logistic support.

Next came Ethiopia, where the revolutionary regime turned away from the USA and toward the Soviets for aid. When Somalia, the original Soviet client in the area, chose to invade Ethiopia, Russia condemned the aggression and threw its weight behind the defenders, even though this meant giving up base rights at Berbera, with no certainty of replacement. The final straw for America was the occupation of Afghanistan, a country that had lain within the general orbit of the Soviet Union for many years, but which had tilted sharply toward them after the 1978 coup, drawing in a significant Soviet presence. But the new Afghan regime progressively lost control and the Soviets chose what they saw as the lesser evil of moving in to sort out the situation, an action which they recognize as demonstrating a serious failure of policy.

American opinion chose to characterize these involvements as an "unchecked advance" and the betrayal of détente. It defined the Soviet invasion of Afghanistan as a radical shift toward more aggressive behavior, rather than recognizing it as the same policy that prompted the invasion of Hungary and Czechoslovakia, reflecting Soviet concern about control of their national security zone. American opinion failed to take account of the loss of Chile in 1973, the eviction of 20,000 Soviet troops from Egypt in 1972, or the loss of Egyptian naval bases in 1975 and Somalian ones in 1978, and of reconnaissance staging in Guinea. Nor did it consider how Kissinger had skillfully exploited détente to squeeze the Soviets out of Middle East negotiations, and to persuade Egypt to switch to the U S side.

American opinion ignored the progressive loss of Soviet influence in Iraq and the way that Moscow was reviled almost as much as Washington by the Iranian revolutionaries. It discounted the political impact of Afghanistan on the Moslem world and the loss of Soviet influence implied by the emergence of Eurocommunism. And it did not take into account the growing normalization of Sino-American relations during this period and, equally important, the rapprochement between China and Japan, developments which were matched by a steady deterioration in Sino-Soviet relations. In other words, the Soviets won some but lost more. They gained access to Vietnamese bases after China invaded the country, but on balance they had not done particularly well in other areas.

From the overly alarmist presentation of the Soviet expansionist threat which was being painted at the end of the Carter Administration, the Reagan Administration moved to open confrontation, with talk of economic warfare and horizontal escalation. And it was this that brought the disagreement about how to handle Russia to a head. But although this disagreement tended to be expressed as an argument about the level of the threat presented to Western interests by the Soviet Union, in reality it was a disagreement about objectives.

It is a truism that if you choose the wrong objective, you get the wrong result; selection of the aim is a critical element of all policy planning. A basic rule is to locate the main objective as high up the causal tree as practical, stopping short of a level that is so general as to be empty of policy guidance. One is dealing with a hierarchy of objectives and missions, and the lower down the tree, the more restrictive each individual objective and the narrower its supporting missions.

As a result of the swing in threat perceptions, the US made a sharp downward adjustment of its policy objectives toward Russia in the direction of "containment." The Europeans, meanwhile, continued with the wider objective implicit in a limited adversary relationship, one that might be formulated as "persuading the Soviets to cooperate with the existing international system." Persuasion involves sticks as well as carrots, so "containment" continued as a mission in support of this objective. But the broader European objective allows a whole range of other less negative missions, such as "increase trade interdependence," "foster inter-institutional links," and even "raise the Soviet standard of living," and it does not rule out cooperation in the settlement of disputes such as the Iran–Iraq war, or in dealing with other world problems.

But the fact that the American objective is pitched at a lower causal level than the European one has broader implications than the loss of flexibility that comes from denying oneself certain policy options. Inevitably, these options will be replaced by additional missions designed to further containment, and containment becomes an end in itself, rather than a means to an end. The concept will therefore be interpreted very literally and the definition of what is covered by the term will be very extensive.

In other words, European and American policy are now directed toward different and increasingly divergent objectives, which implies that the policies will be increasingly in conflict. More important in terms of this discussion is that a policy whose primary objective is containment will inevitably be confrontational, and probably bellicose.

I suspect that the widespread concern about nuclear weapons reflects an intuitive awareness among the concerned body politic of the flaws in current policy that I have sketched out above: the silent assumption that nuclear war cannot happen; the logical inconsistency of increasing the scale of deterrence, although the level of temptation has dropped; the fallacy of ignoring Soviet interests and intentions when deciding Western defense policy; and the choice of the wrong objective in our dealings with Russia.

They are also expressing a judgment on current policy that appears to be founded on three basic convictions. One, that the physical threat of assault by the Soviet Union is negligible, given a manageable level of conventional defenses. Two, that the notion that the Soviet Union could somehow use its superior military power to "Finlandize" NATO Europe is nonsense. And three, that the best way to reduce the threat of nuclear war is through arms control and not through arms racing.

They consider that East–West tension creates conditions which make nuclear war more rather than less likely, and it is widely believed that the steady rise in tension over the last four or five years can be traced to ill-advised policies which are seen as completely counterproductive. Many would argue that it is better to risk the remote possibility of Soviet occupation by adopting a different defense posture and style of foreign policy than to face the virtual certainty of nuclear incineration if we carry on along this road.*

In these respects, the "commonsense of the people" would seem to have it right. But this same "commonsense" tolerates a rather mindless anti-Sovietism that serves to justify the very policies that commonsense rejects. This anti-Sovietism certainly exists in Britain, where it has its roots in the prewar fear of Bolshevism and the enmity between Communism and Socialism, and reaches back to pre-revolutionary imperial competition. And it is especially strong in the USA, where it is a long-standing phenomenon. This visceral dislike is not confined to decision-making elites, but pervades the American people at large. One can understand the reasons for it: ethnic and religious sympathies for oppressed groups; conflicting political, socio-economic and religious values; and, of course, superpower rivalry. But this pervasive anti-Sovietism results in a style of foreign policy which concentrates on "punishing" the Soviet Union, rather than managing relations and trying to shape its future action.

It is the attitude of the magistrate toward the criminal, rather than that of an entrepreneur toward a tough competitor. It is a dangerous attitude, because it fosters a bellicose and moralistic style which can only raise East–West tensions. This alarms the concerned body politic because, as tension rises, so does the likelihood of intentions being misread and of one side embarking on that dangerous chain of demonstrating resolve to the other.

* It is unfortunate that this sensitive assessment of probabilities, costs and benefits has been compressed into the slogan "Better red than dead."

It is also dangerous because it leads to the comforting assumption that if it were not for the Soviets, everything in the world would be fine. The Catholic bishops were reluctant to tackle this question of our share of responsibility for the perilous state of East–West relations, over the long and the short term, a reluctance, I suspect, that stemmed from their condemnation of the very real evils of the Soviet political system. But reading across from domestic to foreign policy distorts the analysis. It encourages the comforting notion that because in the West our domestic policies are (on the whole) acceptable, therefore our foreign policies are unexceptionable. And since there are aspects of Soviet domestic policy that are appalling, their foreign policy must therefore be the same. But, as Roy Medvedev has pointed out (and he is ruthless in his criticism of Soviet domestic oppression), Russia is far more sensitive to the dangers and horrors of nuclear war than America appears to be, and behaves much more cautiously in this area of foreign policy.

Indeed, among the criticisms that could be levelled at the bishops' Pastoral Letter was that while it focused on the morality of threatening nuclear war to deter aggression, it never addressed the more pressing problem of how to avoid stumbling into such a war by way of more lowly sins. One batch comes under the heading self-indulgence: indulging our latent anti-Sovietism by using the Russian scapegoat to explain all the problems of the world, including the erosion of Anglo-Saxon predominance; indulging the temptation to pursue every technological military option, without heed to the dangerous long-term implications; indulging our hankering for total security, a chimera in any circumstance, but a deadly one when pursued with nuclear weapons; and perhaps the ultimate self-indulgence of treating arms control as an aspect of Alliance and domestic politics.

But there are also the sins that stem from hubris, which fosters the urge for moralistic crusades, never mind the dangers of heightened international tension, and encourages the self-righteous attitude that whatever we choose to do is justified by the ends. And this leads to the major ethical question, which the bishops did address but we prefer to ignore, namely, what right do *we* have to place the rest of humanity at risk of extinction as we pursue our sectional interests and respond to our emotional and fluctuating perceptions of the Soviet threat.

This brings us back full circle to the bishops' challenge to the role of nuclear deterrence as the keystone of Western defense, a moral challenge that can be supported on strictly pragmatic grounds. For a start, we should reject the claim that "nuclear deterrence has kept the peace for thirty-five years." This assertion can be neither proved or disproved, but it can be dissected, although only briefly here.

The claim rests on two assumptions: one, that the Soviets have a strong urge to territorial expansion; the other, that any lesser threat would have been unable to deter them from invading Western Europe. The first assumption is not supported by historical analysis of Soviet behavior during the last sixty years, nor by their dogma concerning the inevitable collapse of capitalism from its own internal contradictions. As for the second assumption, are we to believe that the Soviets could not have been deterred by some lesser cost, such as the threat of conventional war? And what of other costs, such as the standing of the Soviet Union in the competition for world influence, or the progress of the world Communist movement? And what of other objectives directed at building the power, and the prosperity, of the Soviet Union itself?

But the real problem is that deterrence has become a buzz-word, a political pacifier that is used to explain all kinds of policy, to justify any weapons program or operational deployment, and to stifle all dissenting argument. Deterrence is not, however, an all-purpose concept. It is only applicable to a specific set of circumstances, and in other circumstances a policy based on deterrence theory is liable to produce results that are quite different, and could even be the opposite of those intended. Even where the appropriate circumstances do exist, nuclear deterrence is not cost-free, since the theory (and its outgrowth, reassurance theory) provide an incentive for arms racing that leads to heightened antagonism and (if war nevertheless comes) would lead to even greater devastation. It is, therefore, no accident that deterrence provides the nexus to the main strands of the debate: the argument about the nature of the primary threat; and the argument about how to deal with the Soviet Union.

A key assumption of deterrence is that one's opponent is strongly tempted to take an action one seeks to deter. But if the existence of such temptation is in doubt, are we just over-insuring, or can misplaced deterrence actually endanger us? What if Soviet policy is *not* driven by an urge to military conquest, but is primarily concerned to avoid the calamity of world war? And what if, in the event that such a war is inescapable, the seizure of Western Europe is seen as a strategic imperative, an essential course of action if the socialist system is to survive in a postwar world? In other words, what if we have misread the motivations underlying the Soviet military posture, and they are not tempted by Europe in normal circumstances, but believe they would have to occupy it in the event of war? In these circumstances, what does a policy of deterrence do for Western security?

If we believe that the probability of war is in some way related to the level of international tension, then we can only conclude that misplaced deterrence makes war (and hence the occupation of Europe) more, rather than less, likely. Deterrence, as formulated in the West, is not just a matter of hedging against temptation by locking the door and barring the windows. It is an active policy that asserts hostile intent and threatens wholesale punishment. It relies on the capability to inflict such punishment and on the will to do so. But the prerequisite for this (in democracies, at least) is a high perception of threat. A policy of deterrence therefore tends to encourage exaggerated rhetoric, to favor intransigence (as a demonstration of resolve), to discourage serious negotiation and the search for compromise, and to value a bellicose posture. Moreover, while creating the conditions that make war more likely, it fosters the delusion that war itself is not the danger. And in that delusion lies the *real* danger of deterrence.

Deterrence has given us an excuse for sloppy thinking, but we can no longer accommodate two conflicting perceptions of threat. We cannot acknowledge that the greatest calamity is war and at the same time hedge against the "worst case" of unprovoked aggression in Europe, because the appropriate response to one set of perceptions is wholly inappropriate to the other. It is essential to establish the nature of Soviet motivation by analysis, and not by mere assertion.

If we are faced by an "intentions threat," then arms control negotiations are worse than useless, as Hitler taught us in the 1930s. But if the threat we face is a "capabilities" one, then arms control and arms reductions become practical propositions. Although the *structure* of Soviet forces is determined by their military requirements in the event of world war, the *scale* of resources they allocate to meeting these requirements is determined by two sets of perceptions. One is the likelihood of such a war. The other is the extent to which US military power is a primary instrument of superpower competition. Both these perceptions are strongly influenced by the style and the content of Western policies.

If we are, indeed, faced with a "capabilities threat" we must renounce the attractive simplicities of a deterrence theory, with its built-in assumptions of threatening intent. Instead, we must revert to the well-tried process of assessing the costs and benefits to our opponent of the various courses of action open to him, and then working out how best to influence the calculus in our favor. In other words, it is as important to dismantle the intellectual edifice we erected over the last thirty years as the structure of armaments we built up during the same period.

This suggests that the way out of our defense dilemma is not to be found in different military postures or force structures, although undoubtedly they will play a part. Clearly, we must also go to the root of our immediate problem: East–West relations in general and Soviet–American relations in particular. But I suspect that the breakdown in the consensus on foreign policy and defense reflects something much more fundamental, namely the accumulation of counter-instances of the kind that precedes a paradigm shift in the world of scientific theory,* and we may be coming up to an equivalent shift in our perceptions of national and international security. If this is the case, then it is not a sudden phenomenon, and the accumulation has been in progress for most of a hundred years. But the introduction of nuclear weapons and the development of nuclear deterrence theory has sharply accelerated the process, and the contradictions are now too blatant and too numerous to be ignored.

This assessment may be too sanguine, but one thing is certain. Should there be a possibility of moving from the "Ptolemaic" stage of international relations to some new "Copernican" stage whose paradigm has yet to be discerned, its actualization will depend on our capacity to identify and challenge the assumptions underlying our present policies and postures, and our ability to perceive the world in all its human diversity. Unless enough of us can escape the perceptual tunnel we are condemned to remain prisoners of the misanthropic paradigm described so acutely by Machiavelli, Carr and Morgenthau, with its built-in potential for global self-destruction.

* "Paradigm" is the term chosen by Thomas S. Kuhn in *The Structure of Scientific Revolutions* (1962) to describe the prevailing "model" of reality used by scientists in their work. The classic "paradigm shift" was from the Ptolemaic view of a universe centered on the earth to Copernicus' sun-centered model.

7 WORST-CASE ASSUMPTIONS: USES, ABUSES AND CONSEQUENCES

Raymond L. Garthoff

Professor Raymond L. Garthoff is a Senior Fellow in Foreign Policy Studies at the Brookings Institution, Washington, DC. He was a member of the Rand Corporation between 1953 and 1957. Subsequently he served as a senior analyst in the Office of National Estimates in the Central Intelligence Agency from 1957 to 1961. He was Special Assistant for Soviet Bloc Politico-Military Affairs in the Department of State (1961–8), Counsellor in the US Mission to NATO (1968–70), and Deputy Director of the Bureau of Politico-Military Affairs at State (1970–73). After serving as Senior Service Inspector until 1977, and then as Ambassador to Bulgaria, he retired at the end of 1979. Among his published studies are Soviet Military Doctrine, Soviet Strategy in the Nuclear Age, Soviet Military Policy, *and a forthcoming major study*, Détente and Confrontation: American–Soviet Relations from Nixon to Reagan.

Since World War II there has been a dangerous tendency on the part of military planners—and later politicians—to overstate the potential of the enemy. This tendency stems from something the military planners call the "worst-case assumption"—that is to say, the worst possible outcome of an engagement with the enemy. Yet the concept of "worst-case assumption" is a two-edged sword. It has its origin in the task of the tactical military planner, whose objective is to seek the most prudent way in which to counter a given hostile military force (usually called a "capability"). Little attention is given in this process to gauging the opponent's intentions; nor would it be appropriate for this purpose.

Of course, there are many other uncertainties in any "scenario" of a military conflict and its outcome. These are almost invariably resolved in favor of the opponent in order to avoid unwarranted optimism and to test the adequacy of one's own forces and plans against the worst contingencies. Where there is doubt—as there often is—it seems to be commonsense to play safe: to the extent that events prove subsequently that the threat was less than originally thought, there is a margin to one's own advantage. Maximum aggressiveness by the opponent is therefore assumed.

However, in the postwar years, as the Cold War set in, the worst-case assumption was drawn up from the important but clearly circumscribed context in which it had developed into the diplomatic and strategic sphere of international relations. The prominence of deterrence theory in the nuclear age was largely responsible for this, for it was in this way that a military strategy came to be elevated into a principle of global politics.

The worst-case assumption is extremely ill-suited to the demands of coherence and effective diplomacy; yet it has acquired a growing importance and is now promiscuously employed. In this chapter, I shall investigate and illustrate the proper and improper uses of this analytic device and shall point to the consequent dangers inherent in its abuse.

The logical, prudent basis for worst-case assumptions in operational analysis is reinforced, and often inextricably mixed, with more or less conscious calculation that the capability and "threat" of the putative enemy should be accented and dramatized in order to persuade political leaders, legislatures and the public of the need to maintain and build forces and capabilities to deter and counter that threat.

This context of worst-case assumption in strategic planning, in public discourse on the strategic balance and concerning the requirements for one's own military programs, also operates in the Soviet Union. Of course, there the importance of public opinion is much less; on the other hand, more attention is given to propaganda about the enemy threat for purposes of military indoctrination and morale-building.

Worst-case assumptions have, however, a tendency to infiltrate the thinking of their users and even their originators, and to affect assumptions, estimates, perceptions and beliefs where they should not. This adversely affects judgments of the intelligence community, the military planning community, the foreign policy community, the political leadership, and the public.

The most obvious, but not necessarily the most pernicious, adverse effect of worst-case estimating is that its political propaganda effect wears down through constant overuse—even when alarmist, it no longer alarms. It also contributes to the cyclical oscillation between hysteria and complacency in public threat assessments. These effects are much less in strategic planning.

Overestimated threats based on worst-case assumptions may stimulate not the desired support for measures to increase one's own capabilities, but conclusions that the task is hopeless. This has been one widespread effect of the many years of Western emphasis on the Soviet and Warsaw Pact threat to overrun Western Europe in a conventional war. It may soon have the effect also in current stress on Soviet theater nuclear capabilities.

In more limited cases as well, worst-case assumptions about opposing capability may lead military and political leaders to neglect options for countering military or military–political moves because they accept an inflated image of the adversary's capability. In the extreme, this could lead either to dangerous escalations or disadvantageous acceptance of defeats because of an inability to gauge a realistic range of other options.

A very important, and frequent, negative consequence of worst-case estimating of capabilities is its insidious infiltration (or, less often, conscious misuse) in estimates of the *intentions* of an adversary. This consideration relates not only to overall attitudes of the enemy (for example, to seek superiority, to seek a first-strike capability), but also to views about why the opponent is pursuing policies or taking actions (e.g., why deploy the SS-20—or the Pershing II?).

Highly important, although among the least appreciated dangers of worst-case estimating, is the impact on the adversary. Conceivably, this could persuade an enemy that he had capabilities which in fact he did not, and lead him to act on the basis of that assumption. Dire estimates could thus *undermine* deterrence and lead either to an unexpected attack, or, since the incorrect estimate was shared, it could lead to acceptance of an objectively avoidable reverse. Such cases would, however, be rare. The adversary himself would be wary of such estimates, especially when they did not accord with his own (frequently overstated) estimates of the other side's capabilities. More basically, neither side is inclined to take the risks or incur the broader costs of military action based on *any* capabilities estimate.

But there is, however, a more subtle form of impact on the opposing side. For reasons which require psychological analysis, although both sides are aware of the phenomenon of worst-case estimating, and to some extent practice it knowingly, both are also very unlikely to credit it to their opponents. Instead, inflated worst-case estimates by the other side are seen solely as propaganda devices, while one's own are in large part accepted. The effect of this differential treatment is that in many areas—political assessment, military planning and arms control negotiations, in particular—worst-case estimates held by the other side are seen not for what they are, but as cynically presented conscious distortions intended to have political effect. At its worst, gross overestimates of the military capabilities of the other side may be taken as evidence of hostile intentions.

The effects of worst-case estimating on arms control negotiations are little appreciated, and of relatively new significance. Overestimates of the adversaries' capabilities and underestimates of one's own are brought to bear in establishing both negotiating objectives and negotiating positions. Such estimates reinforce the tendency to demand concessions from the other side while avoiding them on one's own, and encourage inflexibility in negotiation. This further inflames a domestic political atmosphere which is already highly sensitive. Hence both the negotiators and the critics who are waiting to pounce upon them (for various reasons including some having nothing to do with the matters under negotiation) develop a stake in justifying their own overestimates for bargaining (and derived political and bureaucratic) reasons. An agreement is thus made difficult to achieve.

The broadest impact of the worst-case approach in political estimating is its ability to turn on its head even a benign or friendly development. For example, advocacy of détente is a sham and a snare; arms control initiatives are intended to lull; rejection of assertions of enemy superiority or offensive goals are disinformation; friendly approaches to allies are intended to split the alliance, etc. In some cases this may be a partly or even completely correct assessment, but in many it is partly or completely incorrect—yet a worst-case approach by definition makes *any* and all actions or courses of action by an adversary or putative adversary dangerous.

Finally, there is a danger that worst-case overestimates can be self-fulfilling prophecies. If one side's own actions are predicated on certain perceived or anticipated policies or actions of the other, what is intended as a deterrent or defensive *response* the other side may well see as an offensive *challenge*. Its own response is in turn seen by the first side as the anticipated hostile action by the other, and as confirmation of its own line of action. When this occurs on both sides, the disadvantage to both is compounded and a vicious spiral of hostile interaction is engendered and, as it proceeds, reinforced.

From this overview, it may be useful to look more closely at some elements of the problem of devising a proper defense posture and policy which may be affected by worst-case assumptions. These can be conveniently grouped into three categories: intelligence assessment, strategic/operational analysis, and political decision-making (which includes both diplomacy and other negotiation).

Intelligence

Intelligence on enemy capabilities, and on basic long-term intentions, tends to be heavily influenced by worst-case estimates. For a number of reasons, there is much less of a tendency to make worst-case estimates of short-run intentions. Without judging the reasons here, it seems likely that the main reason for the differential application in long- and short-term estimates is functional: the very act of positing an enemy and of considering the possibility of war is necessary to the military planning process, but the prediction of near-term hostilities is not only prone to be soon proven wrong but also would call for militarily (and politically) disruptive actions; and the military process requires stability and steadiness.

There are also particular problems raised in coalition assessment. A massive annual intelligence estimate of the Warsaw Pact threat has been prepared in NATO for many years. While nominally intended to provide a coordinated and agreed starting point for military planning, this estimate also serves as the basis for public statements. For both purposes, when discrepancies appear in the data or estimates provided by individual NATO members, the standard practice has been to resolve them conservatively, either by adopting or at least by including the highest (that is, most threatening) estimate of Soviet and other Warsaw Pact forces and capabilities. New intelligence information reducing estimates of Warsaw Pact forces and capabilities is usually very slow to be brought forward and even slower to be adopted in these estimates. (When such information is based on very sensitive sources, the country providing the information is also likely to be reluctant to divulge the basis for the lower estimates, reinforcing reluctance by others to accept a change.) The inherent bias is toward worst-case intelligence estimates of military capabilities.

In the United States and in NATO during the past thirty years (and in some respects undoubtedly for much longer and in many countries) there has been a proclivity in the military intelligence communities to proclaim a strong preference for estimating only capabilities, not intentions. However, in practice this means not a neutralization of the tendency to worst-case estimates of intentions, but its indirect enthronement. The United States does not of course estimate possible attacks by the French and British nuclear forces, despite undoubted "capabilities" for such attack, for the obvious reason of friendly intentions. On the other hand, with respect to the Soviet Union as well, the United States does not look only at capabilities—current intelligence warning reports correctly do *not* predict imminent Soviet attacks on the United States, although the "capability" is there. Most estimates concern future capabilities—and it is not possible to divorce intentions of some kinds from any exercise in prediction. The dictum "estimate capabilities, and not intentions" conceals a smuggled assumption. It really means "estimate capabilities to build up military forces *assuming implicitly an intention to maximize capabilities*;" usually it also assumes—and sometimes imputes—hostile intentions. There is also a tendency, even stronger in Alliance assessments, not to estimate the political morale and combat effectiveness of the forces of the opposing coalition—that is, to assume at full value the worst case: that all potentially opposing forces will be at maximum effectiveness. While there have been some exceptions in recent years, the usual tendency has been to equate unrealistically the military value of all Warsaw Pact forces, counting a Czech unit, for example, as equivalent to a Soviet one.

But American and NATO worst-case intelligence assessments do deal directly with Soviet intentions though interpretation of their capabilities. The most striking example is the frequent assertion that since the Soviet Union has built up both strategic nuclear forces and Warsaw Pact conventional forces in the European theater, and since we judge them to be in our opinion greater than those needed for deterrence or defense, their aims must therefore go beyond those objectives.

There are a number of serious problems with such assertions. In the first place, the West does not concede that the Soviet Union and the Warsaw Pact need *any* deterrent or defense, because we pose no threat. Beyond that, the United States and NATO have *never* estimated Soviet deterrence or defense requirements, or even what the *Soviet* military and political leaders might see as their force requirements for those missions. If NATO were to do so, it is highly unlikely that it would (or, given possible leaks or espionage predictions, that it *should*) posit a NATO or American first strike. Yet it should on a moment's reflection be evident that a conscientious Soviet military planner would be derelict in his duty if *he* did not assume such a Western attack. An analysis beginning from that premise would not necessarily find Soviet forces greater than needed for deterrence and defense.

Strategic analysis and military plans

There is no sharp dividing line between intelligence assessments and other assumptions used in strategic analysis. But use of worst-case intelligence and operational assumptions in military contingency planning is a more difficult matter to judge. It may have a useful role, but it should not be over-used. Excessive hedging to assure a favorable outcome may mean that "requirements" are set which are so demanding, or appear so out of keeping with the purpose of a contingent employment, that a given military planning option may be discarded when more realistic assumptions would have made it feasible.*

Worst-case assumptions in military planning also tend to generate or to support conservative (that is, inflated) requirements for one's own military forces. Thus quite apart from use of worst-case threat assessments to justify and mobilize public support for desired military programs, such estimates and other worst-case assumptions about the performance of one's own forces also affect the process of military analysis leading to the establishment of "requirements" for forces. When the other side, in turn, sees military programs geared to meeting those requirements, it is often prone to misread the purpose and to make its own worst-case judgments as to the significance of those programs. The use of worst-case assessments and assumptions thus tends to have a dynamic interactive effort contributing to arms races.

Worst-case assessments may also lead to misallocation of attention, efforts and resources. An exaggerated concern over nuclear threats may, for exampie, lead to responses at the expense of strengthening conventional forces, not only weakening conventional capabilities but also reducing options.

It should, of course, be recognized that in most cases military planning and related political–military assessments do *not* involve resort to worst-case planning with respect to the key question of current and operationally predictable prognoses of hostile attack. Worst-case assumptions do not dominate military or political expectations. But they do occupy an important place in both "balance of power" intelligence estimates and in strategic and operational military analysis. Because worst-case calculations do have a useful role to perform, they cannot simply be foresworn. But it is necessary to weigh carefully their proper application and to guard against inappropriate uses and pernicious effects.

* For example, when in October 1962 President Kennedy was seriously considering a "surgical strike" on Soviet intermediate-range missiles in Cuba with conventional bombs, the cautious US Air Force estimate was that 500 sorties would be required, with considerable collateral damage, and still without assurance that all missiles would be eliminated before they could be fired; that estimate killed the option—a response neither expected nor desired by its advocates.

Political decisions

Worst-case assumptions and judgments with respect to military capabilities may seriously affect a wide range of political and diplomatic decisions and actions. Exaggerated fears may lead to a resort to arms that could and should have been avoided, or it may lead to a decision against resorting to military action when that course would be appropriate. This is true of both military and political decisions in crises.

For example, in 1914 both Kaiser Wilhelm and Tsar Nikolai II wanted to order partial mobilizations, but were told that only full mobilization was possible. In 1936, the British and French overestimate of German capabilities led to acquiescence in the German military occupation of the Rhineland; only after the war was it learned that the German High Command had feared their reaction and obtained Hitler's reluctant advance agreement to draw back if Britain and France took a firm position. And in 1938, the British Cabinet concluded that it had no alternative to reluctant acceptance of the Munich Agreement in light of the British General Staff's appraisal of the military balance.[1]

In general, worst-case estimates thus lead to more conservative or even timid diplomacy. In negotiation, they tend to give the adversary more bargaining power and to lead to less advantageous outcomes. In some cases, on the other hand, they may lead to holding back from objectively advantageous agreements. Such effects are most pronounced in arms limitation negotiations. Since the other side would rarely share overestimates of its own forces, and if there is doubt would also hedge by overestimates of the first side's forces, the problems in reaching a mutually acceptable agreement are likely to be compounded by mutually excessive demands based on reciprocated conservative overestimates.

Finally, one important aspect of the impact of worst-case assumptions on political decisions is the need to take account of the perceptions of others—one's own public, the leadership (and perhaps the public) on the other side, and various third parties.

Publicly aired worst-case or other overestimates of the capabilities or intentions of the other side may make it difficult or impossible to gain public support, and thus seriously constrict policy options. One cannot readily differentiate by playing up the military power of the other side in order to gain support for arms programs, and then play it down again to justify balanced arms control agreements. More basically, it is difficult to argue that an adversary breaks arms control agreements and other treaties, lies and cheats, is out to do one in, and is the focus of evil in the world, and then carry out a policy of compromise accords and steps to improve relations.

A capsule case study: intermediate-range nuclear forces

the current case of the reciprocal build-ups of land-based intermediate-range nuclear systems in the European theater provides a useful example of a number of the points we have been discussing.

The Soviet decision in the early mid 1970s to deploy the SS-20 intermediate-range ballistic missile on a large scale was based on several considerations. Above all it was seen in Moscow as a much-needed modernization of a long-standing deployed capability, an overdue replacement of the aging SS-4 and SS-5 missiles (deployed since 1959 and 1961, respectively). Without reviewing the Soviet considerations further here,[2] suffice it to say that they were based on a perceived military requirement, grounded in turn on Soviet worst-case assumptions (including the need for substantial redundancy to allow for heavy attrition from a possible American first strike).

In the West, however, the SS-20 deployment was perceived as representing a "new threat," and one that ominously seemed to imply a political purpose of intimidation. The *military* capability of the Soviet theater missile force was increased by the modernization with SS-20s, and while this may have been somewhat overstated in military assessments it was a real consideration. But the evaluation of the Soviet *intention* in making the SS-20 deployment was a "worst-case" judgment, more pernicious for not being recognized as such. Accordingly, NATO decided after extensive deliberations to deploy a new land-based intermediate-range missile in Europe to assure "coupling" of the Alliance deterrent forces.*

The Soviet reaction, in turn, was to see the NATO decision to deploy 572 new missiles in Europe not as a Western response, even a misguided one, to a political challenge (since they did not see their own deployment as presenting such a challenge), but rather as American use of the pretext of the SS-20 deployment to gain NATO acceptance of the deployment of American missiles capable of striking key strategic targets deep in the

* See Raymond L. Garthoff, "The NATO decision on theater nuclear forces," *Political Science Quarterly*, Vol. 98, No. 2 (Summer 1983), pp. 197–214. The American leaders did not, in fact, see a need for new missile deployment in order to bolster deterrence or for other military purposes, but supported—and indeed took a lead in developing a NATO consensus on—the new deployment in order to be responsive to perceived allied concerns.

Soviet Union—indeed representing a new capability, not modernization of an existing one. Moreover, this new American deployment, following on the heels of the signing of the SALT II treaty—which still lay unratified—to them represented a deliberate circumvention of the limitations of that accord, which had provided parity in American and Soviet strategic forces capable of striking the territories of the USA and the USSR. This worst-case judgment was reinforced when the United States after long delays finally presented an arms-control proposal which called not for limiting or even neutralizing the enhanced capability provided by the SS-20 modernization, but for the complete elimination of the 600 Soviet medium- and intermediate-range missiles which had been part of the acknowledged military balance for twenty years as the price for non-deployment of the new American missiles.

It is not necessary for present purposes to carry this analysis further, but it illustrates the ability for worst-case estimates of the intentions of the two sides in military deployments to generate additional plausible worst-case evaluations of diplomatic and arms limitation proposals as well.

Conclusion

The implications of our findings on the dangers of conscious and unconscious misapplications of worst-case assumptions are broad. They extend to the entire range of defense planning, including especially the basic political and political–military foundation for military policy. They extend as well to public expressions of policy and of public propaganda intended to generate support for military programs. And they extend, too, into military planning and intelligence assessment where, because there is a use for worst-case assumptions, it becomes all the more necessary to be wary of possible misuse.

NATO and its members have not been sufficiently aware of this problem, and they have not avoided unfortunate consequences. The fact that the Soviet Union is afflicted by the same failure is no consolation or reason for not seeking to adjust our own thinking and action. Nor is the fact that excessive Soviet secrecy stimulates worst-case capability estimates. Thus, joint consideration of the mutually corrosive impact of the abuse of worst-case calculations would be an excellent candidate for a confidence-building dialogue. At present, the political will for such an endeavor is lacking, and indeed has receded compared with the situation a decade ago. But unilateral Western attention to the problem, and use of available means quietly to draw Soviet attention to it as well, is both possible and necessary.

The urgent reason which commends this course of action is that, without change, worst-case outcomes are the possible and fatal result of failing to recognize and to attend to the problem of misuse of worse-case thinking.

8 SOVIET POLICY AND THE ARMS RACE *David Holloway*

Dr. David Holloway is a Senior Lecturer in Politics at the University of Edinburgh. He has been a Visiting Professor to the Peace Studies Program at Cornell University, and is currently Senior Research Associate at the Center for International Security and Arms Control, Stanford University. His writings on Soviet matters include, most recently, The Soviet Union and the Arms Race.

When Leonid Brezhnev died in November 1982 he received only perfunctory praise at his funeral, and this was quickly superseded by an almost total oblivion. The Soviet press, which lavished praise on him during his lifetime, now mentions his name only rarely. There may be many reasons for this particular instance of the transience of earthly glory, but one is surely that Yuri Andropov had little reason to be grateful for the legacy that Brezhnev left him.

This judgment may seem surprising, for we are constantly being reminded about the massive build-up of military power that took place under Brezhnev. The Soviet Union attained strategic parity with the United States, built up its forces along the frontier with China, and extended the deployment of its navy to all the oceans of the world. But in spite of this impressive accumulation of military power, the Soviet Union has not been able to translate its increased might into commensurate political gains.

Brezhnev left Andropov armed forces that were more powerful than ever before, but he also passed on to him a foreign policy that had failed to achieve its most important goals. At home he bequeathed a corrupt and sluggish bureaucracy, and an economy whose rate of growth had been declining steadily. Andropov tried to tackle these problems. He had some success with his drive against corruption and indiscipline, but in foreign policy the legacy he passed on to Konstantin Chernenko in February 1984 was if anything worse than that which he had inherited fifteen months before.

This is an appropriate time to take stock of the problems the Soviet Union faces, and of the implications of these for the East–West competition in nuclear arms. This chapter will look at three main elements of Soviet policy: Soviet thinking about nuclear weapons and nuclear war; the relationship between military power and foreign policy; and the domestic politics of military power.

Nuclear weapons and military doctrine

Stalin decided to launch an all-out effort to develop the atomic bomb as soon as the United States had shown that such a weapon could be built, and had demonstrated its destructive power on Hiroshima and Nagasaki. He had already initiated a project early in 1943 to determine whether atomic energy could be used for military purposes, but this was small compared with the effort that he now undertook to eliminate the American nuclear monopoly. Stalin's decision to build the atomic bomb was automatic. It did not depend on the specific conjuncture of international relations in 1945. It sprang from the deeply rooted belief that the Soviet Union should be a great military and industrial power, and play a leading role in world politics. The first Soviet atom bomb test took place in August 1949, but it was not until the mid 1950s that the Soviet armed forces began to receive nuclear weapons in any number.

Stalin gave the highest priority to the development of Soviet nuclear weapons, but he permitted no serious discussion to take place about the implications of nuclear weapons for the conduct of war. Only after his death in 1953 did the military begin to reassess doctrine. In the late 1950s and early 1960s the General Staff and the military academies, working under the direction of the Party leadership, revised military doctrine to take account of the development of nuclear weapons and long-range missiles. When he outlined the new doctrine in January 1960, Khrushchev declared that a world war would be fought with nuclear-armed missiles, and would begin with missile strikes deep into the enemy's interior.[1]

The new doctrine stressed that the Soviet Union did not want war with the United States, and that such a war could be prevented. But a nuclear war might be "unleashed by the imperialists," and the Soviet Union should prepare to wage it, and to win it. Deterrence was not seen as something separate from the preparation for war: the best way to prevent war was to prepare for it. There is some evidence, though it is not conclusive, that Khrushchev believed that the requirements for fighting and winning a nuclear war did not need to be met, and that war could be prevented through the threat of nuclear retaliation. But the High Command seems to have had no doubts about the need to prepare for war, even though there were different schools of thought about the forces that would be required.

Khrushchev claimed in the same speech in January 1960 that the Soviet armed forces had already gone over to a considerable degree to nuclear-armed missiles, and that these would continue to be improved until they were banned. The United States, he said, would try to catch up in missile production, but the Soviet Union would hold onto its leading position until agreement was reached on disarmament. These boasts were premature, however, for the Kennedy Administration's strategic weapons programs soon left the Soviet Union far behind, and by the time of Khruschev's fall from power in October 1964, the United States had a lead of about four to one over the Soviet Union in strategic weapons.

The Soviet Union now felt impelled to expand its missile programs in response to the Kennedy Administration's policy. These programs, which began under Khrushchev and were perhaps augmented by his successors, reflected a deeply rooted determination not to accept a position of inferiority to the United States. The speed and scale of the Soviet build-up came as a surprise to many officials in Washington.[2] By the end of the 1960s the Soviet Union was approaching strategic parity with the United States.

The Soviet leaders now faced an important question of policy. Should they strive for significant superiority in strategic arms, the better to ensure victory in a nuclear war? Or should they accept that mutual deterrence—in the sense of mutual vulnerability to devastating retaliatory strikes—was the only possible relationship with the United States at present? This was not an issue of principle, for superiority would clearly be desirable, but a matter of practical policy, for the pursuit of superiority might prove extremely costly, and ultimately unsuccessful.

The issue was posed most sharply by antiballistic missile (ABM) systems. In the mid 1960s the Soviet Union had already begun to deploy such a system. Defense against ballistic missile attack fitted well into the Soviet conception of nuclear strategy, for it would lessen the damage caused to the Soviet Union by nuclear war. Moreover, it reflected a basic desire not to let Soviet security depend on the balance of terror. In 1964 Major General Talensky, one of the leading military theorists, wrote that "the creation of an effective antimissile system enables the state to make its defenses dependent chiefly on its own possibilities, and not only on mutual deterrence, that is, on the goodwill of the other side."[3] But soon afterward an intense debate broke out about the effectiveness of such systems and their consequences for the Soviet–American strategic balance.

By the late 1960s Soviet military writers acknowledged that ABM systems could disrupt the strategic balance, and that if the United States deployed an effective—or comparatively more effective—ABM system, the balance would tilt in the American favor. The American decision to build an ABM system is likely therefore to have played an important part in convincing the Soviet leaders of the desirability of a treaty to limit such systems. But this was hardly the only factor in the Soviet decision. The Soviet leaders were also aware that the deployment of ABM systems would stimulate the further development of offensive forces, since the other side would develop countermeasures designed to improve the penetration of its offensive missiles.[4]

The ABM Treaty of 1972 was based on the recognition that, for the time being at least, the Soviet Union and the United States would remain vulnerable to retaliatory strikes by the other, no matter which side struck first. This recognition has remained central to the Soviet conception of the Soviet–American strategic relationship. Marshal Ogarkov, the Chief of the General Staff, wrote in September 1983:

> "With the modern development and dispersion of nuclear arms in the world, the defending side will always retain such a quantity of nuclear means as will be capable of inflicting 'unacceptable damage,' as the former Defense Secretary of the USA R. McNamara characterized it in his time, on the aggressor in a retaliatory strike . . . In contemporary conditions only suicides can wager on a first nuclear strike."[5]

The SALT Agreements of 1972 signified that the Soviet Union had now caught up with the United States in strategic nuclear power. The Soviet leaders apparently believed that nuclear war was now less likely because the Soviet Union was stronger, and therefore less likely to be attacked. In their view, the United States was now forced to recognize that it could not win a nuclear arms race, and was thus willing to pursue serious negotiations to limit arms. But while the Soviet leaders evidently believed that strategic parity would bring them important strategic and political benefits, they did not accept that Soviet security could be guaranteed merely by possession of the capacity to inflict unacceptable damage on the enemy in the event of war. After 1972 they continued to improve Soviet strategic forces, within the terms of the Interim Agreement on Offensive Missiles, by deploying new weapons systems with considerably enhanced operational characteristics.

The military doctrine worked out under Khrushchev called for superiority over the potential enemy, but it did not take account of the need to manage the strategic relationship with the United States or to assess the effect of Soviet actions on American policy. Brezhnev had to face this issue, now that the Soviet Union, for the time being at least, would have to live with the United States in a relationship of mutual deterrence. During the last years of his rule he elaborated a defensive and deterrent rationale for Soviet strategic policy. This appears to have been intended to assuage Western anxieties, and to guide Soviet policy in managing the relationship of parity with the United States.

This rationale, which has not been changed since Brezhnev's death, was set out in various speeches and documents in the late 1970s and early 1980s.[6] Its basic elements are quite simple and can be summarized as follows: Soviet strategic forces are intended to prevent an attack on the Soviet Union and its allies. If such an attack is launched, the attacker will receive a "crushing rebuff." The present strategic relationship is one of rough parity, and neither side can outstrip the other in the arms race. The Soviet Union is not striving for superiority, but neither will it allow the United States to attain superiority. Nuclear war would be immensely destructive, and it would be suicidal to start one. It is dangerous madness to expect to win a nuclear war.

These statements introduced some important changes of emphasis into the military doctrine worked out under Khrushchev. The explicit commitment to parity was new, for the pursuit of superiority was implicit, and sometimes explicit, in earlier doctrinal formulations. Parity is an imprecise term, but not altogether without meaning. It clearly excludes superiority in the sense of the ability to launch a disarming strike at the other side; and it excludes inferiority in the reverse sense. Parity is, therefore, a relationship in which each side is vulnerable to a retaliatory strike by the other: in which each side possesses the capacity to inflict extensive damage on the other, irrespective of who strikes first. In other words, parity is the relationship normally described in the West as "mutual assured destruction" or "mutual deterrence."

Although the Soviet leaders accept that mutual assured destruction is an objective phenomenon, they have not adopted a *strategy* of assured destruction, in the sense of seeking only to destroy American cities in a retaliatory strike in the event of war. Even within the confines of strategic parity, Soviet military thinking still focuses on the problem of how to fight and win a nuclear war, if such a war should come. Party leaders have stressed the defensive nature of Soviet military doctrine, but Soviet military strategists have given primary importance to offensive operations in war, and the combination of a defensive doctrine and an offensive strategy seems at best ambiguous, and at worst threatening, to Western governments.

The new formulation of doctrine under Brezhnev has been greeted with considerable skepticism in the United States, where the prevailing official view appears to be the one expressed by President Reagan at a press conference in October 1981, when he said that "the Soviet Union has made it very plain that among themselves they believe [a nuclear war] is winnable."[7] Some skepticism about the new Soviet doctrinal statements may certainly be in order, especially since it remains unclear what practical implications they have for operational doctrine and weapons procurement. But it is a mistake to dismiss them out of hand, for they can be understood as part of an attempt by Brezhnev to adapt Soviet policy to the relationship of strategic parity with the United States. Brezhnev may well have believed that the pursuit of clear superiority would merely stimulate further costly and dangerous competition, in which the Soviet Union might well emerge worse off. Moreover, the new formulations of Soviet doctrine do not appear to be directed only at a Western audience, for they reflect intensive debate and discussion inside the Soviet Union about the course of Soviet policy. It appears, therefore, that an important shift in doctrine has taken place that may have significant consequences for policy.

One effect of the changing attitude to nuclear war has been a new conception of the relationship between nuclear and conventional warfare in Europe. In the early 1960s Khrushchev assumed that a Soviet–American war would be nuclear from the outset, and would start with missile strikes deep into the enemy's interior. Khrushchev's conception had its critics in the Soviet High Command who rejected the idea of "one-variant" war. In the late 1960s Soviet forces began to train for non-nuclear as well as nuclear operations, apparently in the belief, which was no doubt encouraged by NATO's adoption of the policy of flexible response, that an East–West conflict in Europe would not necessarily go nuclear at the very outset.

It now appears that this trend away from the preoccupation with "one-variant" nuclear war has continued to the point where the Soviet Union may believe that its nuclear forces could deter NATO from resorting to nuclear weapons, and thus keep a conflict in Europe at the conventional level. Recent organizational changes in the ground forces and air forces tend to support this interpretation, for they point to a determination to achieve the goals of war in Europe as quickly as possible with conventional arms.[8]

This determination is of course quite compatible with the often expressed Soviet view that nuclear war in Europe could not remain limited. Indeed, if the Soviet Union accepts, as it appears to do, that general nuclear war would be catastrophic for all concerned, and that nuclear war in Europe would be difficult, if not impossible, to limit, then it follows that it should try to keep the nuclear threshold as high as possible. In this context the Soviet commitment not to be the first to use nuclear weapons makes a great deal of sense.[9] Of course the announcement of that commitment was designed to enhance the Soviet Union's image as a peace-loving state, and to embarrass NATO, but it may also reflect a genuine strategic preference.

The Soviet leaders appear to have reconciled themselves in the late 1960s to living, for the time being, in a relationship of mutual assured destruction with the United States. But that relationship was called into question by President Reagan in his "Star Wars" speech of March 23, 1983, when he held out the hope that new defensive systems could be developed that would render nuclear weapons "impotent and obsolete."[10] In his reply to Reagan, however, Andropov made it clear that he thought the President had a more sinister aim in view. He said that a plan to render the Soviet Union "incapable of dealing a retaliatory blow is a bid to disarm the Soviet Union in the face of the United States' nuclear threat." Defenses against ballistic missiles might appear attractive to the layman, Andropov said, but "those who are conversant with such matters" could not view them in the same way. The SALT I agreements had been based on the realization that an "inseverable relationship" existed between offensive and defensive strategic systems, and the implementation of Reagan's plan would "open the floodgates to a runaway race involving all types of strategic weapons, both offensive and defensive."[11]

Ironically, the arguments Andropov used were akin to those that the United States had advanced in the late 1960s when the Soviet Union was deploying an ABM system of its own. In 1967 Kosygin spoke in much the same terms as Reagan used in 1983: defensive systems, he said, were not "a cause of the arms race but designed to prevent the death of people."[12] But in spite of Kosygin's assurances, the United States was alarmed by the Soviet ABM deployment, and feared that if the Soviet

Union could make itself invulnerable to an American retaliatory strike, it might well be tempted to launch a nuclear attack. In the late 1960s the Soviet leaders took the point that defensive systems could play an offensive role, and Andropov repeated it in his reply to Reagan in 1983.

Even if it does prove possible to develop defenses that are highly effective against ballistic missiles, it will be a long time before they are deployed. At least until the end of the century the Soviet Union and the United States will be locked into a relationship in which each is vulnerable to devastating retaliatory strikes by the other. The race to develop defensive systems will complicate an already complex strategic relationship, but will not change its basic character in the next fifteen to twenty years, and may not do so after that.

Soviet military theorists have struggled to come to terms with nuclear weapons, and to turn them into effective instruments of policy in war and in peace. The context in which they have approached these problems has had its own special character. For much of the nuclear age, the Soviet Union lagged behind the United States in nuclear weapons; the military have had a more important role in thinking about nuclear strategy; and the commitment of the Soviet Union to Communism has engendered a reluctance to concede that nuclear war might reverse the course of history. But in spite of these differences, this brief survey suggests that the Soviet leaders do not have answers to all the problems raised by nuclear war and nuclear weapons. The answers they have arrived at are not very different from those given in the West: nuclear weapons are at one and the same time instruments of power and influence, and the potential agents of catastrophic destruction on a global scale. The Soviet leaders have not been able to escape from the danger of annihilation that hangs over the world.

Military power and foreign policy

The Soviet leaders have sought to exploit their growing military power for foreign policy purposes. Two of the most important Soviet foreign policy conceptions—peaceful coexistence and détente—are related in Soviet thinking to growing Soviet military power.

In 1956 Khrushchev gave new meaning to the idea of peaceful coexistence between states of different social systems when he declared that war between capitalism and socialism was no longer "fatalistically inevitable."[13] The Soviet Union and its allies, he said, were strong enough "to prevent the imperialists from unleashing war, and if they actually try to start it, to give a smashing rebuff to the aggressors and frustrate their adventurist plans." This was an important new position, and it has remained central to Soviet thinking ever since. War was less likely because the Soviet Union was increasingly able to prevent an attack on itself and its allies. This ability did not rest, according to Khrushchev, on military power alone, but Khrushchev's reference to a "smashing rebuff" suggests that he had military power, including nuclear weapons, in mind when he stated that war was no longer inevitable.

Soviet success in testing long-range ballistic missiles in the late 1950s apparently convinced Khrushchev that the balance of power in the world—or the "correlation of forces," to use the Soviet term—was moving in the Soviet favor. He tried to capitalize on this in a series of crises in the late 1950s and early 1960s. But Khrushchev's missile diplomacy proved unsuccessful: he failed to achieve his aims in Berlin, and he helped, by his claims of Soviet superiority, to push the United States toward a rapid expansion of its strategic forces. The Cuban Missile Crisis finally exposed the recklessness of Khrushchev's attempt to exploit Soviet military power for political purposes.

Khrushchev's successors evidently thought that his military policy had not provided adequate support for his policy toward the West, and that, as a consequence, he had been forced to choose between risky adventures on the one hand, and passivity on the other. This mismatch between military power and foreign policy was evidently one of the reasons why they continued to increase their strategic nuclear forces, and decided to expand their conventional forces. Brezhnev and his colleagues apparently felt that their policy toward China also needed a new military basis, for they proceeded to build up their forces along the Chinese frontier, thus providing themselves with a powerful instrument of diplomatic pressure, and an effective fighting force in the event of war.

The build-up of Soviet military power was designed not only to meet the requirements of military doctrine, but also to provide strong support for Soviet foreign policy. This is especially evident in the Soviet conception of détente. The Soviet leaders claimed that détente followed from an increase in Soviet power and a shift in the correlation of forces toward socialism. The attainment of strategic parity by the Soviet Union would prevent Western governments from trying to deal with the Soviet Union from a position of strength, and would encourage them to adopt more "realistic" policies.

Détente also provided a favorable context in which to pursue Soviet objectives, some of which entailed cooperation with the West, and some of which entailed conflict. The Soviet leaders rejected the idea of linkage, which was a central part of American policy. They argued that cooperation in such areas as arms control and trade was mutually beneficial and that the Soviet Union should not be expected to pay an extra price by changing its political system or modifying its foreign policy to conform to American ideas about the norms of international behavior. They must have been aware that the elements of cooperation and conflict in their relationship with the United States could not remain isolated from each other. But their belief that détente rested on growing Soviet military power may have encouraged them to think that the continuing growth of that power, and the use of it in support of Soviet policy, would not undermine cooperation with the West.

The elements of cooperation in Soviet–American détente were always under threat from the conflicting interests of the two sides. This was demonstrated by the Middle East War of 1973, and by the Soviet abrogation of the Trade Agreement in 1975, after the Senate had adopted an amendment linking Soviet–American trade to Jewish emigration from the Soviet Union. In the late 1970s the continuing growth of Soviet military power and the increasingly assertive use of that power in the Third World were more and more seen by the United States as incompatible with détente.

The Soviet interventions in Angola and Ethiopia were taken by the United States as signs that the Soviet Union was a global superpower, willing and able to use military force around the world to further its political ambitions. Since it was a major aim of American policy to restrain Soviet expansion by linking cooperation in arms control and trade to Soviet behavior abroad, Soviet activities in Africa inevitably undermined American faith in cooperation in other areas.

The expansion of Soviet power provoked closer cooperation among the Soviet Union's adversaries. As Soviet relations with the United States deteriorated, so American ties with China grew stronger. After Mao's death in 1976 the Soviet Union put out feelers to see whether the new leadership was ready for an improvement in relations. But it was soon clear that, in spite of major changes in domestic affairs, hostility toward the Soviet Union would remain a feature of Chinese policy. In August 1978 China and Japan signed a Treaty of Peace and Friendship, which included an "anti-hegemony" clause that, in spite of disavowals, was clearly aimed at the Soviet Union. In December of the same year China and the United States announced that they had reached agreement on the vexed question of Taiwan, and that they would now proceed to establish normal diplomatic relations. Although the Soviet Union concluded a

Friendship Treaty with Vietnam in the same period, and saw Vietnam occupy Kampuchea some weeks later, the events of late 1978 marked a serious setback for Soviet policy in Asia.

It was now clear that a potential or quasi-alliance, based on anxiety about the growth of Soviet power and the assertiveness of Soviet policy, was being formed between the Soviet Union's chief adversaries. The Soviet invasion of Afghanistan gave additional impetus to this realignment, for both the United States and China saw it as further evidence of Soviet expansionism. President Carter abandoned the now hopeless effort to have the SALT II Treaty ratified by the Senate, and he imposed economic sanctions on the Soviet Union. He also continued to move toward closer relations with China.

The closer alignment of the United States, China and Japan prompted Marshal Ogarkov to declare in a speech to military leaders in June 1980:

> "A serious threat to peace is presented by the strengthening military–political rapprochement of the USA, China and Japan, the attempt to form a unified anti-Soviet front in which the military might of the USA and the European countries of NATO in the West would be united with the manpower resources of China and the industrial potential of Japan in the East. By widening military contacts with China, and increasing deliveries of military machinery and equipment, the Western powers are calculating on pushing Beijing into open aggressive actions against our country and the states of Southeast Asia."[14]

Ogarkov claimed that it was now the policy of the United States to undermine, by any means possible, the growing influence of the Soviet Union and the socialist community, and to achieve a crushing military superiority over them. The ultimate goal of imperialist policy was "to change the correlation of forces in favor of imperialism."

In spite of Ogarkov's warnings, no major modifications were made in Soviet foreign policy at the 26th Party Congress early in 1981. Brezhnev acknowledged that the previous five years had been a "complex and stormy" period in international affairs, but he produced no significant new initiative to deal with the problems that now beset the Soviet Union.[15] The general impression he gave to the Congress was that the Soviet Union's problems were manageable, and that the basic line of policy was correct. He did little more than attempt to portray the Soviet Union as the champion of peace in a troubled world.

In the last months of Brezhnev's life, however, the tone of Soviet policy changed and there were signs that a new assessment of the international situation had been made. The Soviet leaders' initial complacency that the Reagan Administration would prove to be more accommodating than its rhetoric was by now dispelled. In July 1982 Marshal Ustinov, the Minister of Defense, accused the United States of striving for military superiority, of trying to set up military blocs to encircle the Soviet Union, and of orchestrating an economic and technological war against the socialist countries, with the aim of destroying socialism as a socio-economic system.[16] In October, less than three weeks before his death, Brezhnev told a gathering of 500 military leaders that the United States and its allies had unleashed an unprecedented arms race with the aim of achieving military superiority, and were trying to isolate the socialist camp politically and weaken it economically.[17]

The Soviet leaders apparently concluded in 1982 that there was little prospect of better relations with the Reagan Administration. They tried to improve their international position by continuing to play on differences between Western Europe and the United States on the issues of intermediate-range nuclear forces (INF) and trade policy toward the Soviet Union. They may have hoped to influence American policy through the European members of NATO, or to salvage détente with Western Europe, even though that with the United States had collapsed; failing that, they may just have wanted to sow dissension in NATO. The Soviet Union also tried to forestall encirclement by seeking a rapprochement with China, whose relations with the Reagan Administration had worsened over the issue of Taiwan. Three times in 1982 Brezhnev expressed interest in improving relations with China, and a very limited relaxation of tension began before his death.

During Andropov's rule the Soviet Union suffered further setbacks. Relations with the United States continued to deteriorate, to the point where Andropov could state in September 1983 (only weeks after a Soviet air defense interceptor had shot down a South Korean airliner) that "if anyone had illusions about the possibility that the policy of the present American administration would evolve for the better, then the events of the recent period have finally dispelled them."[18] With the failure of the INF talks to reach an agreement before the start of the NATO deployment in December 1983, Soviet–American relations entered their worst phase since the Cuban Missile Crisis.

Soviet efforts to improve relations with China, and to exploit Sino-American differences over Taiwan, have not, by the spring of 1984, yielded significant results. There are still serious obstacles in the way of a Sino-Soviet rapprochement. One of the main obstacles is, ironically, the presence of large Soviet forces in Mongolia and along the frontier with China—forces that were supposed to make China more tractable in its dealings with the Soviet Union.

In Europe Soviet policy has suffered a serious setback with the start of NATO's deployment of Pershing II and ground-launched cruise missiles. The Soviet Union tried strenuously to prevent this deployment. The Soviet leaders may have thought in 1979 and 1980 that Western Europe was the weakest link in the chain of encirclement, and believed that NATO would be unable to deploy the new missiles. But the deployment demonstrated that the main Western European governments were united with the Reagan Administration on this issue. When the NATO deployment began in November 1983 the Soviet Union withdrew from the INF negotiations and refused to set a date for the resumption of START (Strategic Arms Reduction Talks).

By the time of Brezhnev's death in November 1982 the Soviet Union faced a range of difficult problems. The United States, alarmed by the growth of Soviet military power, and by the use of that power in Angola, Ethiopia and Afghanistan, had embarked on a major build-up of its armed forces. The Soviet Union's chief adversaries—the United States, China, Japan and Western Europe—had drawn closer together to resist the expansion of Soviet power. The Soviet Union was still embroiled in a war in Afghanistan, while the Soviet-backed governments in Angola and Ethiopia continued to face internal opposition. Several partial expedients were taken in 1982 and 1983, but these have not proved to be successful, and the time would seem to have come for a major reassessment of the Soviet Union's international position. It is difficult to judge what the effect of Andropov's death will be. It may make it easier for the Soviet Union to move away from some of the positions it has taken recently, notably on arms control talks. But the emergence of an apparently transitional leader may make it more difficult to chart a new long-term course in foreign policy.

It would be wrong to exaggerate the problems that face the Soviet Union. It remains a powerful state, and is already taking steps to counter the Reagan Administration's military build-up. There are many tensions and disagreements among the Soviet Union's adversaries, and the Soviet Union will try to exploit these. But the failures of Soviet policy show that the Soviet Union has not been able to translate its military power into commensurate political gains. Soviet military power did not make détente irreversible. Indeed, it contributed to the ending of détente, for the growth of that power and its exercise abroad inspired widespread anxiety in the Soviet Union's major adversaries. If the Soviet Union now finds itself in a difficult international position, that is at least partly the consequence of its own policies in the 1970s.

Military power and domestic politics

The "Soviet military build-up," which has received so much attention in the West and played such an important role in the domestic politics of the United States, had its origins in the transition to a nuclear-based defense policy under Khrushchev. According to CIA estimates, Soviet military expenditure remained steady from 1952 until the end of the decade, but then it began to rise. This growth continued under Brezhnev as all elements of the armed forces were strengthened.[19]

In 1976 the CIA produced a new estimate of Soviet military outlays. It concluded that the Soviet Union was spending 11 to 13 percent of its GNP on defense, twice as large a proportion as had been previously estimated. It also concluded that this expenditure had been growing at the rate of 4–5 percent a year since the mid 1960s. This new estimate was based on a new assessment, not of the size of the armed forces, but only of their cost to the Soviet Union.[20] It did, however, greatly increase Western awareness of the size of the Soviet military effort, and even led some people to believe that the Soviet Union had in fact doubled its military outlays in the mid 1970s.

Until 1983 the CIA continued to state that Soviet defense expenditure was growing at the rate of 4–5 percent a year. Early in 1983, however, it came to the conclusion that Soviet military outlays in the late 1970s and early 1980s had not grown as fast as it had estimated. The CIA now thinks that Soviet military expenditure grew at no more than 2 percent a year from 1976 to 1981 (the latest year for which estimates are now available), and that expenditure on weapons procurement did not grow at all during that period.[21] The new estimate is of course subject to all the same uncertainties and qualifications as the earlier one. It is ironic, however, that it points to a slackening of the rate of growth in the Soviet defense effort in 1976, the very year in which the revised CIA estimates aroused such strong anxieties in the United States.

The slowdown in the rate of growth of defense expenditure has lasted too long to be plausibly explained as a lull caused by the phasing out of old programs and the introduction of new ones. It seems more reasonable to interpret it as resulting from a policy decision on the part of the Soviet leaders. It coincides with the decline in the rate of growth of the economy as a whole. Since the 1950s the rate of growth has fallen steadily, whether measured in Soviet national income statistics or in Western estimates of Soviet GNP. From 1956 to 1960 Soviet national income grew at 9·1 percent a year; from 1975 to 1979 it grew at an annual rate of 4·5 percent. According to CIA estimates, Soviet GNP grew at an annual rate of 5·8 percent from 1956 to 1960, and at 2·8 percent from 1976 to 1980.[22] The slowdown in the rate of growth of defense expenditure can be interpreted, therefore, as a response to the more general slowdown in economic growth and the pressures on resource allocation that have followed from this.

The slowdown in the growth of defense expenditure also coincided with Ustinov's appointment as Minister of Defense in April 1976. When the previous Minister, Marshal Grechko, died in April 1976, the Politburo moved quickly to replace him with Dmitri Ustinov, an old associate of Brezhnev's who had spent most of his career in managing weapons development and production. Although hardly the archetypal civilian, Ustinov is not a professional soldier, and his appointment marked the first time in twenty-one years that a non-military man had held the post of Minister. Ustinov's appointment thwarted the ambitions of the then Chief of the General Staff, Army General Kulikov, a protégé of Grechko's who had hoped to succeed his patron. Within nine months Ustinov removed Kulikov from the General Staff and gave him the less important post of Commander-in-Chief of the Warsaw Pact. Ustinov replaced him with his own protégé, and Kulikov's rival, Army General Ogarkov, who is still Chief of the General Staff.[23]

Within a month of Ustinov's appointment, Brezhnev was made Marshal of the Soviet Union, and his chairmanship of the Defense Council (the top defense policy-making body) was revealed. In the following year it was made known that he was Supreme Commander-in-Chief of the Armed Forces. These moves symbolized the assertion of his—and of the Party's—authority in military affairs. This assertion was soon followed by Brezhnev's reformulation of military doctrine. In January 1977, in a speech in Tula, he declared that superiority was not the goal of Soviet policy. Marshal Ogarkov later pointed to this as an important statement of military doctrine.[24]

These circumstances—the slowdown of economic growth, Ustinov's appointment as Minister of Defense, the assertion of Party authority, and the reformulation of doctrine—all coincided with the reduction in the rate of growth of defense expenditure. This suggests that that reduction was the result of a conscious policy decision. If this interpretation is correct, it helps to set the context for the choices the Soviet leadership now faces. Marshal Ogarkov's warnings about the international situation and the policy of the United States can be read as an argument that military preparations should not be neglected, and that military expenditures should grow more rapidly, in order to match the United States' military build-up.

But the Party leaders have not, so far as can be judged, responded eagerly to Ogarkov's warnings. In 1981 and 1982 Ogarkov stressed the dangerous and aggressive nature of American policy, and its search for global military superiority.[25] But the assessment of American policy that Ustinov gave in 1982 was different in emphasis. He portrayed the American threat not merely in military terms, but as an all-round political, ideological and economic challenge. The implication of this analysis was that the Soviet response must have a similarly all-embracing character: more military expenditure by itself would not solve the Soviet Union's foreign policy problems.

Brezhnev delivered the same message when he met military leaders in October 1982. At this extraordinary meeting Brezhnev tried to assuage military disquiet about the policies being pursued in the face of the worsening international situation. But he gave little comfort to the military. He painted a rather bleak picture of world politics, but he seemed to suggest that the Soviet Union had room for diplomatic maneuver, for he noted that the Reagan Administration's policies were causing alarm even among American allies, and he pointed to the possibility of an improvement in relations with China. He also stressed the importance of industrial development at home, and spoke of the "exceptional significance" of the Food Program which had been adopted in May, thus implying that only limited additional resources would be forthcoming for the military. He spoke of the support that the armed forces were already receiving, and said that it was up to the military leadership to ensure that they were capable of discharging their responsibilities effectively.

Brezhnev died within three weeks of giving this speech. Ustinov appears to have played a key role in Andropov's emergence as Brezhnev's successor, and this presumably meant that Andropov had the support of the military too. But Ustinov's role under Brezhnev suggests that he should be regarded not merely as a mouthpiece or creature of the military, but as a powerful Party figure in his own right. Ustinov's support for Andropov did not mean that Andropov was beholden to the military. Nor does the support that he seems to have given Chernenko imply that Chernenko is the creature of the military. On the contrary,

Chernenko's emergence as General Secretary shows the key role of the Party's central apparatus in the political system.

While he was General Secretary, Andropov gave no clear sign that he had made a major increase in military expenditure, though it is possible that some additional funds were allocated in order to match the Reagan build-up. Andropov made it his most urgent priority to restore some vigor to the economy. He tried to improve labor discipline and productivity by cracking down on absenteeism and corruption, and launched limited experiments in economic reform. The emphasis on economic problems did not mean that international politics had lost its significance for the Soviet Union. On the contrary, a major reason for the effort to revitalize the economy was the fear that economic and technological weakness would undermine the international position of the Soviet Union and its future military power.

Since 1981 the Soviet leaders seem to have felt beleaguered by their international problems, and to have turned inward to deal with problems at home. They have not withdrawn from world politics, of course, but they have concentrated on consolidating their power rather than on trying to expand it. They may come to feel, however, that their competition with the United States requires further increases in the rate of growth of defense expenditure, and a more assertive foreign policy.

Conclusion

The Soviet Union does not have all the answers to the questions posed by nuclear weapons and nuclear war. The Soviet leaders have regarded nuclear weapons both as instruments of war and political pressure, and as the potential agents of catastrophic destruction. This duality is evident in the Soviet acceptance of the objective reality of the relationship of mutual assured destruction and in the simultaneous preparation for nuclear war.

Soviet attempts to exploit military power for political purposes have met with only partial success. Khrushchev's missile diplomacy failed to achieve its most important goals, and helped to provoke a massive build-up of American strategic forces. Under Brezhnev the growth of Soviet military power, far from making détente irreversible, contributed to its collapse. The need for a new Soviet conception of the relationship between military power and foreign policy seems clear. Brezhnev tried to address the problem with his stress on parity, but this is a vague and ambiguous concept, and in any event came too late to halt the deterioration in détente.

The Soviet Union faces difficult problems at home and abroad, and these will confront the Soviet leaders with hard choices throughout the 1980s. Strong pressures exist for a far-reaching reassessment of domestic and foreign policy, but Andropov's death and the emergence of what looks like another transitional leader suggest that there may be a long period of debate and hesitation before any major changes of policy are forthcoming. The sense of immobilism that marked Brezhnev's last years were only partially dispelled by Andropov, and may return with the election of Chernenko, Brezhnev's close political friend and ally, as Andropov's successor. It may be, nevertheless, that the failure of their defense policy will force the Soviet leaders to reassess the basis for good relations with the West, and to define more clearly what they are seeking.

It is important, however, not to exaggerate the problems that face the Soviet Union. The growth in Soviet military power since the 1950s has been real, and the Soviet Union is now a military superpower in a way in which it was not in Khrushchev's day. Moreover, it has the capacity to prevent the United States from attaining any significant degree of military superiority. Similarly, although the economy faces serious problems, it is not likely to collapse or to suffer from negative growth in the next twenty years; in 1983 the rate of economic growth underwent a modest revival. It is wrong, therefore, to suppose that the Soviet Union will cease to play a major role in world politics in the foreseeable future.

There has been a tendency, especially in the United States, to shift from the image of the Soviet Union as a monstrously powerful state to the view that it is vulnerable to strains at home and pressure from abroad. The myth of Soviet weakness—that the Russians are only two feet tall—may be just as harmful as the exaggeration of Soviet strength. What both judgments have in common is that they make it less likely that the West will seek to conclude agreements with the Soviet Union—the one because it suggests that such agreements are unnecessary, the other because it suggests that they are impossible to obtain on an equitable basis.

The conclusion that this paper points to is precisely that this is a time for Western governments, and especially for the United States, to work out the basis for cooperative efforts to bring the nuclear arms race under control. In spite of the present poor state of Soviet–American relations, there are several important features of Soviet policy that suggest that this is an opportune time for pursuing serious arms limitation and reduction agreements. The changes in Soviet doctrine, the setbacks in Soviet foreign policy, the problems of resource allocation, and the continuing uncertainty about the political leadership all point in this direction. But for the West to take advantage of these developments, a political strategy is required that aims at cooperation and agreement, and directs the normal techniques of foreign policy—both toughness and conciliation—toward that political goal. The mere application of pressure, if it is not directed toward a realistic political goal, is likely to do little more than produce hostility and truculence on the part of the Soviet Union. The mere assertion of the desire for better relations, if it is not accompanied by concrete measures, will do little more than add to the suspicion and cynicism that characterize East–West relations at present.

No one should suppose that agreements will be easy to reach. Negotiating with the Soviet Union has always been an intensely frustrating experience. But a determined effort should be made to explore some of the arms control proposals that the Soviet Union has put forward in recent years to see whether some accommodation can be reached. Unilateral measures by the West—such as the adoption of a "no first use" policy—do have an important part to play in changing the political climate and demonstrating a determination to bring the arms race under control. But in the end, the prevention of nuclear war and the survival of the human race cannot be secured without the cooperation of the Soviet Union.

9 THE STATE OF US–SOVIET RELATIONS: BREAKING THE SPELL *George Kennan*

Professor George Kennan, Hon. LL.D., Hon. D.C.L. (Oxon), is Emeritus Professor at the Institute for Advanced Study, Princeton. Between 1926 and 1952 he held many posts in the Foreign Service of the United States, culminating in service as US Ambassador to the USSR in 1952–3. He returned to public service to become Ambassador to Yugoslavia during J. F. Kennedy's presidency. A member of long standing, Professor Kennan has served as President of the American Academy of Arts and Letters. He is the author of many books on diplomacy and Soviet affairs, and has recently published a collection of his writings on the nuclear question entitled The Nuclear Delusion. *He was awarded the Albert Einstein Peace Prize in 1981. He is currently co-chairman of the American Committee on East–West Accord.*

Soviet–American relations, in consequence of a process of deterioration that has been going on for several years, are today in what can only be called a dreadful and dangerous condition. Civility and privacy of communication between the two governments seem to have largely broken down. Reactions on each side to statements and actions of the other side have been allowed to become permeated with antagonism, suspicion and cynicism. Public discussion of the relations between the two countries has become almost totally militarized, at least in the United States: militarized to a point where the casual reader or listener is compelled to conclude that some sort of military showdown is the only conceivable dénouement of their various differences—the only one worth considering and discussing.

Can anyone mistake, or doubt, the ominous meaning of such a state of affairs? The phenomena just described, occurring in the relations between two highly armed great powers, are the familiar characteristics, the unfailing characteristics, of a march toward war—that, and nothing else. The danger would be intolerable even if the two countries were armed only with what are called conventional weapons. The history of the past century has shown that the damage produced by armed conflict between highly industrialized great powers in the modern age, even without the use of nuclear armaments, is so appalling that it is doubtful whether Western civilization could survive another such catastrophe. But this danger is now increased many times over by the nature of the weapons that the two countries hold in their hands. Either of these two factors—the nature of the weaponry, the state of the political relations—would be a danger in itself. The two in combination present a shadow greater than any that has ever before darkened the face of Western civilization.

Is this state of affairs really necessary? Is it unavoidable from the standpoint of the American policy-maker? Is there no way we could hope to cope with it other than by a continuing and intensified weapons race of indefinite duration? The casual reader or listener is led to believe that there is not. If, however, there is something that could be done, what is it? There are those in Washington who would argue that the present situation flows automatically from the nature of the regime that confronts us in Moscow, and is therefore unavoidable. To support their view, they would point to a given image of that regime. Goethe's Mephistopheles observes cynically, in the second part of *Faust*, that "in the end we are all dependent on monsters of our own creation." And so it is with the image of the Soviet regime which has come to inform American policy. It is an image of unmitigated darkness, with which we are all familiar: that of a group of men already dominating and misruling a large part of the world and motivated only by a relentless determination to bring still more peoples under their domination. By those who cultivate this image, no rational motivation is suggested for so savage and unquenchable a thirst for power. The men who suffer this thirst, one is allowed to conclude, were simply born with it—the products, presumably, of some sort of negative genetic miracle. In any case, since they were born with it and are unable to help themselves, there is no way—or so we are told—that they could be reasoned with; no basis on which they could usefully be approached; no language they could be expected to understand other than that of intimidation by superior military force. Only by the specter of such a force—an overwhelmingly superior nuclear force, in particular—could these men be "deterred" from committing all sorts of acts of aggression or intimidation with a view to subjugating other peoples and eventually to conquering the world. There are alleged to be no other inhibitions, no other considerations, no other interests that could be expected to restrain them from such behavior.

Well, if this image had been applied thirty or forty years ago to the regime of Joseph Stalin it might have been nearer to reality (although even then it would have been in some respects wide of the mark). Applied to the Soviet leadership today, it is seriously overdrawn: a caricature rather than a reflection of what really exists, and misleading and pernicious as a foundation for national policy. Beyond that, it is deeply and needlessly offensive to the people in question. But how much truth, if any, is there in it?

The Soviet regime has always been marked by a whole series of characteristics that complicated, and were bound to complicate, its relations with the West. Some of these were inherited. Many-sided estrangement from the West was nothing new in Russian history. It was an outstanding feature of the old Grand Duchy of Moscow—pious, xenophobic, eternally suspicious of the heretical foreigner. Two hundred years of Petersburg rule broke down this estrangement only in part, and primarily among the educated classes: the nobility, the gentry, commercial circles, and the liberal intelligentsia. And then the Russian Revolution, occurring in all the agony of the First World War, and marked, as it was, by the return of the capital to Moscow and the political destruction or elimination of precisely the more cosmopolitan elements of the population, intensified the estrangement enormously, substituting a militant ideological antagonism for the onetime religious abhorrence of the West, and discovering a new form of dangerous heresy in the Marxist vision of capitalism. This militancy, to be sure, soon began to fade under impact with reality; but the rhetoric, in itself an impediment to normal relations, remained. And the years of Stalinist horror were no help. This fearsome Stalinist despotism, a grotesque anomaly in the modern world, could no more stand free association with the Western countries than could the court of old Muscovy in the days of Ivan the Terrible. And the traces of Stalinism, while today much faded and partly obliterated, are still not wholly absent from the Soviet scene.

All in all, then, the Soviet regime never was, and is not today, one with which the United States could expect to have anything other than a complex and often difficult relationship. It is a regime marked by a relatively high sense of insecurity. It has a tendency to overdo in the cultivation of military strength. It is unduly sensitive to the slightest influence or involvement of outside powers in regions just beyond its lengthy borders. It has a neurotic passion for secrecy and, as a product of that passion, a positive obsession with espionage, both offensive and defensive—an obsession that has interfered with its relations with the West, and has even damaged the regime's own interests, more often and more seriously than the regime has until lately brought itself to recognize. The penetration by a Soviet submarine into sensitive Swedish waters and the shooting down in 1983 of the Korean airliner are striking examples of the over-indulgence in this obsession; and one hopes that the Soviet leaders will learn from the world reaction to these events what harm they do themselves when they let military considerations ride roughshod over wider interests.

To continue with this listing of the negative factors: Soviet negotiating techniques often appear, particularly to those not familiar with them, to be stiff, awkward, secretive and unpredictable. Above all, they are lacking in the useful lubrication that comes from informal personal association and exchanges among negotiators. And there are, too, specific Soviet policies that grate severely on Western sensibilities. The Soviet leaders do indeed make efforts to gain influence and authority among the regimes and peoples of the Third World. While the methods they employ do not seem to differ greatly from those of other major powers, including us, and while other efforts in this direction have not met, generally speaking, with any very alarming measure of success, these practices naturally arouse concern and resentment in large sections of our official community. And then, of course, there is the fact that the Soviet leaders insist on maintaining a monopoly of political power in their own country and proceed harshly against those who appear to challenge or threaten that monopoly; and, beyond that, they unquestionably use their military hegemony to support and to maintain in power in Eastern Europe, insofar as it is possible, regimes similarly inspired and similarly resistant to liberalizing tendencies. All this is obviously a constant thorn in the flesh of much Western opinion.

And, finally, there is the phenomenon, familiar to all foreign representatives and observers in Russia, of the curious dual personality that the Soviet regime presents to the resident foreigner: the façade that is composed of people—often amiable and charming people—authorized to associate and communicate with the outside world; and, behind that façade, never visible but always perceptible, the inner, conspiratorial personality, of whose inscrutable attitudes and intentions the foreigner is never quite sure, and which for that reason probably incurs more suspicion than it deserves.

Now, these, and others that could be named, are formidable difficulties. Of course they limit the relationship. And of course they have to be taken into consideration by Western policy-makers. But there are certain aspects of them that deserve to be kept in mind. First, most of them are not new. Some have been there since the outset of the Soviet–American relationship. All of us who have served in Moscow have had to contend with them. We were taught, in fact, to regard them as the more intractable parts of the problem. General George Marshall, I recall, used to say to us, "Don't fight the problem," by which he meant, I believe, "Don't fight against the problem as a whole, for it includes elements that you cannot hope to change; find out which elements, if any, are susceptible to your influence, and concentrate on them." Second, many of these difficulties are actually less acute today than they were many years ago. This shows that they are not theoretically unsusceptible to change. Perhaps, if they are approached with patience and understanding, they can become even less pronounced in future years. Third, the negative factors are counterbalanced by a number of encouraging ones in both the psychology and the situation of the Soviet leadership.

Of these, the most important consists of the many persuasive indications that that leadership, however complicated its relations with the West may be, does not want a major war—that it has a serious interest in avoiding such a war, and will, given a chance, go quite far together with us to avoid it. The term "interest" does not mean, in this case, an abstract devotion to the principle of peace as a moral ideal. It means a consciousness on the part of these men that certain of the things they most deeply care about would not be served by Russia's involvement in another great war. Anyone who tries to put himself in the position of the Soviet leaders will at once recognize the force of this point. Even if they should be as evilly motivated as they are sometimes seen to be, these men are not free agents, wholly detached from the manifold complexities and contradictions that invariably go with the exercise of vast power. They constitute the government of a great country. They have a direct responsibility for the shaping of its society and its economic life. It is from the successful development of this society and this economy that they derive their strength. They cannot play fast and loose with either. Beyond that, they live and operate in a highly complex international environment. There is no single consideration that would serve to persuade these men that their interests would not be served by opening the Pandora's box of another world war; rather, there are dozens of considerations—and these quite aside from any so-called "military deterrence"—that would dissuade them from such a venture. The view that sees them as supremely independent, wholly on top of all their other problems, and madly riveted to dreams of world conquest to the point where it is exclusively by the interposition of overwhelming opposing military force that they could be dissuaded from striking out in all directions with acts of aggression or intimidation—this view is, if one will forgive my language, simply childish, unworthy of people charged with the responsibility of conducting the affairs of a great power in an endangered world. Surely American statesmen can do better than this in penetrating, with their imaginations and their powers of analysis, the true complexity of the forces that come to bear on the decisions of another great government, and in forming a realistic idea of the motivation of that government's conduct? And surely if they were to make this effort what they would then see would be more reassuring than what, in the absence of it, they are led by their fears to assume.

Nor is the area of common interest between the Soviet Union and the United States limited to the need of both countries to see world peace preserved. Both are great industrial powers. As such, they have a growing number of common problems. Prominent among these are the environmental ones. Both countries occupy major portions of the environmentally endangered Northern Hemisphere. The Soviet leaders are no less aware than we are of the extent to which this hemisphere, if it escapes nuclear disaster, will still be threatened in the most serious way by environmental pollution and deterioration. They know that these problems will not be mastered just by measures taken within any single country—that the solution will require international collaboration, particularly between the two greatest industrial powers of the hemisphere.

And the environmental questions are only examples of the many problems and challenges that all the great industrial societies of this age, including the United States and the Soviet Union, are coming to have in common. There are the truly revolutionary effects, in some ways promising and in some ways terrifying, of the present revolution in communications on education, on the organization of life, on the human spirit and the human fiber. The Soviet Union is no less affected by this revolution than we are. It is such problems that unite—they are the ones on which we and the Soviet Union *can* collaborate. And they are the problems of the future. The others—the ones flowing from the ideological conflicts of the turn of the century which produced the Russian Revolution—are the problems of the past.

Those are some of the pros and cons of the Soviet–American relationship; and if these pros and cons are stacked up against each other what one gets is, naturally, a mixed pattern, embracing serious differences of outlook and interest but also embracing positive possibilities that are not negligible. It is a pattern that, of course, leaves no room for exaggerated hopes, or for fulsome and hypocritical pretenses to a friendship that does not, and cannot, fully exist. The pattern embraces problems that will not be solved by just any summit meeting. But it also affords no justification for some of the extremes of pessimism we see around us today; no justification for the conclusion that it is only by some ultimate military showdown that the various Soviet–American differences can be resolved; and no justification for the overdrawn image of the Soviet leadership to which reference has here been made. Americans lived for more than a century at peace with the empire of the czars. Despite the addition of several seriously complicating factors during the present century, they have lived for some six and a half decades at peace with the Soviet Union. In the mixed pattern we have just had occasion to note, there is nothing to suggest that these two countries should not be able to continue to live at peace with each other for an indefinite number of decades into the future.

This cannot, of course, be assured by the state of relations we have before us today. The prospects for a peaceful development of Soviet–American relations are not theoretically hopeless, but they could easily become just that if we are unable to rise above some of the morbid nuclear preoccupations that now seem to possess us—if we are unable to see the positive possibilities behind the negative, military ones, and are unable to give to those positive ones a chance to take shape and to realize themselves. No one questions the fundamental importance of the outstanding questions of arms control. These represent the greatest and most urgent single problem we have before us in our relations with the Soviet Union. Without progress in this respect, there can, of course, be little hope of a peaceful future. But it is vitally important to remember that there are other dimensions to the Soviet–American relationship than the military one; and that not only are these other dimensions of sufficient importance to warrant attention in their own right but unless they, too, can be recognized, and cultivated, and their favorable possibilities taken advantage of, the arms talks themselves are unlikely to have any adequate and enduring success. The two aspects of the relationship are complementary. Progress in the one is indispensable to progress in the other.

What could be done, then, to place this relationship on a sounder, less frightening, and more hopeful basis than it rests on today? One starts, of course, from the recognition that as of this moment things are royally fouled up. Any effort to straighten them out would unavoidably take time. There are some who believe that nothing that could be undertaken from the American side in the short term could restore the atmosphere necessary to provide prospects for success. Possibly. In any case, to remove all those sources of tension which are theoretically susceptible of removal would certainly be a task of years, not months. But it is never too early to make a beginning; and nothing prevents us from considering what sort of agenda might be necessary if one wanted to embark on that course.

Some of this flows, by implication, from what has already been said. We could try, first of all, to restore the full confidentiality and the civility of communication between the two governments. And we could cease treating the Soviet Union as though we were, out of one pocket, at peace with it and, out of the other, at war. We could lift the heavy dead hand from Soviet–American trade and proceed, with the usual, minimal security precautions, to permit that normal and useful branch of human activity to develop in response to its own economic requirements. We have no need to be trying to set back the economy or depress the living standards of any other great people; nor is such an effort in keeping with the American tradition.

We could take a much bolder, more hopeful, and more promising position in matters of arms control. This does not mean embracing in any way the principle of unilateral disarmament. We could acknowledge (and it is high time we did) that the nuclear weapon is a useless one: that it could not conceivably be used without bringing catastrophe upon whatever country initiated its use, along with untold millions of people elsewhere. Acknowledging this, we could reject all dreams of nuclear superiority and see what we could do about reducing existing nuclear arsenals, with a view to their eventual elimination. A number of approaches have been suggested: a freeze, deep cuts, the so-called "build-down," a comprehensive test-ban treaty, others as well. These are not alternatives. They are complementary. Any or all of them would be useful. But to get on with any of them we would have to learn to treat the problem as a whole in our negotiations with the Russians, not cut up into a series of fragmented technical talks; to treat it at the senior political level where it belongs, not in periodic encounters between politically helpless experts; and to treat it—initially, at least—in an atmosphere of complete confidentiality, not in a series of public posturings before various domestic political constituencies.

And then, while we were working on the more positive and hopeful possibilities, we could set out to take advantage of those areas where the peaceful interests of the two powers do coincide and where possibilities for collaboration do exist. What have we to lose? If my memory is correct, we once had thirteen separate agreements for collaboration and personal exchanges in a whole series of cultural and scientific fields. A number of them proved fruitful; some, we are told, did not. I hold no brief for the retention of the ones that did not. But many of the thirteen, including certain of the useful ones, have been allowed to lapse. These could be restored, and others could be added. There are many possibilities in the scientific field, some of which exist in rudimentary form and all of which could be extended: possibilities of collaboration on environmental problems, on the study of the Arctic and the Antarctic, on oceanographic research, on public health, on nuclear fusion. The entire great area of the uses of outer space—this vast umbrella that protects every man, woman and child on our planet—ought to be not only demilitarized but genuinely internationalized; and these two great countries could well be taking a major collaborative part in that internationalization, rather than each speculating how it might exploit this medium to the detriment of the other party, and perhaps to the detriment of humanity as a whole.

There are those who will say, "Yes, we once had such agreements, but we did not get as much information out of them as the Russians did." The answer to this objection is clear. If the acquisition of military intelligence is the only reason one can see for entering into such agreements with another country, then they had better be omitted. But if one is prepared to place one's hopes on their long-term effects—their effects in bringing people together in a collaborative relationship and helping them to see one another as human beings, not as some species of demon—then many of these arrangements will prove a more hopeful perspective than the most ambitious of our efforts to learn how to destroy each other.

Such collaborative arrangements require, as a rule, formalized agreements. There are some who question whether we can trust the Soviet government to live up to such agreements when it makes them. When I hear this question asked, I am surprised. We now have six and a half decades of experience to go on, and the answer provided by this experience is reasonably clear. You *can* conclude useful agreements with the Soviet side, and they *will* respect them—on condition, however, that the terms be clear and specific, not general; that as little as possible be left to interpretation; that questions of motivation, and particularly professions of noble principle, be left aside; and that the other contracting party show a serious and continued interest in their observance.

Finally, there is the question of "human rights." American sympathies are, of course, engaged in behalf of people who fall foul of any great political police system. This neither requires nor deserves any concealment. But if what we are talking about is the official interrelationship of great governments a choice must be made between the interests of democratization in Russia and the interests of world peace. In the face of this choice, there can be only one answer. Democracy is a matter of tradition, of custom, of what people are used to, of what they understand and expect. It is not something that can be suddenly grafted onto an unprepared people—particularly not from outside, and particularly not by precept, preaching and pressure rather than example. It is not a concept familiar to the mass of the Russian people; and whoever subordinates the interests of world peace to the chimera of an early democratization of the Soviet Union will assuredly sacrifice the first of those values without promoting the second. By the nature of things, democratization not only can but must wait; world peace cannot. If what we want to achieve is a liberalization of the political regime prevailing in the Soviet Union, then it is to example rather than to precept that we must look; and we could start by tackling, with far greater resolution and courage than we have shown to date, some of the glaring deficiencies in our own society.

These, then, are the directions in which we could move, if we wanted to ease the situation. We have, I reiterate, so little to lose. At the end of our present path of unlimited military confrontation lies no visible destination but failure and horror. There are no alternatives to this path which would not be preferable to it. What is needed here is only the will—the courage, the boldness, the affirmation of life—to break the evil spell that the severed atom has cast upon us all; to declare our independence of the nightmares of nuclear danger; to turn our minds and hearts to better things.

The foregoing observations flow from an involvement with Soviet–American relations on this writer's part which goes back over a longer span of years than that of anyone else now in public life on either side, except for that of Averell Harriman. In the course of these years—there are fifty-five of them—I have seen this relationship in some of its better times: particularly at the time of the establishment of diplomatic relations, just a half century ago; and again during our association with the Soviet Union in the waging of the Second World War. I have also seen it in some of the most bitter and disheartening moments it has known—

have not only seen it in such moments but felt some of its more painful effects upon my own person. Precisely for this reason, I think I know as much as anyone about the difficulties that the relationship involves. Yet at no time in the course of these fifty-five years have I lost my confidence in its constructive possibilities. For all their historical and ideological differences, these two peoples—the Russians and the Americans—complement each other: they need each other; they can enrich each other; together, granted the requisite insight and restraint, they can do more than any other two powers to assure world peace. The rest of the world needs their forbearance with each other and their peaceful collaboration. Their allies need it. They themselves need it. They can have it if they want it. If only this could be recognized, we could perfectly well go forward to face the challenges that the true situation presents, and to shoulder, soberly but cheerfully, and without all the melodramatics of offended virtue, the burdens it imposes.

PART III *Arguments from principle*

10 THE MORALITY OF NUCLEAR DETERRENCE *K. D. Johnson*

Chaplain (Major General) K. D. Johnson, US Army (ret.), served as a Heavy Mortar Company Commander in the Korean War. After the war he attended Princeton Theological Seminary and was ordained a minister of the Presbyterian Church, re-entering the army as a Chaplain in 1960. His service took him to Germany and Vietnam. He graduated from Command and General Staff College and the US Army War College before being appointed Deputy Chief of Chaplains in 1978. The following year he became Chief of Chaplains, a post he held until his retirement in 1982. He is currently an Associate Director of the Center for Defense Information, Washington, DC.

There was a time when the validity of nuclear deterrence was widely assumed, and its relationship to the search for real security and the pursuit of peace was unquestioned, and through the twists and turns of US declaratory policy in the nuclear age, deterrence has remained the basis of nuclear policy.

The reason for this is easily seen. After all, it was argued by nuclear strategists, nuclear weapons could not be disinvented, so nuclear deterrence was believed to be a way of managing their existence peacefully. At the same time, nuclear weapons were declared to be the bedrock of national security. Their existence would "deter" a potential enemy by the threat of retaliatory use. One of the original nuclear strategists, Bernard Brodie, stated the appeal of deterrence that resulted from that view:

"The first and most vital step in any American security program for the age of atomic bombs is to take measures to guarantee to ourselves in case of attack the possibility of retaliation in kind. The writer in making that statement is not for the moment concerned about who will win the next war in which atomic bombs are used. Thus far the chief purpose of our military establishment has been to win wars. From now on its chief purpose must be to avert them. It can have almost no other useful purpose."[1]

this well-known statement, repeated in various forms over three decades, has held public support and acquiescence. Philosophers and theologians have often been party to this, arguing that this course held moral virtue because it simultaneously favored national defense and averted nuclear incineration. I shall return to examine this view later in the chapter. However, recently doubts about nuclear policy have been reflected in the increasing strength of the peace and anti-nuclear movements. The fact that it took three and a half decades for an anti-nuclear peace movement to materialize was noted by the prominent pro-nuclear strategist Colin S. Gray when he speculated that the anti-nuclear movement "might have been weakened fatally in advance" had government leaders "taken the trouble—and indeed invited the trouble—to educate the public about some of the basic premises underlying its nuclear strategic thinking . . ."[2]

The condescending belief among ruling circles that mass anti-nuclear movements represent a temporary aberration which can be "solved" by government education, manipulation and cooptation is, in fact, an essential reason why they exist. Increasingly, the public resists being viewed as a passive instrument of support for established policy but instead seeks active and intelligent participation in the nuclear debate. Increasingly the general public does not accept or acquiesce in nuclear annihilation as a fact of the age about which it can do nothing; and people are not at all sure that the President and his advisers will do what is best to prevent it.

The memory of the Vietnam War still lives powerfully in the American public consciousness. Repeatedly in that experience they were asked to trust their leaders, all of whom saw "light at the end of the tunnel." But light was not seen until people began to dig the tunnel for themselves. The comments on eighteenth-century warfare by Clausewitz fit precisely the Vietnam experience: "war was still an affair for governments alone, and the people's role was simply that of an instrument . . . the people's part had been extinguished . . . War thus became solely the concern of the government to the extent that governments parted company with their peoples and behaved as if they were themselves the state."[3] That this should not happen in the battle for nuclear survival appears to be a basic axiom of the widespread anti-nuclear sentiment. The pleas by political, military and civilian nuclear strategists to "trust us" are likely to fall on the deaf ears of substantial sections of the population. That is the strong message from the public at large.

From the standpoint of ethics, this means that ordinary citizens now refuse to recognize the "off limits" signs posted around the hermetically sealed world of nuclear "experts." One of the politically appointed officials at the Defense Department once complained to me about the involvement of American Roman Catholic bishops in nuclear issues, saying they were "tampering in geopolitical areas." Whether trespass onto holy nuclear ground be a deliberate moral intrusion, as in the case of the bishops, or a vague sense on the part of laypersons that something is wrong, the significance for ethical judgments cannot be overemphasized.

This is because in any sphere—medical, legal or military—ethical judgments are not simply a function of professional expertise. Albert Speer spoke of "the phenomenon of the technician's often blind devotion to his task."[4] In the Third Reich, Speer recalled, no word was used more frequently than "loyalty;" he discovered too late "that there is only one valid kind of loyalty—toward morality."[5] Outside scrutiny is essential to the maintenance of clear limits upon the autocratic tendencies of inbred technocratic loyalty. Public participation in nuclear policy is needed to maintain a humane perspective. Nuclear theorists wage "war on the cheap" in the labyrinths of strategic abstraction, but ordinary people emphasize the high cost of nuclear war and question whether any political objective can be worth it. Increasingly they resent euphemisms or evasions which conceal this truth. Yet nuclear strategists still speak of the irrational and naive assumptions of the general public. They even discuss whether the public ought to be involved or informed in nuclear issues at all. Here is an example:

> "It might be that only a highly specialized cadre of invisible technocrats can carry on with these matters in secret, because of public abhorrence of the subject. Like the death camps of Germany in the 1940s, perhaps the planning and analysis for nuclear war should be an invisible issue."[6]

Such arrogant—indeed amoral—thinking is additional proof of the urgent importance of informed popular concern as a countervailing check upon this unhealthily closed elite.

Ordinary citizens are also alarmed when it appears that government leaders are insensitive to the perils of nuclear war. The US President does not inspire confidence when he speaks casually about the possibility of a limited nuclear war or when he dismisses European peace rallies as "bought and paid for by the Soviet Union." The public becomes concerned about the prospects for arms agreements when they hear the President say, "the argument, if there is any, will be over which weapons, not whether we should forsake weaponry for treaties and agreements."[7] In fact, the public has had to come to grips with a whole range of troubling and sometimes outrageous statements by Administration officials. And Administration positions on nuclear questions cannot be excused as "clumsy rhetoric." The public now knows better.

The upshot has been just the opposite of Colin Gray's thesis. Greater public awareness has fueled anti-nuclear opinion. Recognizing this, Administration officials have become more circumspect. But it is too late. Concerned Americans and Europeans are searching out the essential facts of U S nuclear policy and attempting to influence its direction.

A confluence of threatening prospects is a second reason that a thorough scrutiny of deterrence doctrine is appropriate. The resurgence of the Cold War and the meager political dialogue between the superpowers is painfully evident. The refusal by President Reagan to consider ratification of the Salt II Treaty or to continue the twenty-year effort for a Comprehensive Test Ban Treaty throws a revealing light upon his dual-track plan, simultaneously to build up and scale down the nuclear arsenal. The $1·8 trillion, five-year defense build-up which increases nuclear expenditures to over 20 percent of the total military budget speaks for itself. The present low ebb of political imagination and creativity seems to be inversely correlated with the rising tides of the arms race. The arms race is not only a result of ideological obsession with a "potential enemy," it is also a product of the circular reasoning which convinces believers that this fixation is necessary.

So a poisoned political relationship between "potential enemies" stands behind the nuclear threat, and in that environment, nuclear weaponry and strategy appear to lead lives of their own. Weapons accuracy with new missiles (MX, Trident II, Pershing II) has now developed to the point where, for the first time, a nuclear war-fighting strategy is both supportable and declared as stated policy.

In a revealing exchange of letters in 1983 between Secretary of Defense Caspar W. Weinberger and Theodore Draper, Mr. Weinberger was unable to extricate himself from the contradiction that on the one hand nuclear war is unwinnable, yet on the other, if fought, the plan is to "prevail:"

> "Neither is there a contradiction between our view that there could be no winners in a nuclear war and our planning to prevail, if war is forced upon us, in denying victory to the Soviet Union."[8]

Thus the concept of deterrence retains its value as an emotive word, sparking feelings of security and safety, but has lost any precise meaning.

This is clear even in the authoritative study of nuclear deterrence by a pro-nuclear strategic theorist, Laurence Freedman, when he concluded (rather strangely) that "The Emperor Deterrence may have no clothes, but he is still Emperor."[9] The loss cannot be restored through word-playing ("extended deterrence," etc.). Nuclear deterrence today means whatever the speaker wishes it to mean. It is a blank check. The Scowcroft Commission Report, which Mr. Weinberger uses for support in his letter exchange with Draper, removes deterrence from any accountable real-world meaning.[10] To the extent that President Reagan's view of the Soviet Union holds sway, that is, that they are "the focus of evil in the modern world," one would surmise that the blank check of deterrence will be written out on the high side.

After nuclear deterrence is redeployed to cover every conceivable threat, actual or perceived, and every belief or determination in the minds of Soviet leaders, absolutely any weapons system can be justified in terms of the blank check of deterrence. As a result a whole panoply of hard-target kill-capable weapons can be developed and justified: the MX, Trident II and Pershing II missiles.

A curious "selling point" advanced for the new war-fighting and winning strategy is that it is a more moral policy than mutual assured destruction. Henry Kissinger in September 1979, in a ringing call for counterforce targeting at a conference in Brussels on the future of NATO, spoke of "bloodthirsty strategies" and the need to "move away from the senseless and demoralizing strategy of massive civilian extermination and try to develop some credible military purpose for the tactical and theater nuclear forces . . ."[11] But with 40,000 designated military targets in the Soviet Union, sixty of which are in Moscow, it is clear that not much of a case can be made for moral superiority due to greater discrimination in targeting. The increased emphasis on targeting Soviet political and command leadership centers in and around major cities means that a counterforce attack would be little different from a countercity attack. Therefore the high degree of accuracy in nuclear weapons does not make a "surgical" attack possible.

It is precisely because the strategy of "nuclear deterrence" allows for the kind of weapons necessary to carry out a war-fighting strategy that the claim for the morality of deterrence on the grounds that it was a policy which, while obnoxious, was at root intended to ward off a greater evil, falls. That this argument is still put by some churchpersons, in good faith, shows how they have not grasped the magnitude of the change in circumstance. Superaccurate, hard-target kill-capable weapons like the

MX are not placed in vulnerable silos in order to be used to strike empty silos. The very nature of the weapons currently being developed makes a sham of stable deterrence. The new weapons unmask nuclear deterrence as a game of advantage. Their sophisticated capabilities are proof that the real, concrete and inescapable effect of nuclear deterrence has been to legitimize the arms race. That particular moral argument is now as bankrupt as the tendentious ex post facto claim for the "morality" of counterforce. Both should be removed from the debate forthwith.

After nearly four decades, at this late stage of deterrence theory, the true nature of the strategy is being exposed. Albert Einstein said that "the unleashed power of the atom has changed everything except our way of thinking."[12] A war-fighting strategy which plans employment of nuclear weapons as if they were conventional weapons dramatically and openly demonstrates that "our way of thinking" has not changed.

Continuation of old ways of thinking was made easier because nuclear weapons slipped onto the stage of history under the positive guise of salvation. That memory is still with us. The bombings of Hiroshima and Nagasaki were welcomed in a positive light, seen as a way to shorten the war and save American lives (though substantial historical evidence suggests that a Japanese conditional surrender could have been obtained diplomatically without use of the atomic bomb).[13] After that unilateral first use during the period of the American monopoly, the continued possession and development of the atomic weapon was justified by a succession of further "good reasons" relating to the deepening Cold War between the USA and the USSR and as a cheap means of deterrence for NATO. There will always be "good reasons," and good theories, for having and using nuclear weapons. That is what the strategy of nuclear deterrence is—a "good reason." In fact, as the American Trappist contemplative Thomas Merton reminded us, there will be "perfectly good reasons" when "the sane ones, the well-adapted ones . . . press the buttons that will initiate the great festival of destruction."[14]

But there is another dimension of the strategy of nuclear deterrence which represents an unchanged "way of thinking." Its roots are found in the extermination bombing of World War II developed by the RAF and the USAF, which Lewis Mumford termed "unconditional moral surrender to Hitler." The Allies exceeded Hitler's destruction of Warsaw, Rotterdam and London with the "area" bombings of Hamburg, Dresden and Tokyo. David Lilienthal, the first chairman of the Atomic Energy Commission said, "The fences are gone. And it was we, the civilized, who have pushed standardless conduct to its ultimate."[15]

This "standardless conduct" has never been squarely faced. Since the end of World War II, it has always been shrouded in and protected by "good reasons," chiefly the strategy of deterrence itself. But to "deter" means to "frighten" or to "strike terror." Winston Churchill's eloquent definition of nuclear deterrence described "safety" as "the sturdy child of terror, and survival the twin brother of annihilation." These inevitable attributes of deterrence the great statesman made plain.[16] What tragic irony. The threat of "terror" and "annihilation" that would be a crime for individuals is made a virtue as policy for the nation. The 1983 United States Military Posture Statement spells it out in straightforward fashion: "Deterrence depends upon the assured capability and manifest will to inflict damage on the Soviet Union disproportionate to any goals that rational Soviet leaders might hope to achieve."[17] In advance of any nuclear holocaust, under certain unstated conditions there is a willingness to use genocidal weapons against our enemy. In other words, there is a willingness to do things which—in the threat and the execution—fly in the face of all that we hold to be most noble and civilized in our society. What are our children to make of such double standards? Which standards should they adopt? What defense have we against their charge of grotesque hypocrisy? This is the immoral basis of nuclear deterrence which I shall spell out in a moment. But before that, I must clear two other obstacles, one a disquiet, the other a confusion.

Without doubt, some readers may feel distressed by the one-sided application of this judgment. "What about the Russians?", they will ask. To them I must answer that whatever the nature of Soviet society, however different from our own in its values and however distasteful and sad we may find it, the statement stands. It is absolute, within the context of our Judeo-Christian heritage—unless we are prepared to abandon civilization's values for relativism.

The second point is a confusion. Continually, the advocates of nuclear deterrence justify it in terms of defense. To be sure, the defense of a nation is recognized as a moral cause. But nuclear weapons have nothing to do with defense. As Henry Kissinger said, "It simply does not make much sense to defend one's way of life with a strategy which guarantees its destruction."[18] A policy of national suicide is more than a problem of "sense" or logic—it is immoral.

The formal basis for indicting the "standardless conduct" inherent in the willingness to threaten with and to use nuclear weapons resides in "Just War" criteria. Now, in Just War literature there is ample and detailed condemnation of nuclear war and weapons. But some Just War theoreticians attempt to make room for the use of nuclear weapons. When they do, there is a heavy dependence on "best case" constructions using highly theoretical possibilities, naive assumptions concerning the control and effects of nuclear weapons, the assumption that escalation can be controlled, and that an enemy would "play the game" the way we wish it to be played. A good example of this is the recent collection by a group of conservative British churchmen entitled *The Cross and the Bomb*.

So how should the Just War criteria be applied? Let us take them in turn. To meet the definition of justice:

1. *War should be declared as a last resort.* If this is so, why are we developing "first strike" nuclear weapons and why will we not forswear "first use"?
2. *War should be declared by legitimate authority.* Do we really believe a hot-line message will go out saying. "We're going to nuke you"? Wouldn't that political authority lose legitimacy if he decided to push the button? Should any human being on the face of this earth have that kind of authority?
3. *War should have a just or justifying cause.* What injury, what cause could possibly justify the mutual destruction of two nations and indeed jeopardize life on the planet?
4. *War should have a justifiable goal.* How could mutual destruction satisfy the goals of survival, justice and peace?
5. *War should be conducted in due proportion.* How could the good possibly outweigh the evil? What assurance is there that catastrophic escalation will not take place? What "good" is there after mutual suicide?
6. *War should be conducted in a just attitude using just means.* How can extermination, vengeance or revenge be a just means or attitude?
7. *War should be fought only if there is a reasonable possibility of success.* What is success in an "unwinnable" nuclear war? What does Secretary of Defense Weinberger mean by "prevailing"? Would there be any winners in a nuclear war?
8. *War should be conducted so as to provide discrimination between combatants and noncombatants or immunity for noncombatants.* In a nuclear exchange, would there be any reasonable limits to "collateral damage"? What are the chances of "a limited nuclear war"?

In a careful two-year study, the United States Roman Catholic bishops linked "expert" testimony to the Just War criteria and in all instances judged that nuclear weapons could not be used on a moral basis. But the bishops were confined within the boundary set by Pope John Paul II when he said:

"In current conditions 'deterrence' based on balance, certainly not as an end in itself but as a step on the way toward a progressive disarmament, may still be judged morally acceptable."[19]

The highly tentative and qualified support which the bishops give to a "moral" deterrence leaves the Pope's judgment hanging by a very slender thread.

The key question is obviously, under what real-world circumstance would the bishops allow for the actual use of nuclear weapons? A close reading of their Pastoral Letter on War and Peace would render the answer "never": "There must be no misunderstanding of our profound skepticism about the moral acceptability of any use of nuclear weapons."[20] The spirit of the Pastoral Letter is reflected in the words of Cardinal Krol in a sermon at the White House in 1979: "possession yes, for deterrence . . . but use, never."[21] Then on what basis does the Pastoral Letter support the Pope's statement that deterrence is provisionally "morally acceptable"? On the basis of *possession* of nuclear weapons only, *not* on any contemplated use. What on earth does that mean?

Cardinal Basil Hume and others following the line of the Pastoral Letter have suggested that an intellectually legitimate distinction can be drawn between "intention to use" and an "opponent's perception that one has an intention to use." This is because the credibility of the nuclear threat is, in their opinion, based upon a judgment of what the opponent believes to be your intention, not upon what your intention actually is. This distinction is of the greatest importance to them, for they then construct a complicated ethical justification upon the presumption of bluff. It goes as follows.

The conditional moral acceptability of nuclear deterrence depends upon it "working" (which really means that, for whatever reason, no nuclear weapons shall explode). If the deterrent threat is the reason why no bombs explode (and for the purposes of this argument they assume that it is), then it restrains the trigger fingers by remaining always a credible threat. For the threat to be credible, the opponent must believe that you would use the nuclear weapons in some circumstance. But the moral acceptability has another essential prerequisite: your private knowledge that, in fact, you never would use the weapons. This ethical case therefore rests inescapably upon bluff, because if you admitted to yourself an intention to use, by the established ethical principle that moral error lies first in the intention and not in the act, it would be impossible to maintain the claim to moral conduct.

Jesuit ethicist Francis X. Winters regards the case for possession of nuclear weapons linked with a prohibition against their use as a tenable position based on a scholastic nicety. But the case is not as delicate as Winters and other advocates of the bluff suppose. The "possession yes, use never" position allows the clergy the luxury of appearing to be moral while in fact lending support to the deterrence policy which is in place. And that policy, as they must surely know, does not rest on pure moral intention. Our present policy is not a policy of bluff. Indeed Albert Wohlstetter, the nuclear theorist, has described bluff as "an invitation rather than a deterrent."[22] But if, in fact, the clergy do not believe that the Soviets will believe their "possession yes, use never" policy—indeed, count upon them not doing so—why propose it? Is it not perverse to depend upon Soviet distrust in order to try to move toward higher moral ground rather than to attempt to break down distrust? How is it moral to advertise a declaratory policy which is wholly at variance with operating policy?

To their credit, the bishops and cardinals have served notice that deterrence, however defined, can only be an interim strategy on the road to disarmament. Unfortunately, this notice comes at a time when the newest upward spiral of the arms race has already well begun, and when governments look upon deterrence as a permanent institution. One cannot help wondering how long the clergy can continue along a precarious path of tentative approval in the face of absolutely no evidence of governmental preparedness to alter course.

The US Catholic bishops' "profound skepticism about the moral acceptability of any use of nuclear weapons" needs to be carried to its logical conclusion that nuclear deterrence itself is immoral. Let a case be made for the necessary forms of nuclear posture (such as that of minimum deterrence) as we begin to escape from the nuclear trap, but let it be made in purely pragmatic terms; and let no one claim that even such a changed policy has moral virtue. The time has come when the churches acting in concert and in the spirit of repentance must withdraw *all* moral sanction from the strategy of nuclear deterrence. I expressed this view to one of the architects of the Pastoral Letter along with my wonder as to why the bishops did not arrive at the same conclusion. The response was: "That's too Niebuhrian for us" (after the theologian Reinhold Niebuhr, who emphasized political realism). Perhaps so. Perhaps I too readily admit that Christians participate inevitably in the evil of this world. But the history of nuclear deterrence and the church's acquiescence or approval indicates that this is precisely the case.

The strategy of nuclear deterrence has always had its "Peace through Strength" proponents in and out of the church. And for them, the Pope's tentative imprimatur "morally acceptable" on a " 'deterrence' based on balance" lends a vital measure of moral support. The perpetuation of the arms race and the drive for military advantage will continue as long as a shred of moral legitimacy is provided; and apparently moral legitimacy is very important for the support of nuclear policy. Why else would the leaders of the Reagan Administration use the word so often in relation to nuclear policy? In 1982 in Chicago Elliot Abrams, Assistant Secretary of State for Human Rights and Humanitarian Affairs, gave a speech entitled "Nuclear weapons: what is the moral response?" He indicated he was speaking in view of his "responsibility . . . to insure that American values are adequately weighed in our foreign policy." The essence of the speech comes near the end, in three words, "Deterrence is moral." This is followed immediately by the quotation of Pope John Paul II's assessment of the morality of "deterrence based on balance."[23]

But Pope John Paul II has had other things to say on the subject. When he visited Hiroshima in 1981 he said: "From now on it is only through a conscious choice and through a deliberate policy that humanity can survive."[24] I believe that that "conscious choice" should begin by tearing away the remaining thread of moral acceptability which still surrounds the strategy of nuclear deterrence. Only then can a "deliberate policy" emerge, based on a paradigm shift from terror and annihilation to survival and peace.

So what are we to do? There is no easy moral escape from the "nuclear box" in which we find ourselves. We are all involved. There are no leaps of faith available to take us instantly out of the box or fudged moral reasoning to permit possession or use of nuclear weapons on a moral basis. The most hopeful direction is that of moving away from dependence on nuclear weapons through bilateral phased reductions and independent initiatives. This has virtue because it provides a realistic way of building trust, moving to safer levels where multilateral talks can take place, and may eventually open up the possibility of getting out of the "nuclear box." But no one should be deluded into thinking this is a "moral" position, not when anywhere along the downward path to disarmament a nuclear holocaust could still happen.

To a society which can possess nearly 30,000 nuclear weapons and plan to spend $400 billion in the next five years for more and "better" nuclear weapons, and still claim that this is "moral"—to such an optimistic culture, unmasking the sinister side of deterrence may seem excessively pessimistic. To an activist culture, not to offer concrete "plans" or "solutions," but simply to clear ground for a "new way of thinking," may seem too theoretical and modest an undertaking. But at this late hour, to propose yet another solution based on the presupposition of nuclear force is merely to continue rearranging deck chairs on the *Titanic*.

At the age of ninety, the renowned psychiatrist Dr. Karl Menninger is wrestling with "the single greatest mental health problem in the world today" expressed in the tentative title of a book he is writing, *The Suicidal Intention of Nuclear Armament*. Asked if America is going to "self-destruct," he said recently, "Of course we're going to self-destruct. At the present rate we're going, that's the plan. Piling up rocks is no way to settle a dispute. One side gets rocks so the other side gets bricks. Then they boast, 'My pile is bigger than your pile.' That's the way children talk. If a patient did that, do you know what a psychiatrist would say? Why destroy yourself?"[25]

Today, if public opinion polls are even a rough indication, the patients feel with Dr. Menninger the same sense of inevitability about self-destruction. But this grassroots anti-nuclear sentiment means that people are not prepared simply to cower under thickening clouds of terror. They stand up and ask "*Why* are we about to destroy ourselves?" The menacing clouds which the nuclear age has brought to the world can only be dispelled when people are resolved to do so. It will not be easy, but it certainly can be done if we have the moral courage and the political will to do it.

Arthur Koestler did not see aggression as the major trouble of human beings, but rather "an excess capacity for fanatical devotion." Yet the two need not be mutually exclusive. The record of human history appears to document amply the trail of aggression. The myths and ideologies which nations have used to transform personal devotion into national egoism can also be historically traced. The task of demythologizing and desacralizing these myths is a painful process. It will not be easy to tear away the "good reasons" which have provided a measure of comfort and coherence during the nuclear age. Nor will it be easy to face squarely the reality that there never has been a more dangerous myth than the present one, that the most destructive military means ever devised should be the bulwark of our security. Open admission of the moral bankruptcy of the strategy of nuclear deterrence is admittedly a difficult first step in turning from this danger. But, as Socrates said, a knowledge of one's error and ignorance is the beginning of wisdom.

Twenty years ago President John Kennedy gave a speech in which practical action went hand in hand with openness to a "new way of thinking." He announced his unilateral decision to stop atmospheric testing, a first step toward adoption of the Limited Test Ban Treaty of 1963. That substantive political agreement came out of President Kennedy's deep reflection upon questions of war and peace after the shock of the Cuban Missile Crisis. Those close to him recall how the last months of his life were preoccupied with this issue, as the President mulled over what was to be the greatest speech of his career—what he called "The Peace Speech," delivered at the American University. In it, he spoke of the conclusions which he rejected: "the conclusion that war is inevitable," the conclusion "that we are gripped by forces we cannot control." He refused to be immobilized by the underlying assumption of nuclear deterrence, that we are permanently faced by an implacable enemy who deserves day by day to be threatened with nuclear destruction. He emphasized that "history teaches us that enmities between nations, as between individuals, do not last forever. However fixed our likes and dislikes may seem, the tide of time and events will often bring surprising changes in the relations between nations and neighbors."[26]

That last observation sets forth the identity of the "conscious choice" still not yet made: to humanize our perception of world politics and to apply the highest and best of our civilization's standards. It also shows how swift and dramatic could be the consequences of that. The nature of that choice is clear: "Confident and unafraid, we labor on—not toward a strategy of annihilation but toward a strategy of peace."[27]

This is the challenge. It is to our generation alone. It cannot be dodged. Have we the courage, faith and humanity to take it up?

11 NUCLEAR WEAPONS AND INTERNATIONAL LAW *John Griffith*

Professor John Griffith, Hon. LL.D. (Edinburgh and York, Ontario), LL.M., F.B.A., is Professor of Public Law at the London School of Economics and Political Science in the University of London. From 1940 to 1946 he served in the British and Indian armies. Subsequently he became successively Lecturer and Reader in Law and Professor of English Law at the LSE. He became a Fellow of the British Academy in 1977. Professor Griffith is the author of several works on issues of public law and civil liberties.

The laws governing the relationship between the state and the individual, or between individuals, within a society are generally understood to be found in rules made by or under statute or in the pronouncements of judges in particular cases. These rules say what activities are criminal and punishable by imprisonment, by fines or other forms of constraint or penalty. They also confer legally enforceable rights to compensation on individuals who suffer loss or damage in certain defined situations as, for example, where contracts are broken or accidental injuries incurred.

The reason why non-lawyers are often puzzled by the notion of international law as a system governing the relations between states and are skeptical about its existence is that they think of law as a set of rules having rule-makers. They feel that in the absence of a supreme World Authority which could lay down the rules governing the relations between states there can be no law in any easily recognizable sense. But if two or more states come to a specific agreement on certain matters and promise to be bound by its terms, it may be said, without abuse of language, that they have created a piece of law for themselves (as individuals do when they enter into contracts). And if they further agree that any dispute arising about the agreement should be settled by an independent body, even an international court, that reinforces the proposition that they are now in legal relations with one another.

So treaties (including conventions, protocols and declarations) between states are a primary source of international law. If the claims stopped there, much of the controversy would disappear. But another major source is appealed to as giving validity, authority and legitimacy to particular rules of international law.

This other source is custom. This is shorthand for what the International Military Tribunal at Nuremberg in September 1946 called "the customs and practices of states which gradually obtained universal recognition." The claim is often put in somewhat stronger terms than this and it is argued that it is sufficient if the recognition is widespread though short of universal. It has also been suggested that in the contemporary age of highly developed techniques of communication and information, the formation of a custom through the medium of international organizations is greatly facilitated and accelerated; the establishment of such a custom would require no more than one generation or even less than that.[1] On the other hand, even widespread recognition is not always convincing evidence of the establishment of a custom if the leading participants do not subscribe to it. This might be the case if the USA and the USSR, on a matter of outer space law, were in the minority.[2]

To a considerable extent, custom has become codified in treaties. But partial codification of a custom should not carry any implication that the uncodified part has ceased to be a custom. In 1899, the Preamble to the Hague Conventions in the famous Martens clause provided:

> "Until a more complete code of the laws of war is issued, the High Contracting Parties think it right to declare that in cases not included in the Regulations adopted by them, populations and belligerents remain under the protection and empire of the principles of international law, as they result from the usages established between civilized nations, from the laws of humanity, and the requirements of the public conscience."

These words were repeated with minor additions in the Hague Convention of 1907. (A caveat must be entered about the last two phrases in that declaration. I am here concerned only with "the usages established," not with the wider claims to humanity and public conscience.)

It is often asserted baldly that the resolutions of the General Assembly of the United Nations, and of its predecessor under the League of Nations, do not have the status of international law. Clearly many of them do not. But those which are passed by the great majority of nations, especially if major powers are in support, provide strong evidence of the existence of a custom or of a custom in the making. It will be obvious that such a formulation carries within it an element of doubt. At what point does continuing practice or continuing acknowledgment of a principle become part of customary international law? How is the support for the principle to be assessed? If universality is not required, by how much may support fall short? Can a practice become a legal custom if not followed by one of the major states? But some principles have certainly become so widely accepted that their status as customary law can be denied only if the whole claim of custom as a source of international law is denied.

Similarly, written agreements between states, especially large numbers of states, may be considered as expressions of widespread consensus and so be regarded as binding on all states. Such agreements may therefore help to create customs, reversing the more usual process whereby customs become codified into written agreements.

So treaties between states, and customary practices, established over time and accepted by the great majority of states, including the most powerful, are the principal sources of international law. To these may be added pronouncements by international courts, though these are of much less significance. As already noted, some writers cite general principles of justice, the laws of humanity and the requirements of the public conscience as sources of international law. These seem to me to be at one remove from agreements and custom. They may indeed be the basis for an agreement or, even more, for that progressive development which leads to the creation of a custom. But I find them too vague to be acceptable as sources of international law in their own right.

The development of the laws of war

In their introduction to *The Laws of Armed Conflicts*,[3] Schindler and Toman suggest that three factors led to the codification of the laws of war in the second half of the nineteenth century. These were the introduction of compulsory military service, the great increase in the horrors of war (especially the number of victims), and what is now the curious and touching belief that "the progress of civilization should have the effect of alleviating as much as possible the calamities of war."

These words were contained in the Declaration of St. Petersburg in 1868, which further recorded the view that the only legitimate object which states should endeavor to accomplish during war was to weaken the military forces of the enemy, that for this purpose it was sufficient to disable the greatest possible number of men, that this object would be exceeded by the employment of arms which uselessly aggravated the sufferings of disabled men or rendered their death inevitable, and that the employment of such arms would, therefore, be contrary to the laws of humanity. The nineteen signatories to the Declaration (which included France, Great Britain and Russia) agreed mutually to renounce the use of any projectile below 400 grammes in weight which was either explosive or inflammable. So was born in modern times the limitation on the weapons of war.

In 1874, a conference of fifteen states adopted a Russian draft on the laws and customs of war, but it was not ratified. The draft on the laws of war did not recognize in belligerents an unlimited power in the adoption of means of injuring the enemy. Amongst the means specifically forbidden were the use of poison or poisoned weapons, the use of arms, projectiles or material calculated to cause unnecessary suffering, and attacks on undefended towns.

Limitation of war weapons was the object of the First Hague Peace Conference of 1899. That object was not achieved. But one Declaration was made prohibiting the use of weapons diffusing asphyxiating gases; and another prohibited the use of expanding (dum-dum) bullets. The Second Hague Conference in 1907, at which forty-four states were represented, revised three Conventions which had been agreed in 1899 and adopted ten other Conventions. The delegates signed the Final Acts, but the states did not ratify. A third international peace conference was forestalled by the outbreak of war in 1914.

The Second Hague Conference recorded in its preamble, echoing the sadly archaic sentiment of 1868, that it was "animated by the desire to serve even in this extreme case the interests of humanity and the ever progressive needs of civilization." Article 22 restated the principle that the right of belligerents to adopt means of injuring the enemy was not unlimited, and following Articles expressly forbade the use of poison or poisoned weapons, the use of weapons calculated to cause unnecessary suffering, the destruction of enemy property unless imperatively demanded by the necessities of war, attack on undefended towns, and on other buildings such as churches, museums and hospitals.

These Hague Convention rules on land warfare of 1907 were said by the Nuremberg International Military Tribunal in 1946 to be "recognized by all civilized nations and were regarded as being declaratory of the laws and customs of war."

As wars increased in ferocity and terror from 1914 to the present, the attempts to contain their practice have diminished. Those with an apocalyptic vision may see 1907 as the last serious effort by the politicians of Europe and North America to hold back the drive to self-destruction. The First World War of 1914–18 saw massive slaughter of members of the armed forces. World War II added to this the massive slaughter of civilians also. Today we are poised on the edge of a third world war with weapons in our hands that will admit of no discrimination, no distinctions, no humanity at all. The "progress of civilization" has not lived up to its nineteenth-century expectations.

This is not to suggest that there have been no developments in the aftermath of the world wars. One most directly relevant to our subject was the Geneva Protocol of 1925 which restated the prohibition of the use of asphyxiating, poisonous or other gases and added bacteriological methods of warfare. Over 100 countries ratified or acceded to the Protocol. Since 1945 the United Nations General Assembly has several times called for its strict observance.

In 1948 came the Convention on the prevention and punishment of the crime of genocide defined to mean specified acts committed with intent to destroy, in whole or in part, a national, ethnical, racial or religious group, as such. The acts included killing and causing serious bodily or mental harm to members of the group. It was also made punishable to conspire, to incite and to attempt to commit genocide, and complicity in genocide.

In 1949, a Diplomatic Conference at Geneva approved four Conventions, subsequently ratified by many states. Convention IV related to the protection of civilian persons in time of war and was the first international agreement in the laws of war exclusively to address their treatment. The Convention was comprehensive and contained 159 Articles. The provisions of Articles 13–26 cover the whole of the population of the countries in conflict, without any distinction based on race, nationality, religion or political opinion, and are intended to alleviate the sufferings caused by war. They relate to hospitals, neutralized zones, the wounded and the sick, evacuation, medical supplies, child and family welfare. In these and other Articles, an attempt was made to protect in part the position of civilians generally, not only those who are citizens of neutral countries. To the Final Act of the Conference the USSR appended its regret that a resolution it had submitted, condemning the use of methods of mass extermination, was rejected. Roberts and Guelff observe that the Convention builds on pre-existing codified provisions but substantially supplements them.[4]

In 1950 the International Law Commission of the United Nations set down the principles of international law recognized in the Charter of the

Nuremberg Tribunal and in the judgments of the Tribunal. Principle VI itemized the following, among others, as crimes under international law: planning, preparation, initiation or waging of a war of aggression or a war in violation of international treaties, agreements or assurances; participation in a common plan or conspiracy for the accomplishment of any of those acts; wanton destruction of cities, towns or villages or devastation not justified by military necessity; murder, extermination, enslavement, deportation and other inhuman acts done against any civilian population, when such acts are done in execution of or in connection with any crime referred to above.

It cannot be said that the revolution in warfare caused by the explosion of the atom bombs over Japan in 1945 has so far resulted in any significant reaction in international law. In 1956 the International Committee of the Red Cross produced a set of draft rules for the limitation of the dangers incurred by the civilian population in time of war. These began with a restatement of the principle (which was beginning to look little more than a hope) that the right of combatants to adopt means of injuring the enemy was not unlimited. One draft rule was that the combatants should confine their operations to the destruction of the military resources of the enemy and leave the civilian population outside the sphere of armed attacks. The draft rules prohibited the use of weapons whose harmful effects "could spread to an unforeseen degree or escape, either in space or in time, from the control of those who employ them, thus endangering the civilian population." It is plain that weapons producing radioactivity came within this definition. The draft rules were submitted to governments, who did not respond.

However, in 1961 the General Assembly of the United Nations passed a declaration (resolution 1653(XVI)) on the prohibition of the use of nuclear and thermonuclear weapons. The declaration recalled that the use of weapons of mass destruction, causing unnecessary human suffering, had in the past been prohibited, as being contrary to the laws of humanity and to the principles of international law. The resolution declared that the use of these weapons (a) was contrary to the spirit, letter and aims of the United Nations and, as such, a direct violation of the Charter; (b) would cause indiscriminate suffering and destruction to mankind and civilization and, as such, was contrary to the rule of international law and to the laws of humanity; and (c) was a war directed against mankind in general, since the peoples not involved in such a war would be subjected to all the evils generated by the use of such weapons. The resolution further declared that any state using such weapons was to be considered as violating the UN Charter, as acting contrary to the laws of humanity and as committing a crime against mankind and civilization. Finally the resolution requested the Secretary-General to consult the governments of member states with a view to convening a conference for the signing of a convention on these lines.

The declaration was adopted by a vote of 55 in favor, 20 against and 26 abstentions. The USSR voted in favor. France, South Africa, Turkey, the USA and the United Kingdom were amongst those who voted against. Of the 62 member states which replied to the Secretary-General, 33 were in favor of a conference. Not surprisingly, no such conference was held.

The XXth International Conference of the Red Cross in Vienna in 1965 restated four major principles of international law: (1) that the right of combatants to adopt means of injuring the enemy was not unlimited; (2) that it was prohibited to launch attacks against civilian populations as such; (3) that distinction must be made between combatants and civilians so that the latter were spared as much as possible; (4) that the general principles of the Law of War applied to nuclear and similar weapons. The first three principles were affirmed by the General Assembly of the UN in resolution 2444 (XXIII) in 1968.[5]

In the next year the General Assembly restated the illegality under international law of the use of chemical and bacteriological weapons (resolution 2603A (XXIV)). This was adopted by 80 votes in favor (including the USSR), 3 against (Australia, Portugal and the USA) and 36 abstentions (including the UK).

Article 2, para. 3, of the Charter of the United Nations provides: "All members shall settle their international disputes by peaceful means in such a manner that international peace and security, and justice, are not endangered." This is not, of course, the whole story. For example, Article 51 protects what it calls an "inherent right" to self-defense. But the general principle of the non-use of force is fundamental. In 1972, resolution 2936 (XVII) of the General Assembly applied this principle specifically to nuclear weapons, by renouncing the use or threat of force and declaring "the permanent prohibition of the use of nuclear weapons." This was adopted by 73 votes to 4; there were 46 abstentions (including the USA and the UK).

A further group of provisions was adopted by the Diplomatic Conference at Geneva on the Reaffirmation and Development of International Humanitarian Law Applicable in Armed Conflicts in 1977. The First Protocol was additional to the Geneva Conventions of 1949 and related to the protection of victims of international armed conflicts. Three basic rules relating to methods and means of warfare were stated. The first, once again, was that the right of parties to the conflict to choose methods or means is not unlimited. The second prohibited the employment of weapons, projectiles and material and methods of warfare of a nature to cause superfluous injury or unnecessary suffering. The third prohibited the employment of methods or means which are intended, or may be expected, to cause widespread, long-term and severe damage to the environment. This important Protocol, which none of the major powers has yet ratified, is discussed in more detail below.

This last provision is to be distinguished from a United Nations convention, also of 1977, by which states undertook not to engage in military or other hostile use of "environmental modification techniques" having widespread, long-lasting or severe effects, as the means of destruction, damage or injury to any other state. This was concerned not with damage to the environment but the use of those techniques as weapons. Examples were methods of forest and crop destruction in Vietnam, and attempts by the US to manipulate weather in Indochina with a view to muddying or flooding land routes.[6] The techniques were described as those for changing, through the deliberate manipulation of natural processes, the dynamics, composition or structure of the earth, including its biota lithosphere, hydrosphere and atmosphere, or of outer space. The UK, the USA and the USSR were among the first of many signatories.

For the protection of the environment, a number of treaties have been entered into. In 1963 a treaty banning nuclear weapon tests in the atmosphere, in outer space or under water was sponsored by the USSR, the UK and the USA and signed by a large number of states. In 1971, the same three countries agreed on the prohibition of the emplacement of nuclear weapons and other weapons of mass destruction on the sea bed and the ocean floor and in the subsoil thereof. This treaty also was widely acceded to by other states. So also was a convention of 1972, similarly sponsored, on the prohibition of the development, production and stockpiling of bacteriological and toxin weapons. The parties agreed also to destroy any existing stockpiles and means of delivery of such weapons.

In 1981, agreement was reached at the United Nations on a convention and three protocols prohibiting or restricting the use of certain conventional weapons which might be deemed to be excessively injurious or to have indiscriminate effects. Protocol I related to fragments not detectable by x rays; Protocol II to mines, booby traps and other devices;

Protocol III to incendiary weapons. These provisions are intended primarily for the protection of civilians, not combatants, and are so understood.

On December 9, 1981, the General Assembly approved a resolution proclaiming that states and statesmen that resorted first to the use of nuclear weapons would be committing the gravest crime against humanity; that there would never be any justification or pardon for statesmen who would take the decision to be the first to use nuclear weapons; that any doctrines allowing the first use of nuclear weapons and any actions pushing the world toward a catastrophe were incompatible with human moral standards and the lofty ideals of the United Nations; that it was the supreme duty and direct obligation of the leaders of nuclear-weapon states to act in such a way as to eliminate the risk of the outbreak of a nuclear conflict; and that nuclear energy should be used exclusively for peaceful purposes and only for the benefit of mankind. In favor were 82 states (including the Soviet Union); against were 19 states (including the USA and the UK); abstaining were 41 states; 13 states were absent and 1 state announced that it was not participating in the vote.

In June 1982 Mr. Brezhnev, then President of the Presidium of the Supreme Soviet of the USSR, sent a message to the General Assembly of the United Nations which stated: "Guided by the desire to do all in its power to deliver the peoples from the threat of nuclear devastation and ultimately to exclude its very possibility from the life of mankind, the Soviet State solemnly declares: the Union of Soviet Socialist Republics assumes an obligation not to be the first to use nuclear weapons. This obligation shall become effective immediately.'

The use of nuclear weapons

From this historical survey, we must now consider in more detail those rules of international law of particular importance to the use of nuclear weapons.

International customary law recognizes three principles. The first is that the right of belligerents to adopt means of injuring the enemy is not unlimited; the second is that the use of weapons or tactics which cause unnecessary suffering or destruction of property is forbidden; the third is that civilians not engaged in war work are entitled to special protection. None of these principles is so clear that it can be applied as a yardstick of legality without elaboration or further specification. As we have seen, some of these principles, along with others, have, with more particularity, been codified in treaties, conventions, protocols and declarations.

None of these codes has stated in terms that the use of nuclear weapons is contrary to international law.

At first sight, the strongest and the most recent set of relevant provisions are those in the 1977 Geneva Protocol I. This concerns the protection of civilians, builds on the 1949 Geneva Convention IV, and contains 102 Articles. The history of this Protocol is instructive.[7] In 1946 a Preliminary Conference of National Red Cross Societies recommended the prohibition of the use of atomic energy for war purposes. In 1948 the International Red Cross Conference passed a similar resolution and in 1950 the International Committee of the Red Cross (ICRC) requested the states who had taken part in the 1949 Geneva Conventions to prohibit atomic weapons. The USA, however, considered that the UN Atomic Energy Commission was the appropriate forum. I have referred to the fate of the draft rules prepared by the ICRC in 1956 for the protection of civilians, and to the resolution of the International Red Cross Conference of 1965 stating that the general principles of the law of war applied to nuclear weapons. The Red Cross persisted in its efforts, drafts were prepared and four diplomatic conferences were convened between 1974 and 1977. These culminated in the two Protocols signed by more than 60 states, including the USA and the USSR.

Articles 48 and 51 of Protocol I provide:

"*Article 48—Basic rule*
In order to ensure respect for and protection of the civilian population and civilian objects, the Parties to the conflict shall at all times distinguish between the civilian population and combatants and between civilian objects and military objectives and accordingly shall direct their operations only against military objectives."

"*Article 51—Protection of the civilian population*
1. The civilian population and individual civilians shall enjoy general protection against dangers arising from military operations. To give effect to this protection, the following rules, which are additional to other applicable rules of international law, shall be observed in all circumstances.

2. The civilian population as such, as well as individual civilians, shall not be the object of attack. Acts or threats of violence the primary purpose of which is to spread terror among the civilian population are prohibited . . .

4. Indiscriminate attacks are prohibited. Indiscriminate attacks are:
(a) those which are not directed at a specific military objective;
(b) those which employ a method or means of combat which cannot be directed at a specific military objective; or

(c) those which employ a method or means of combat the effects of which cannot be limited as required by this Protocol; and consequently, in each such case, are of a nature to strike military objectives and civilians or civilian objects without distinction.

5. Among others, the following types of attacks are to be considered as indiscriminate:
(a) an attack by bombardment by any methods or means which treats as a single military objective a number of clearly separated and distinct military objectives located in a city, town, village or other area containing similar concentration of civilians or civilian objects; and
(b) an attack which may be expected to cause incidental loss of civilian life, injury to civilians, damage to civilian objects, or a combination thereof, which would be excessive in relation to the concrete and direct military advantage anticipated."

Even with the greatly improved targeting possibilities of some nuclear weapons, almost all nuclear attacks, with their consequential effects, would be indiscriminate within the meaning of Article 51. Article 52 gives general protection to civilian objects and limits attacks to military objects as defined. Also protected are cultural objects and places of worship (Article 53) and objects indispensable to the survival of civilians (Article 54). Article 55 requires care to be taken to protect the natural environment against widespread, long-term and severe damage, and Article 56 prohibits attack against dams, dikes and nuclear electrical generating stations even where those objects are military objectives "if such attack may cause the release of dangerous forces and consequent severe losses among the civilian population." As Ellen Collier says: "Nuclear war would almost certainly have effects which would violate or infringe upon these articles and the purpose of distinguishing between combatants and the civilian population."[8]

The earlier history of this Protocol has shown that it originated in concern about the fate of civilians in nuclear war, and this was reflected in many resolutions of the General Assembly of the United Nations including resolution 2444 (XXIII) of 1968 already referred to. Yet, in the event, from the beginning of the 1970s the control of nuclear weapons began to be excluded from the discussions at Geneva. It was at about the same time that meetings began which led to the 1981 UN Convention on conventional weapons.

From the outside, these developments looked unreal to the point of absurdity. Over a period of thirty years and most recently over an intensive period of some six years, detailed discussions had taken place, seeking, however idealistically, to put something on paper which might have some effect on the treatment of civilians in a future modern war. Yet it was then decided to exclude the central and overwhelming consideration of the human condition: the effects of nuclear weapons.

Many countries signed the Protocol with specific reservations. But the USA signed on the understanding that "the rules established" by the Protocol "were not intended to have any effect on and do not regulate or prohibit the use of nuclear weapons."

The UK made an almost identical reservation, but spoke of "the new rules introduced by the Protocol," suggesting that this reservation applied only to those rules that could not be considered pre-existing and in force before 1977.[9] The UK indeed made nine other reservations. In relation to Articles 51 to 58, one reservation was that "military commanders and others responsible for planning, deciding upon or executing attacks necessarily have to reach decisions on the basis of their assessment of the information from all sources which is available to them at the relevant time." In relation to Article 52, the reservation was that "a specific area of land may be a military objective if, because of its location or other reasons specified in the Article, its total or partial destruction, capture or neutralization in the circumstances ruling at the time offers definite military advantage." Other UK reservations were of a similar kind.

The position of the USA was explained during the negotiations. At the 1975 session of the Diplomatic Conference, the US representative said:

> "An acceptable rule of law designed to be applicable to the use of weapons of mass destruction would, almost certainly, provide little or no protection in conventional war. Conversely, rules, such as the ones on which we are working in this Conference, are designed for conventional warfare and would not fit well in the context of the use of weapons of mass destruction."

In June 1977 the US representative, Ambassador Aldrich, used the words of the reservation already quoted. He also said:

> "We recognize that nuclear weapons are the subject of separate negotiations and agreements, and further that *their use in warfare is governed by the present principles of international law*" (italics added).

Ellen Collier has said: "Since the Geneva Protocols codify some of the customary and older conventional principles of international law, such as the rule of proportionality, the ambiguity about their relevance to nuclear war has not been ended."[10] But while that ambiguity may remain, it is clear that the USA and the UK are agreed that Protocol I does not apply to nuclear weapons. The USSR and its allies have made no stated reservations.

The reservations made by the USA and the UK to the 1977 Geneva Protocol I do not of themselves negate the rule of international law that unnecessary suffering should not be inflicted. And it is here that proportionality becomes critical. The 1907 Hague Convention IV forbade the employment of arms, projectiles or material calculated to cause unnecessary suffering. If it is to be argued that the use of nuclear weapons in any circumstances is contrary to international law on this ground then it must be asserted that the suffering inflicted by their use can never be militarily necessary.

The argument is sometimes heard that the humanitarian rules of armed conflict do not apply because, for the most part, they predate the invention of nuclear weapons or fail to mention them by name. In a recent and comprehensive article, Burns Weston dismisses this as failing to heed the multifaceted nature of the international law-creating system and as disregarding the fact that legal rules typically are interpreted to encompass matters not specifically mentioned and often not contemplated by their formulators.[11] This seems to be a sufficient dismissal. If the principle of the avoidance of unnecessary suffering is an accepted rule of international law, as I take it to be, then it cannot be argued that the use of nuclear weapons can never infringe that principle because when that principle was first adopted mankind had not invented this particular means to inflict suffering.

We are still left with the argument from military necessity. Warfare, as such, is not an illegal activity. The Laws of War exist to impose certain limits on the activity. Whether a particular military action is "necessary" so that it cannot be said to cause "unnecessary" suffering is a matter of judgment. The level of civilian morale is a matter of military significance. If a state carries out bombing raids on cities with the intention of reducing civilian morale and so preparing the way for invasion, can we say that the suffering which results from those raids is, in military terms, "unnecessary"? On the other hand, was the extent of the bombing of Dresden and Hamburg, carried out by the Western allies in World War II, "necessary"? For our present purposes, we may pose the question in simple terms. Are there any circumstances in which thermonuclear attack in the 1980s could be justified in international law on the ground that military necessity prevailed over the infliction of suffering on the scale we anticipate? It seems to me that there are no such circumstances.

The strongest case that could be put against that conclusion is where the attack was launched to pre-empt a strike, the likelihood of which appeared to be very great. Since, with the weapons of today, such a strike could be only partially effective and would certainly result in counter-attack of a like kind, I think that case does not justify the first strike.

The provisions of the 1925 Geneva Protocol are often quoted as grounds for declaring the use of nuclear arms illegal. As we have noted, in the 1899 Hague Declaration 2 the contracting powers agreed to abstain from the use of projectiles that had the sole object of diffusing asphyxiating or deleterious gases. And the 1907 Hague Convention IV forbade the employment of poison.

The 1925 Geneva Protocol, endorsed by over 100 states, extended the prohibition to the use of bacteriological methods of warfare. Roberts and Guelff[12] note two flaws in the Declaration and Protocol. The first is that there are divergent interpretations on the use of tear gas and chemical herbicides. The second is that a number of states considered that they ceased to be bound by the Protocol if enemy states failed to respect it.

The 1925 Protocol begins:

> "Whereas the use in war of asphyxiating, poisonous or other gases, *and of all analogous liquids, materials or devices*, has been justly condemned by the general opinion of the civilized world; and whereas the prohibition of such use has been declared in Treaties to which the majority of Powers of the world are Parties; and to the end that this prohibition shall be universally accepted as a part of International Law, binding alike the conscience and the practice of nations . . ."

The argument that these words, especially those I have italicized, are comprehensive enough and strong enough to include the effects of nuclear weapons and so to prohibit their use, is compelling. However, it is argued on the other side that the analogy indicates that the use of nuclear weapons is prohibited only if directed against non-military objectives or against military targets which cannot be destroyed without serious loss of life or injury to health. Alternatively, it is argued that express prohibition is needed for the banning of nuclear weapons.[13] The attempt to limit the prohibition to civilian targets is difficult to justify from either the texts or the intentions of the parties. The argument based on the absence of express provision (which we have met before) denies, as sources of international law, much that is elsewhere accepted without question.

A final major argument for the illegality of nuclear weapons, which flows particularly from the inability to control their use and its effects, concerns the consequence for the rights of neutrals. That their territory is to be regarded as inviolable in time of war is a fundamental rule of international law. Article 1 of the 1907 Hague Convention V so provides and has long been accepted as a statement of general international law. Fallout from nuclear weapons, because of its extent and the impossibility of limiting its spread, is bound to cause suffering and death to the inhabitants of neutral countries.

But the arguments for the legality of nuclear arms do not end here. A particular case is based on the law of reprisals. Part III of the *Manual of Military Law* of the UK[14] contains a comprehensive statement. It defines reprisals as acts of retaliation for illegitimate acts of warfare and claims that by the custom of international law they are a means of securing legitimate warfare. They must not be taken against civilians (except those not protected by the 1949 Geneva Convention IV). An infraction of the laws of war having been definitely established, every effort, says the *Manual*, should first be made to detect and punish the actual offenders. Only if this is impossible may recourse be had to reprisals. The Hague Rules and the 1949 Convention forbid collective punishment in the form of a general penalty. Acts done by way of reprisals must not be excessive but must bear a reasonable relation to the degree of violation—otherwise they will be punishable as war crimes.

The *Manual* clearly contemplates illegitimate acts of an individual kind which can be replied to by reprisals on a similar scale. But a nuclear response to such illegitimate acts is obviously not a legitimate use of reprisal.

Conclusion

If it is accepted that the rules of international law, written and customary, impose limits on the means that may be employed by a belligerent state against its enemy; that these rules exclude, first, the use of asphyxiating, poisonous and analogous materials, and bacteriological substances; that they exclude, secondly, attacks on some civilians in certain circumstances; and that they exclude, thirdly, means which must inevitably result in the death of large populations in neutral countries; it then follows that the use of nuclear weapons is illegal. Much ingenuity is needed to find any exceptions to that general statement. The use of a small "clean" tactical weapon against an enemy ship in mid-ocean, or against a small force in a desert, might not amount to a breach of those rules. But such examples can hardly be said to invalidate the general statement.

I would not wish to base that statement on a more broadly drawn distinction between civilians and combatants, however valuable it may be to have in operation a code to protect civilians. Of course almost all nuclear weapons are indiscriminate in their effects. But in modern warfare civilians are in very large numbers engaged in the direct prosecution of war, in munitions factories and elsewhere, and cannot in law or in logic disengage themselves from the consequences of so doing.

Beginning in the 1930s, there has been a new acceleration in the destructiveness of weapons. The bombing of civilians in London and other cities in the UK was followed by bombing on a far greater scale of civilians in Hamburg, Dresden and other German cities. Some of these, especially in the earlier years of World War II, were spoken of as reprisal raids, as indeed in part they were. Horrifying as were the consequences of those bombings, and of the rocket warfare that followed, the atom bombs that fell on Hiroshima and Nagasaki introduced a new dimension that proved to have an almost limitless range of development. So profound was this change that it brought about one of the strongest statements on the limitation of weapons in the history of international law. I mean the agreement incorporated in the Non-Proliferation Treaty of 1968. This resulted in assurances by the main nuclear powers that they would not use nuclear weapons against non-nuclear states and in undertakings not to assist non-nuclear states to acquire nuclear weapons. Non-nuclear states gave reciprocal undertakings. Over 120 states acceded to this treaty, including several states (such as Canada, Japan, Sweden and Switzerland) who would have little or no difficulty in manufacturing nuclear weapons. With all its imperfections, the treaty is a considerable recognition of the dangers to all mankind that these weapons have created.

It is sometimes argued that this treaty, by controlling the acquisition of nuclear weapons, implies that the possession by nuclear states is not contrary to international law. And it may be assumed that all nuclear states—this is certainly true of the UK—would claim that possession of nuclear weapons is in accordance with international law. Since they have not been heard to admit that their use of these weapons would or might be illegal, this is not surprising.

But if we start from the assumption that the use is illegal, the legality of possession is most doubtful. First, we have seen that a convention of 1948 made punishable any conspiracy or incitement or attempt to commit genocide or any complicity in genocide. Such words easily embrace actions which involve possessing and planning the use of nuclear weapons. But genocide is limited to action against a national, ethnical, racial or religious group as such and, as a matter of interpretation, planning to kill or injure all or some of the inhabitants of an enemy state might not fall within the meaning of such a group. A second, and more firmly based, argument rests on Principle VI of the judgment of the Nuremberg Tribunal as declared by the International Law Commission in 1950. This made punishable, as a crime under international law, the planning, preparation, initiation or waging of a war of aggression or a war in violation of international treaties, agreements or assurances; or participation in a common plan or conspiracy for the accomplishment of any such acts. If, as I have argued, the use of nuclear weapons would be in violation of treaties, then the possession of these weapons as part of the planning and preparation for such a war, or of a war of aggression, would seem to be illegal.

Thirdly, again on the assumption that the use of nuclear weapons would be illegal, any preparation to use them would be a criminal conspiracy.

It can be further argued in the UK that as under English statute law a person may use such force as is reasonable in the circumstances in the prevention of crime, resistance to the manufacture, storing and deployment of nuclear weapons is legally protected.

Since 1946, the USSR has frequently invited Western states to conclude a treaty prohibiting unconditionally either the use of or at least the first use of nuclear weapons. As the USSR has developed over the years its own nuclear strength, such attempts have changed their character and become more realistic and more of a possible bargain between equals. But the Western states have never responded favorably.

An undertaking of "no first use" goes further than the existing rules of international law in two respects.[15] First, it applies to attacks, not prohibited by those rules, against military objects and wherever the effects are not grossly disproportionate. Secondly, it prevents a state from threatening the use of nuclear weapons as a response to an attack by conventional weapons.

This brings us, finally, to the political heart of the argument about the illegality of the use and the possession of nuclear weapons. The NATO and the Warsaw Pact powers each justify their possession of these weapons on the need to deter the other's use. But the NATO powers justify possession also on the grounds that they may need to use nuclear weapons first to resist a "conventional" Soviet invasion of Western

Europe. Since such first use would inevitably result in massive retaliation, it would bring about the full-scale nuclear holocaust.

This threat of possible first use by NATO powers means that nuclear deterrence has a wider significance for those powers than it has for the Soviet Union. For NATO powers, nuclear deterrence has largely replaced negotiation as the way to prevent the outbreak of war. This may now be the view of the Soviet Union also. If so, diplomacy is for present purposes dead and the very idea of international agreements between the major powers is on no one's agenda. The failure to agree on weapons control is part of a much larger and perhaps a final and fatal collapse in international relations.

No one supposes that any group of politicians will be deterred from pushing the nuclear button because to do so would be contrary to the rules of international law. But rules determining legality and illegality are statements about social and moral situations and attitudes. The laws of war represent the best agreements the representatives of the peoples of the world have been able to achieve in the interests of their common humanity. Those laws require the avoidance of unnecessary suffering, of indiscriminate attack and of the use of weapons whose effects are uncontrollable. The use (and I would argue also the possession) of nuclear weapons breaches these rules. This is to be condemned not on the ground that it is wrong to break a law but because these particular laws represent mankind's best effort to contain our destructive instincts. And to break those laws is to forfeit the last protection.

Not only politicians but also military leaders have always been at pains to establish the legitimacy of their own actions, upholding the social order. And they have sought to do this, especially, when those actions seem most contrary to the rule of law. The use of nuclear weapons must bring down the structure of society. And so the use (and only to a lesser extent the possession) is the ultimate breach of the ultimate law.

12 THE MILITARY AND POLITICAL BACKGROUND OF THE NUCLEAR AGE *W. B. Gallie*

Professor W. B. Gallie is Emeritus Professor of Political Science at the University of Cambridge and an honorary Professorial Fellow at the University of Wales. He served in the British Army throughout World War II, and was awarded the Croix de Guerre in 1945. Subsequently he lectured in philosophy at the University College of Swansea before becoming Professor of Logic and Metaphysics at the Queen's University, Belfast. He was Visiting Professor in Philosophy at New York University during the Cuban Missile Crisis. His philosophical writings include Philosophy and the Historical Understanding *and* Philosophers of Peace and War.

One of the most worrying features of the current debate about nuclear weapons is this. The general public is liable to be discouraged by the endless repetition of all-too-familiar arguments from seemingly immovable positions. True, there are occasional changes in the arguments and proposals of nuclear disarmers—and even of nuclear rearmers—but these leave the fundamental oppositions untouched. In this situation, further investigation and debate may well begin to seem pointless. And once this feeling takes over, it quickly attracts support of a most insidiously dangerous kind. The whole question of nuclear weapons and their possible uses, we are sometimes told, is too complex, too technical (the technicalities being at once scientific, military and diplomatic) and above all too rapidly changing for ordinary men and women, no matter how intelligent, to keep up. It really would be wiser, more useful and safer to leave this matter to the experts, military, scientific and political, and to go back to digging our own gardens.

This suggestion presupposes that the experts have all the answers to the questions in hand. And this is far from obviously the case since the experts not only differ in the conclusions and policies which they advocate, but over the fundamental terms in which the problem should be stated. But I want to go further than this and argue that, with respect to the nuclear problem, the experts to date have been incapable of providing the right answers, since, for the most part, they have neglected some of the essential, albeit preliminary, questions which we should all of us—experts and inexperts alike—have been asking long ago. I shall pursue four such questions, which help us to begin to see the nuclear problem "in the round," and thus to feel a more warranted confidence about the interconnections of the theses which we want to urge and the policies which we want to see put into motion. These questions are all, in their different ways, philosophical; they are questions about how we do and might and should think about nuclear weapons. But this does not mean that they are obscurely technical or academic. Here they are:

1. *What is it about the nuclear problem that gives it its peculiar dominance and oppressiveness in serious political thought and discussion today?* This is a question of logical identification, to be pursued, however, not so much within the fields of weaponry, strategy and military destructiveness, as within the ideas and feelings which the new weapons have evoked and in terms of which different justifications of their development have been devised. In particular we need to identify, in its full intellectual context, the moral imperative to be seen so powerfully impelling today's anti-nuclear movement.

2. *How and why*, from what background and by what routes and stages, *has the nuclear peril come to its present position of dominance?* At first sight this might seem to be a question for professional historians to settle. But it is astonishing how little professional historians have done about it. Moreover, what is called for is a broad balanced sketch of international history, political and military, culminating in the currently much discussed militarization of international relations in the nuclear age. And this is a task which, while calling for careful study and reflection, requires few if any of the specialized techniques of research historians. It is a matter of achieving an adequate conception of the nuclear age as it emerges from the many-sided mold of international history.

3. But since all histories are in some degree selective, and make their selection in the light of some particular focus of interest, *what should be the focal or climax point of interest in the kind of history we should here be studying?* This may sound academic, but it is a question of practical importance, since the lessons that we can derive from any history depend upon the focal point of its interest. For example, it was maintained by Kant in the late eighteenth century that our focus, when we study international history, must be the ultimate achievement of world peace and justice, resulting from the elimination of war, if only after the hardest of struggles. Only by assuming that this is the goal of history,

Kant argued, can we begin to make any use of history, that is, begin to see how the hideous crimes and follies which it chronicles could have been avoided or could be forestalled in the future. This requires, as a kind of beacon shining back toward us from the future, the idea that we can ultimately reach the haven of international peace. But, as it seems to me, many of our troubles today arise from the fact that, without appreciating either the subtlety or the dubiety of Kant's argument, we have most of us accepted a vulgar version of his conclusion—that of course we must think of our history as leading us, despite many discouragements, toward an ideal goal of some sort or another. I shall argue that no such general hope or promise is justifiable. Indeed I shall urge the paradoxical view that the more pessimistically we regard the international history of the last hundred years or so, the more likely we are to avoid the dangers which it has bequeathed to us.

4. However, irrespective of our particular selective approach, *what sorts of lessons can we expect a sketch of the historical background of the nuclear problem to provide?* Its lessons will be mainly critical and corrective, restraining and warning—as indeed most principles and maxims for the conduct of international relations must be; but they are not less important for that reason. Indeed, they are indispensable, since they serve to pick out and highlight the danger spots where positive initiatives and experimental leads are most urgently needed. The historical background of the nuclear problem is in no sense an alternative to other practical approaches to it, whether moral, political, strategic or economic. Rather, it is the complement and necessary matrix of them all.

Question 1: Identification

The peculiar oppressiveness of the nuclear problem is not due simply to the horrific destructiveness which it portends, nor to the seeming immobility of the parties that debate it, nor to the callousness, sloppiness or doublethink of some of the debaters. The nuclear problem oppresses us chiefly because its roots and ramifications seem endless. It reaches back to, and reveals inadequacies in a number of our deep-seated habitual beliefs and assumptions—moral, political, military and economic—the questioning of any of which would be irksome, but the questioning of all of which together threatens something close to intellectual vertigo. To suggest that our nuclear peril is rooted in anything as elusive as our thought-habits offends the popular orthodoxy of the age—the belief that our science-based technology can cope with whatever problems we come up against. But faced with the recalcitrance of the nuclear problem this belief is beginning to take on a frantically rigid character, repugnant to the essentially adaptive character of human thought. In this situation we have, therefore, every reason to look for aid in a redirection of our thinking, inwards and backwards, to get clearer bearings on where we are and how we have arrived there, as well as some fresh ideas on the possibilities before us.

As a first step in this direction we can compare our nuclear peril with other conceivable disasters of at least comparable extent and horror such as might arise from natural causes, in outer space or in our planetary environment or within the genetic structure of mankind. Such disasters would obviously be beyond human responsibility, and most likely beyond human comprehension and control. By contrast, our nuclear peril is evidently a result of certain operations of human reason—in the fields of scientific inventions, political and industrial organization, ideological creeds and so on. Whatever disasters nuclear weapons may bring us, it will be a case of the works of man destroying the hand that made them. But it is not the prospect of actually unmaking or refashioning our characteristically human ideas, inventions, artifices and institutions that so greatly discourages and oppresses us. After all, we put them together and should have no great difficulty in redesigning them in somewhat less dangerous forms. What oppresses us, I believe, is the sense that we can no longer place habitual reliance on certain of our inherited ideas and institutions. Our trouble is very much a matter of the old Adam of sloth and inertia, failure of the will to adjust, and a return of the age-old fear of the unknown. In particular we find it hard to conceive how we are to conduct our international relations in a world in which national security can no longer be equated with possession of the latest and most destructive weapons. The prospect of having to defend ourselves, or resist oppression, without the latest, most lethal and indeed genocidal aids that science has given us, fills us with feelings of panic and of outrage which all too easily pass into either despair or devil-may-care self-will. But such feelings as these will get us nowhere. And the sooner they are recognized for what they are, in all their uselessness and stupidity, the better.

This point can be put more positively. Not only is the nuclear peril a problem of our own making, it is one of a sort which the human mind (according to teachers as great and as different as Vico and Kant) has a peculiar capacity for understanding. There is nothing, according to their teachings, which the human mind is more at home with, more capable of comprehending in its wholeness and hence of criticizing, reconstructing, communicating and re-adapting to new purposes, than its own inventions, artifices and institutions. We have a direct understanding of these "human objects," not in terms of their relative magnitudes or their observed concomitants and effects, but inasmuch as they are *expressions*—even if sometimes misleading or outmoded expressions—of interests, aspirations and emotions which are common to us all. Looked at in this way, the nuclear problem begins to appear, not as an oppressive horror pressing down upon us from "out there," but as part of the proper study of mankind: namely human beings in relation to their own characteristic works—especially when these begin to go wrong.

In saying this I am not denying that to think about the nuclear problem—let alone to deal with it—presents enormous difficulties. But what else should we expect from one of the crucial moments of transition, of ostensible discontinuity, in human history? We have come to the end of a familiar, if far from ideal, plateau in human affairs; in place of it we are faced with deep divides, seemingly unending mountains, no doubt pitted with crevasses for which we are unprepared. The essence of this transition is the collapse of the axiom already mentioned (that, for its own security, any political society should possess weapons at least as destructive as those possessed by any of its rivals). Today we all recognize that a number of nations possess not only weapons of a destructive capacity incomparably greater than anything that earlier generations could have dreamed of, but involving a risk of destruction even to their possessors—as well as to innocent third parties the world over—again on a scale beyond the worst nightmare fears of mankind.

This prodigious change on the international horizon might seem to suggest that the past history of war has no longer anything useful to teach us. And this could be true if we were looking simply for the most likely immediate cause of—or the most immediately effective check upon—the outbreak of a nuclear war. But the nuclear problem cannot be identified with any *one* such disaster, considered in isolation, even if that disaster should put paid to the history of mankind. If its seat is in our minds and thought-habits, its eradication—even its containment—is bound, for all its urgency, to be a long-term task and ordeal.

So the exercise of identification yields in sum two paradoxes. First, the nuclear problem is for us something essentially novel; yet its novelty can be coped with only in the light of the historical background from which it has sprung: this is because to cope with it means to *change* certain habits of thought and action which are very clearly identified through their history in the centuries that led up to the nuclear age. Second, the novelty of the nuclear problem has placed a uniquely awesome responsibility on those who have lived since 1945. But we are not the first generation to feel itself specially chosen—or cursed—with such a burden. Moreover, while future generations will not feel the shock of its novelty, they may well continue to feel the recalcitrance of the nuclear problem. And this paradoxical combination of our moral uniqueness and our moral kinship with other generations points to the awesome and unavoidable fact that the nuclear problem is the first great problem to affect, directly and all too materially, the human species *as a whole*. Herein, no doubt, lies the hope of achieving an effective unanimity in face of it. Yet to achieve unanimity across the barriers of mankind's moral, religious, political and economic heterogeneity is patently a daunting task. Not one that can be postponed to a more favorable future; but equally, not a purely technical problem that will yield to a little clever tinkering here and now.

Question 2: From the mold of international history
This calls for a five-stage approach, each succeeding stage dealing with a shorter but more patently relevant period of time than its predecessor.

(a) The premilitary prehistory
Although the evidence, both literary and archaeological, runs out quickly, there can be little doubt that the *prehistory* of mankind was a *premilitary* one. The history of war proper—in the sense of organized armed struggle between rival groups, each seeking to defeat and either disable or dominate or destroy the other—can hardly date back beyond eight or nine thousand years; whereas the history of *homo sapiens* may possibly cover ten times that period. No doubt human breeding and feeding groups—like individual humans—have always been quarrelsome, aggressive, pugnacious and revengeful; but possession of these qualities does not mean war. No doubt, again, earlier human groups would have taken to war as zestfully as their descendants have done, if only they had thought of it—which fortunately they did not, for it is quite possible that if humans had discovered the delights of war earlier than they did, they would have destroyed themselves before they had developed those skills of communication, organization and construction upon which civilization depends. What is certain, however, is that during by far the greater part of the race's history, human beings have walked the earth—have hunted and gathered, raised their children and dealt with their dead, painted and decorated, sung and danced, loved and suffered—without recourse to war. We are, emphatically, not war-

making animals by genetic endowment. But to this suggestion of primal innocence, we must add that in their premilitary phase, human beings were also prepolitical in the sense of knowing neither the benefits nor the costs of continuously operative rule. Which suggests the outlines of an answer to the question: what brought the premilitary phase of human history to an end?

(b) Political society and the state of war

Again, the details are lost beyond recovery. But there is certainly much truth in Montesquieu's famous dictum: "Once in a political society, men lose their feeling of weakness: thereupon their former equality disappears and the *state of war* begins."[1] What makes this dictum at once so astonishing and so persuasive? On the surface it seems to be a boldly simplified account of how the state and war came into existence in a kind of symbiosis. But it also claims to explain the paradox that states provide their subjects with relative security at home only at the cost of almost constant wars with rival states abroad. To expand this point a little: Montesquieu's dictum implies that the burden of continuous government upon any group of people is rendered acceptable by the new sense of corporate strength which it engenders among them. However, this new strength is felt and exercised mainly in face of other competing groups, likewise organized and strengthened through the acceptance of continuous rule. In other words, in becoming political, human beings identify themselves not simply *with* a particular political unit but potentially *against* other competing units: political adhesion turns the subject into a soldier, and the foreigner into a foe.

Yet despite its persuasiveness this answer can be misleading. It presents the state and war as, roughly speaking, two sides of the same coin or as partners in a symbiosis which is permanently and equally necessary to each. But symbiosis on these terms is rare. In human affairs as much as in nature, it is usually confined to certain phases in the life cycle of the forms involved and is also much more evidently indispensable to one form than to another (e.g. to the parasite than to the host). It is easy to see that this is the case with the state and war. The idea of war *logically* requires the idea of the state or continual government—if war is to be distinguished from mere mayhem or brigandage. But the dependence of the state upon war, although unquestionable at many stages in the history of most states, is not of the same logically clear-cut kind. It varies from case to case; it is sometimes problematic; and it has always to be established, not by reference to ordinary linguistic usage, but in the light of historical evidence and of careful historical assessment. Therefore, the upshot is that even if war and the state arose together, and even if the state required war to help it establish itself on the human scene, this particular dependence is not necessarily perpetual. To assume that it must be so is rather like assuming that because good family relations require that children shall learn habits of obedience, such habits must remain the basis of family happiness when the children have grown up.

(c) The "classic" phase

This brings us to what I shall call the "classic" phase in the overall history of war, which stretches from its establishment as the main means of settling differences between political units until approximately 200 years ago. By that time the expansion of Europe was pointing toward the global wars, and the development of science-based industry toward the total wars, of the twentieth century.

But why should we treat such an enormous period of time, replete with wars varying in scale and skill—many of them occurring within areas of the world cut off from and ignorant of each other—as a single phase of warfare? My answer is that during this phase there grew up and hardened a certain way of thinking about war (which could also be described as ways of *not* thinking about war) so widespread that it may have seemed as unnecessary as it would be difficult to indicate them precisely—and which persist to this day, side by side and however inconsistently, with other more sophisticated conceptions of what war is and is not about. The importance of this classic view is that we are all liable to slip back into it because it provides the base line from which any more adequate view of war must be developed. Its essence is the acceptance of war as a necessary half of international life, periodic but ineradicable.

Although markedly affecting the character of all political societies, war in its classic phase was restricted both in its operations and its effects, chiefly through lack of resources and uncertainty of communications. And while, on the classic view, war was accepted as a *general* necessity of civilized life, it went without saying that, in respect of their special motives, methods and magnitudes, particular wars were as various and unpredictable as their long-term effects were impossible to compute.* Less regular than the sequence of the seasons or the rhythms of organic life, but with an irrepressible force of their own, wars, it seemed,

* There was of course some impressive theorizing about the possible *justifications* of the use of war, by the philosophers and jurists of the later Middle Ages and the early modern period.

would always alternate with periods of peace. Even if improvements in weaponry, tactics or methods of supply may have enabled certain powers to secure their conquests for several generations, self-evidently discoveries in military technology cannot be kept secret for long, and usually spread fast and far. Certainly the question whether wars might some day be brought to an end—through world conquest by a single power, through rational agreements between near-equal powers, or through the danger of mutual destruction by war-intoxicated powers—seems never to have been seriously considered during war's classic phase. The only apparent exception to this lies in the Apocalyptic hopes and fears of Judaism and early Christianity.

Given this attitude to war, it is not surprising that no serious study of its inner logic and political dependence should have been attempted before the eighteenth century, and that the first—and to date the only—work of intellectual eminence on this subject did not appear until after the Napoleonic wars. This was Clausewitz's *On War*, a work which owes its interest largely to the fact that it can be read both as an attempt to rationalize the assumptions of the classic attitude to war and as an adumbration of the attitudes that were to come. Clausewitz was properly impressed by the *variety* of the wars which he had studied; a variety which proved the absurdity of trying to wage war by rules that can be learnt from books. Hence his dictum that war is a veritable chameleon. Yet chameleons are animals of a single type; and Clausewitz had to decide what it is that we have in mind when collecting under one name all wars, past, present and future.

War, he eventually decided, consists in all its forms and phases, in "a remarkable trinity": first, the clash of armed forces in violent hostility, each side trying to destroy or at least disable the other; second, the art of directing such forces through a turmoil of accidents and uncertainties, an art which calls for a rapid calculation of probabilities and the ability to take risks subject to a few guiding maxims; and third, the backing afforded by, and the obedience demanded by, the needs and interests of the state or of whatever political unit on behalf of which the war is being waged. There may seem to be nothing remarkable or objectionable in this threefold definition; but as used within Clausewitz's system, it is of the greatest interest. Valid if uninteresting as a précis of the past, it was as pertinent for the future for what it anticipated as for what it ignored.

On the former score, we must ask: on what principle did Clausewitz select the three members of his "trinity"? They are not simply features which he found present without exception in all wars. They also share a property which is essential to the point and purpose of every war: the winning of it. Normally, Clausewitz assumes, wars take place between forces of comparable if not equal strength. What, then, explains which side will win? In essence, he answers: whichever side most effectively and most quickly escalates its efforts in respect of any or all of the three members of his trinity. Thus, in any war, it is possible for one side to enlist, arm, train and throw into battle more soldiers more quickly than the other; or one military commander can choose to take greater, but still well-considered, risks than his opposite number; or, as in the wars of the French Revolution and Napoleon, one state or government can infuse its troops with enthusiasm, based on assured political backing and direction, unknown to their opponents. So the key to success in war is for Clausewitz always an escalation, that is, a deliberately willed change in the intensity of at least one of the three aspects by which every war is recognized to *be* a war. And this means that, although seeking for the few available permanent truths about war (which he assumes to be a permanent feature of the human condition), Clausewitz actually presents it and makes it intelligible as something which, by its very nature, is always on the move; something which only works by changing or adapting its own methods and character to meet the needs of every new military situation. But the question whether there are any essential limits to this process—whether escalation carried too far would have the effect of altering the very nature and function of war—simply did not occur to him.

Leaving this question aside for the moment, let us next ask: why did Clausewitz assume that the three members of his trinity were the *only* aspects of war which can be escalated and are therefore the key to victory in war?

Of course, he knew the importance in war of such factors as weaponry, supply, communications and economic pressure on the enemy. But his experience suggested that the contribution of such factors as these could not be escalated by any feats of will or skill: they were virtually fixed, given the technology and the economic resources available during the classic phase of war. Had Clausewitz written his treatise in the 1860s, or *a fortiori* after 1914, he would almost certainly have given more weight to the organizational and technical aspects of war, and, had he done so, this would no doubt have alerted him to the question raised a few moments ago: namely at what point would further escalation of any of the essential aspects of war have the effect of changing it, not simply in respect of its immediate efficacy or temporary style, but in its total character and role within human life, so that men would come to say, this isn't what was formerly known as war, but something different in kind, something wholly unacceptable whether because of its moral or its physical effects. After the two world wars of our century, and under the shadow of nuclear war, we find this question only too pertinent and pressing. But there is hardly a trace of it in Clausewitz's thought.* Thus, although his analyses of war brought him to the verge of seeing where and why war might some day turn into something other than itself, his viewpoint remained based in the classic phase of war. He assumed that war, though it came in many forms, was an irremovable part of the furniture of the world of nations, and that its logically defining core was as fixed as the defining faculties of mankind.

Remnants of the classic phase of war are still very much with us. It rested on ideas that were natural enough to human groups too distinct and ignorant of each other to cooperate, too interdependent to leave each other completely alone, and economically too weak to impose permanent dominion one upon another. Given these conditions, war easily became as much a way of life as a condition of survival. But these conditions had ceased to hold in eighteenth-century Europe. The liberal aspirations of the Enlightenment, the cult of economy and efficiency in all walks of life, the commercial unification of the world and the applications of science-based industry to war—these developments, as we shall now see, were to render the classically accepted patterns of war less and less acceptable, and its future entirely problematic.

(d) The "problematic" phase

What I call the "problematic" phase of warfare runs from the defeat of Napoleon to the outbreak of World War I. This was the period during which, for the first time in recorded history, men and women of many different nations and walks of life began to ponder and discuss seriously the place of war in human affairs and to devise and dream of ways in which to contain or remove it. It was also a period during which the material character of war, in particular its destructive potential, was beginning to change greatly, although at first in ways that escaped the attention of most politicians, publicists and philosophers.

Serious criticism of war as a means of settling international disputes dates back to the middle decades of the eighteenth century. The leading

* But see Book VIII, Chapter 6, A, final paragraph of *On War* (p. 604 in Howard and Paret's translation). This is a remarkable passage in which Clausewitz considers the possibility of war losing its classic character as a result of gradual *de*-escalation, so that it becomes little more than frontier policing.

thinkers of the Enlightenment found war objectionable on the grounds both of efficiency and of morality: often provoked by trifles, it seldom achieved anything of consequence. Such criticism first took on systematic and constructive form at the hands of Kant and Bentham, both of whom saw war as an unqualified evil and peace as a moral imperative, an imperative which was rendered attractive by the promised rewards of unhampered international trade. During the nineteenth century these highly intellectualist beginnings found popular support from various quarters: from numerous religious bodies in the wake of the Quakers, from middle-class and working-class political parties (on grounds of free trade in the one case and of international solidarity on the other), while intelligent conservatives had learned how easily wars can lead to political and social upheaval. Altogether, throughout the nineteenth century a wide array of opinions and interests came to be ranged against war in all "progressive" nations, most notably in the United States, Britain and France, but also in important circles in militaristic Russia and Prussia.

On the other hand these movements of antiwar opinion and sentiment suffered from two grave weaknesses. Their component elements never pulled together; on the contrary, they commonly distrusted or despised one another, liberals sniping at conservatives, intellectual radicals at churchmen and so on. Moreover, in the intellectual and rhetorical euphoria of the later nineteenth century, antiwar spokesmen too often took their eyes off their proper object: the character and causes of the prospective wars which they were endeavoring to prevent. For the wars they inveighed against were the wars of the mercantile and early capitalist past, not those that were being prepared in the shipyards, railway networks and engineering shops of the Western world. Nor was it simply the impact of industrialization on the means of war that was neglected. Nineteenth-century speculation and rhetoric had created the myth of a new pacific, although commercially expansive, Europe. It was widely believed, by Marxists, Comtists and Cobdenists alike, that the great decisions of the future would be taken not on military but on economic grounds, so that international relations were, for the first time in history, about to be demilitarized. However, the sad truth was that during the long peace from 1871 to 1914 the great European nations, despite the caution of conservatives, the international aspirations of liberals and the boasted solidarity of socialists, were developing a submerged passion for war, an emotional and an economic need and readiness for war, as well as a capacity for organizing, supplying and enduring war, of which their political leaders had virtually no conception. What were the main ingredients of this long-hidden retrogression into war?

They can be collected under two heads. First, the inherent progressiveness of research science and its seemingly endless capacity to produce continuous improvements in all forms of machinery. This last appeared only gradually in the fields of weaponry and military transport and communication; but by the 1860s its significance had become clear, particularly in the American Civil War, and by the 1880s the first serious naval arms race had begun.[2] Competition in weaponry and transport soon led to competing plans of war, offensive and defensive; and by the turn of the nineteenth century these had given rise to panic in diplomatic circles and to a dangerous xenophobia among the masses of the great industrial powers. The idea had been put around that even in time of peace the greatness of a nation was to be measured by its power to outbuild its rivals, especially in the numbers and firepower of its battleships and in the length and efficiency of its railways. Second, the commercial unification of the world immensely enlarged the scale, the stage, the rewards and the motives of wars between industrial nations. From a narrowly European point of view the nineteenth century seemed a period of comparative peace, but from a global point of view it opened up new possibilities of war as the continuation of European politics on far-off colonial shores. Like the crusades and voyages of discovery which preceded it, the commercial expansion of Europe gave expression to all the egoistic rivalries of its component nations. No one of them could have carried through so immense a task on its own: yet that task demanded a readiness on the part of successive front runners to ditch, replace or liquidate any competitors who blocked the road of further and speedier exploitation. The commercial unification of the world was something that had to come; it was an inescapable part of the destiny of mankind. But its short-term effect was to add a new dimension to the European people's strong propensity for war.

Therefore the problematic phase of the history of war culminated in an entirely novel conflict of forces which would decide not so much how the fortunes of war would be distributed on the next occasion, but the future scale, range and effects which war, considered as a worldwide institution, would achieve in so rapidly changing a world. On the one side stood the force of new ideas and ideals—in the main rational, forward-looking and responsible, but in some ways dangerously unperceptive and over-optimistic; on the other side an amalgam of changes in mankind's intellectual horizons, in their constructive and destructive capacities, and in their uncertain sense of social virtues and values. How this conflict of forces would develop was unforeseeable; but the course which warfare has taken since 1914 leaves us in no doubt about which side was the stronger. Even the best ideas offered in the cause of peace could do little to stem the forces making for even greater wars. The principles and projects of successive nineteenth- and early-twentieth-century peace movements today seem like so much genteel litter along the high road of history. By contrast, the advances in war technology during the last seventy years offer an awesome example of what social scientists call "cumulative causation." They have proved, to date, entirely unstoppable.

(e) Global and total into genocidal war

Taken together, the two world wars of this century represent, with terrifying repetitive power, the failure of Western civilization to cope with the problematic condition of war bequeathed to it by the nineteenth century. Or, looked at from a different angle, the two world wars represent an unmistakable advance from the previous problematic condition of war toward a general acceptance of its future total, global and genocidal capacities.

Of course, when considered as ordeals—for the individuals, the families, the regions and the nations most affected by them—the two world wars differed greatly; similarly, when considered as military operations of unparalleled complexity; and similarly again, when we consider the kinds of wrong which they were intended to eliminate or contain, and the kind of leadership, political and military, which they evoked. But these are aspects of the two great wars which reflect the special values and interests of their various participants; and our present concern with them is as two spans of a single bridge that has carried humans' war-making propensity from the uncertainties of the nineteenth century to the terrifying near-certainties of the Nuclear Age. To think of the two great wars in this abstract way may seem distasteful, the more so since it suggests that the principal result of World War I was World War II, and that the principal result of World War II was the nuclear menace that hangs over us all today. But thinking and its results often *are* distasteful, even when they offer the only possible means of avoiding worse horrors to come.

We are so used to hearing World War I described as the end of an epoch—that of Europe's world hegemony—that it is difficult to envisage it as the first span of a bridge carrying mankind toward a much more terrible future. But the task becomes easier when World War I is considered successively at the levels of popular attitudes, of the new military methods which it involved, and of the quality of the leadership which it called out. On the first score we need only recall the mood of (to us) incomprehensibly innocent euphoria with which, in all the combatant nations, men of different age groups, states and cultural levels flocked to the colors; and then contrast this with the moods—dazed, bitter, black and in some cases murderous—of those who eventually returned. Next, we should remember the means by which the war was sustained. At the outset the destructive power of the new automatic weapons took generals and statesmen and the public at large by surprise, as later did the horrors of poison gas, submarine warfare and economic blockade. At each stage in this process, the wits of inventors and the endurance of whole populations were to be strained to the limit, to produce an ever further escalation of war toward "totality." Finally, let us recall the manner of men who found themselves directing the war of August 1914 and compare them with those who were to push it through to its conclusion. Asquith, Viviani and Bethmann-Hollweg were what Gibbon might have called "decent easy men" in comparison with Lloyd George (the wizard), Clemenceau (the tiger) and Ludendorff (the political mentor of Hitler). At each of these levels, World War I afforded proof of Clausewitz's insight that the process of war demands escalation, not only in respect of numbers, moves and stakes, but of the level and order of the ruthless destruction required.

In World War II this pattern of development—the acceptance of continuous escalation of the means of violence—was less immediately obvious but, once appreciated, even more ominous. As so often before, the war began with operations resembling those of its predecessor, but applied this time with more caution. On the Western Front no one wished to repeat the bloodbaths of 1914–18. But very quickly new and more terrifying forms of warfare were to appear. Aerial bombing was developed, first as an adjunct to war on land and sea, and later to economic warfare, concentrated deliberately, in the end, on densely populated areas. It was thus within this existing strategic framework that the decision to drop the two atomic bombs on Japan was publicly situated. More generally, the industrial production of the Unites States, the Soviet Union and Britain on the one side, of Germany and its satellites on the other, was harnessed to service a war effort on five major fronts, each in itself a big war by all previous standards. On the Allied side this effort resulted in important economic and social lessons; but in

German-dominated Europe it took forms more shaming than those of primitive barbarism. It is worth recalling that the worst revelations of the Nazi extermination camps only narrowly preceded the bombs of Hiroshima and Nagasaki, a combination which inevitably sowed the thought: what enormities will mankind next show itself to be capable of?

The present argument could also be usefully developed in terms of the level of leadership, political and military, on the Western side in World War II. What an immense improvement it showed over that of World War I! Yet, in face of the atomic explosions which brought World War II to a close, even the ablest Western leaders—Roosevelt being then dead—were exposed as men unequal to their time. The victors looked out on a future big with dangers vastly more horrific than those which they had just overcome. They lacked the requisite energy, the words and the vision to cope with the Nuclear Age.

That was one short generation ago. How long this phase will last—whether its nearly forty years of existence indicate its durability or its imminent demise—is a question to which no one can give an authoritative answer. It is from this situation, so nerve-wearingly frustrating, that I now propound my last two questions. In the light of what focal point or illuminating end should we regard the history of war as it enters the Nuclear Age? And in what ways should that focal point of interest help us to assess other powerful and more positive initiatives for dealing with the challenge of nuclear weapons?

Question 3: Which focus of historical interest?

Thinking seriously about international relations and war's role in them is an enterprise as recent as it is rare. And as with national and family histories, with which all historical thinking begins, the focus of our interest in international history betrays the elementary and elemental character of our concern with it. Not until the eighteenth century did this area of political thinking take on something like a systematic shape, and, when it did so, international relations were usually presented as drawn to some simplistically dramatic end: a crowning world empire, a permanent balance of freely competing states, an escalation of conflicts leading to Armageddon, a return to—or through—a virtually pre-human jungle. Some of these fragmentary visions no doubt derive from the very dawn of political thinking, embedded in the myths and prophesies of different peoples, such as the ancient Hebrews; and some of them had been formulated with immense intellectual—albeit prehistorical and prescientific—force by St. Augustine. But in the rationally balanced writings of

Kant and his contemporaries they took the form of a choice between three alternatives. Either we should regard international relations, in the light of their history, as essentially improvable if never wholly perfectable; or we should view them as always subject to cyclical or oscillatory forces so that, while international politics were always tending toward an apogee of good or of ill fortune, they would never persist in either; or, finally, it is logically conceivable that they are unalterably set in a downward direction, leading to endless war, chaos and final disaster.

Each of these focal points of assessment admits of a twofold interpretation. On a metaphysical or dogmatic interpretation, each could be taken as a particular brand of fatalism: something in mankind's organizational capacities guarantees in advance either final political salvation, or an endless duel between opposing political tendencies, or total ultimate disaster. But on a critical and pragmatic interpretation, each has to be judged for its contribution to the overall task of rationalizing human thought and endeavor. Kant chose the second interpretation, and, on the basis of it, he argued persuasively that on all major historical issues we should allow our thought to be guided by the first and most cheerful of our three focal points of interest: the possibility—and more than possibility—of mankind's approximating even more closely to, if never securing completely, an ideal international system. Reduced to the barest outline, his position was this:

We have an indisputable duty to work for the continual improvement of international relations (conceived in terms of justice, peace and the happiness of all peoples) in the faith that this can be achieved, even though proof of it can never be provided. However, we can only succeed in this attempt if we recognize, and learn how to control and manipulate, all the egoistic vices and weaknesses which constantly threaten to frustrate it. Any effective program of political action must take into account both the above points; that is, it must leave separate states their liberty of (what we hope will be conscientious) action, whilst inducing in them in every possible way recognition of the mutual ruin which awaits them if they continue in their traditional egoistic ways. More simply, mankind can be saved from its political vices only by a skillful exploitation of them so that vices are made to serve the purposes of reason: a doctrine which shows how much the great philosopher of liberty, duty and humanity owed to the cynical conclusions of Hobbes and de Mandeville.[3]

There are great merits in this part of Kant's teaching. It is tough, astringent and businesslike. But it has three serious failings. It succeeds in being at once excessively—and simplistically—moralistic in its judgments on international history and also excessively—and simplistically—mechanistic in the cures which it commends. Kant neglects the importance in all human affairs of inevitable and tragic ignorance. He could not see that every great human enterprise, such as Western science and its application to industry, or the commercial unification of the world, is bound to involve grave misjudgments, grave misuses and even crimes. Secondly, he assumed that international history had been all of a piece—a scene of constant friction and anarchy which he attributed to a kind of collective original sin. He had no appreciation of the discontinuities, the notably different phases, which my sketch of the overall history of warfare disclosed. Thirdly, although Kant's international optimism was of a most carefully qualified and critical kind, its main effect was to strengthen the belief that international relations could be *de*militarized, given a modicum of ingenuity and goodwill, and so to turn attention away from all the scientific, industrial and sociological factors which pointed in the opposite direction. The dangers inherent in such optimism became plainer in Kant's nineteenth- and early-twentieth-century successors.

What then of the other two possible focuses of our interest in international history—the cyclical or oscillatory and the downright catastrophic? I pass over the first of these because, from the standpoint of our age, it is open to much the same objections as those just made against Kantian optimism. It suggests that, no matter what frustrating cycles or oscillations between peace and war may await mankind, at least the very worst result—total self-destruction or degradation—can never befall us. But this is a message which carries very little conviction in the Nuclear Age. There remains therefore the third possible focus of interest: the possibility, perhaps the probability, that our civilization is headed for total, irreversible self-destruction.

At first blush this may seem the least acceptable of the alternatives. No sane being can live with a doctrine which promises the complete destruction of everything that he or she holds dear even if, logically, this is no more unacceptable than other doctrines which present the future as completely predetermined. Why, then, stop to consider it? The reason is that, in order to learn the main lessons of certain histories, we must read them with an attitude of mind which comes very close to looking for a demonstration of their inevitability. Looking for the all-but-inevitable consequences at every stage of a historical narrative can be a valuable heuristic principle, provided that it is confined to a relatively short period of time and is controlled by a proper appreciation of the inherent conditionality of all prediction based on the lessons of history. In the case of that history which leads into the Nuclear Age, it is of the first importance that we should *feel* the seemingly fatal consequences of our mistaken pursuit of security through destructive superiority into which the world's great powers have slipped: feel them, that is to say, *as if* they were predetermined and inevitable—unless and until we recognize them for what they are and reject them with a will. And this means recognizing that the one valid sense of "nuclear terror" is the fear that we should *already* have relied on our nuclear deterrent strategy for too long.

It is difficult, of course, to get our late-twentieth-century minds, at once dazzled and weighed down by our latest technical advances, to acknowledge that their principal achievement has been to keep mankind steadily accelerating down the suicidal path on which it has so confidently stepped. We have blandly assumed that none of our applications of science can ever cause irreversible harm, and that the aggressively egoistic politico-economic dogmas of post-Renaissance Europe provide mankind with the only possible path of progress. Like all other generations we have no doubt done some remarkable and timely things. But in comparison with the enormity of the *worst result* to which we have been contributing, all our cleverness is indeed but tawdry rags . . . Yet to recognize this does not mean to despair. History offers countless examples, two of which are here surprisingly pertinent. Sir Winston Churchill in the first volume of his World War II memoirs, and General de Gaulle in the opening chapters of his, have given striking accounts of how they saw their respective countries slip, with seeming irretrieveableness, into deeper and more shaming dangers which culminated in June 1940. Yet the sense of all-but-inevitability which their writings convey on this issue in no way inhibits their affirmation of positive personal resolve. A few sentences from de Gaulle's *Mémoires de guerre* illustrate this combination. After describing the collapse of the French front in 1940, and the chaos of refugees pouring south and blocking the roads, he writes: "Faced by this spectacle of a bewildered people and a broken army . . . I felt myself lifted on a wave of rage beyond all limits. What stupidity beyond bearing! The war has begun inconceivably badly! Very well, it must be continued . . . Whatever I have managed to do in the years that followed was decided that very day."[4]

Reading and assessing the historical background of the Nuclear Age from the standpoint of its worst conceivable result gives substance to my claim that the *locus* of the nuclear peril is our own thought-habits and, in particular, the assumption that national security requires in all circumstances possession of weapons as destructive as any of those possessed by the enemy. The Nuclear Age, whatever its other obscurities, has revealed the falsity of that assumption. There are weapons—and it has always been possible that mankind should discover such weapons—as intolerably noxious to those who use them as to those at whom they are directed. It is the consequences of this disclosure that rattles military nerves and induces agonies of politico-military vertigo. How are we to defend ourselves if we abjure the Clausewitzian assumption that victory, even in the most justly defensive of wars, depends upon an escalation of military means—now that these means have come to include weapons of total genocide?

Clear acknowledgment of this situation must not be expected to imply immediate agreement as to what should be done to rectify it. All that the present section of my argument shows is that, for any foreseeable future, highly industrialized nations, when they slip into violent conflict, must admit to themselves and to each other that they are *eo ipso* slipping into the hands of an enemy infinitely stronger and more pitilessly destructive than either of themselves: an enemy composed of the weapons systems, strategies and beliefs in strategies whose destructive power is unlimited so far as human and perhaps all higher life on this earth is concerned . . . Vengeance is mine, says the atom; mistakes at my level allow no reprieve.

Question 4: Lessons from the historical background

I have made the bold claim that, once we have located the nuclear peril within our thought-habits, or as a portentous failure of thought-adaptation, then our approach to it *must* be historical. More specifically, we must try to see how it has come to dominate all our other political concerns, and how its main ingredients, in a process of cumulative causation, continue to accelerate our descent toward self-devised destruction. This, I maintain, is or should be the supreme, all-guiding, all-embracing vision of politically responsible human beings today. Nothing that we cherish is not threatened by the approaching danger: much of what we do and much of what we fail to do facilitates it in its headlong course.

Yet this claim, even while it persuades, may seem to leave a whole area of our concern untouched. It illuminates, it warns, it cries "Stop!" It embodies or suggests reasons for the most moving of protests. But it does not tell us what to do, or even help us in any obvious way to choose, or to grade in order of urgency and importance the many things that we might be doing to forestall a nuclear catastrophe. When propounded in this way, the objection is unanswerable. No history ever tells us, directly and specifically, what we should do in the future, if only because no history can cover or control the future intentions of its readers. But in that case how can history assist us in dealing with the nuclear peril? Let me outline three all-too-often neglected answers.

First, it is quite possible for a warning or a protest, which is entirely lacking in positive suggestions for action, to be nevertheless indispensable for any positive program of action. Our historical approach has presented the nuclear peril as the apogee of a cumulative process, dating back over 100 years, and growing steadily—and ever more rapidly—menacing; a combination of forces whose many-sidedness and unstoppable appearance become all the clearer the closer to us that it comes. To present a danger in this way, as constantly intensifying and accelerating, is, psychologically, much more effective than any account which, no matter how accurately, treats that danger as an inherent part of the furniture of our accepted world. Unlike Everest, the nuclear peril is not simply *there*, it is getting rapidly nearer *here*. And only a historical vision of its titanic advance can convey this vital difference.

Secondly, and from the other side of the question, we should recall how the different strands of the nineteenth-century peace movements failed through lack of cohesion—indeed through lack of appreciation of their common target. The peace movements of today, in so far as their target is the danger of nuclear catastrophe, are equally varied in character and approach and equally liable to suffer from division and dispersal of their efforts. Some of them, for example, owe their pertinence and authority to the specialized knowledge of certain professional groups—medical, scientific, legal, economic, and indeed military. Others speak from the side of religious, humanitarian, educational and cultural interests. Others speak and act with notable effect from the standpoint—as crucial morally as it is biologically—of women. Moreover, as today's peace movements gather strength they will certainly evoke more widespread and organized opposition, in face of which they will have to decide where to find allies, even if partial and uncertain—in political parties, in trade unions, in the "media." Of one thing we may be certain: if the future of today's peace movements is to match their hopes, it is bound to be a stormy, difficult and frictive one. How then are they to keep their unity of spirit and aim?

My answer is simple. Different groups of human beings seldom agree about the kind of future they want to create, but can often agree about the future they want to avoid. But this involves initial agreement about the nearness and line of approach of the danger which threatens them. One of the most confusing features of the present international situation is that the two rival power blocs see the nuclear danger from the standpoint, and in the vocabulary, of their respective radically opposed ideologies. Such opposition is almost certainly irreconcilable through debate; but the two sides to it can nevertheless be subjected to the impartial eye of international history. There can be no question about the main actors—or rather agencies—in the history that has brought us to the edge of nuclear destruction. They have not been individual men or nations or classes or creeds, but the universal availability of physical science and its industrial and military applications, and the unification of the world through the competitive forays of a handful of Western nations, resulting in its reduction to the dimensions of a battlefield. Whatever their ultimate result, these developments mark a discontinuity in human history comparable to that brought about by the last great geological changes. And this discontinuity is the most important truth that is shared by mankind today. At the beginning of our century it was widely acclaimed as the triumph of Western virtues and values. Today it is more widely felt to presage irreversible disaster unless its literal and metaphorical explosiveness evokes efforts of self-discipline, self-correction and mutual forbearance such as national communities have never before been called upon to exercise. Evidently, a sense of that history cannot by itself create or sustain the required understanding and effort. But by acting as a persistent reminder and warning, it can keep our minds steadily directed onto their target: the containment, if not the conquest, of mankind's propensity to self-destruction.

It may be objected to this second answer that the historic inheritance whose lessons it invokes is too general to provide a rallying point for a new and unparalleled effort in international cooperation. It may be argued that every great political advance has been made in relation to particular issues around which strong popular feeling can easily be aroused. (Later, of course, such feeling may find a wider reference, as with the antislavery movement, for example.) This objection has force against political projects based on some abstract formula or set of principles which, it is assumed, no rational mind can reject. But the discontinuity by which we are all bemused is, emphatically, not something derived from a set of general principles. On the contrary, it is a manifestation of their breakdown. To risk a paradox, it is, in spite of its immense complexity, as individual as most individuals are; it is a once-for-all turning point or breaking point in international history, making special—because novel—demands upon those who are involved in it. However, as I have insisted, its speciality is such that it can be coped with only in the light of earlier phases of international history from which it has arisen, and of the alternative possible futures which it gravely if dimly foreshadows for later generations.

Yet here our nuclear predicament presents a further paradox. When we think of it in the short term—in terms of what we might do this week or this year—we are likely to be overwhelmed by its seemingly endless ramifications and by the immensity of the forces, especially of ignorance and inertia, which are ranged against us. But when we think of it in the context of other seemingly impossible tasks which have faced and doubtless will again face humanity, then its weight is surprisingly lightened. We are being called upon to give at most a first difficult but decisive pull in a task which will, on the most hopeful interpretation, make heavy demands upon many generations to come. It is as good for us to acknowledge the smallness of our effort as to affirm its indispensability.

PART IV *Rebuilding security*

13 THE MILITARY POWER
John Kenneth Galbraith

Professor J. K. Galbraith is Paul M. Warburg Professor of Economics Emeritus at Harvard University and the newly elected President of the American Academy of Arts and Letters. During World War II he headed wartime price control activities at the Office of Price Administration, and later he became a director in the State Department Office of Economic Security Policy and of the US Strategic Bombing Survey, receiving the Medal of Freedom and the President's Certificate of Merit for his work. From 1961 to 1963 he served as US Ambassador to India.
J. K. Galbraith's many books include American Capitalism, The Affluent Society, The New Industrial State, The Great Crash, Economics and the Public Purpose, Money *and* The Age of Uncertainty. *His most recent book is* The Anatomy of Power.

We have a political ritual in the United States that all will have noticed. It is that of the politician who essays a criticism of the Pentagon budget, raises doubts as to the need or wisdom of a new weapon or weapons system or otherwise seems to be critical of some part or policy of the military establishment. He then hastens to add that nothing should be interpreted as suggesting that he in any way doubts the need for a strong national defense. One may be critical on military matters in detail; one must never have reservations as to the military purpose or power in general. That is above debate.

My intention in this paper is to examine this politically protected, even sacrosanct, power. I have in mind power as Max Weber defined it—the submission of one, some or many to the will and purposes of other persons or organizations. I have long felt that we disguise matters and learn little when we speak of power in general—that of corporations, trade unions, the Moral Majority, the Catholic bishops or the President of the United States. One must always go more deeply and see the sources of the power in question, and that is my present purpose as regards the modern military establishment.

By the military establishment I have reference to the armed services, the large supporting civilian bureaucracy and the huge outreach to the weapons firms, to related corporations, to the lobbyists and their spokesmen, to the supporting scientists, engineers and politicians. I will be concerned with both strengths and potential weaknesses, and, needless to say, I will have a word on how the military establishment might more effectively be controlled. It is the military power in the American context that I address. I do not suggest that it is here unique; in all countries, East and West and also, sadly, poor as well as rich, the military power is a major fact of modern life.

All power has its origins in one of three sources—in the personality, what Weber called the charisma, of a great leader. Or in property or disposable income. Or in organization. Or in some combination of the three. From these sources of power come, variously, the instruments of its enforcement. Of these, again, there are three. Power is exercised by the threat or reality of punishment—the threat or reality of physical, psychological or moral hurt or damage. And it is exercised by the promise of reward—of pay, profit, praise, contracts or, possibly, a decently discreet bribe. And it is exercised by the existence or successful cultivation of the requisite belief—belief that the submission to the individual or organization in question is necessary, normal, in accord with truth and fact, virtuous, required by immediately exigent circumstance, patriotic or otherwise right or beneficial. In discussing these matters in the past, I have called this last method of winning submission conditioned power. It is of great importance, and particularly as regards the military power.

It is the compelling feature of the modern military establishment that it has, in massive form, two of the three great sources of power, and, almost uniquely, it has access to all three of the instruments for the enforcement of submission.

Personality was the traditional source of military power from Alexander to Caesar to Napoleon to General Douglas MacArthur. It is not now very important. The names of the Joint Chiefs and of their Chairman are widely unknown. So also those of the civilian heads of the individual services. The names of Secretaries of Defense are known, but their public personality is the creation of their office. In all but the rarest cases they disappear into an often well-earned oblivion on the day they leave Washington. In the Vietnam War, in keeping with centuries of past practice, an effort was made to ascribe a personal charisma to the generals of that campaign. It was not successful; they, too, proved highly forgettable. The leaders of the modern military establishment, civilian or military, are the temporary expression of the large and continuing organization they head.

The two other sources of modern military power, property in the form of disposable income and organization, are, however, infinitely impressive. There is the military budget commanding $229 billion for the calendar year of 1984, 6·6 percent of the Gross National Product, 26 percent of all federal expenditures and more for the purchases of goods and services than is available to all other federal agencies combined. There is no similar concentration of disposable wealth anywhere else in our economy; compared with the amounts available to the military establishment the resources of the largest corporations fade into relative insignificance. Curiously it is the archaic tendency of the liberal left to react far more strongly to corporate than to any form of public power and thus to see the Pentagon, to the extent that it arouses concern, as the instrument of private corporate power. This is a minor triumph of traditional attitudes over the modern reality.

The third of the sources of power is organization. Here again the military establishment is transcendent. Organization has two dimensions—size and discipline. The military establishment has both. There are the two million active uniformed persons, the million full-time civilians of the Department of Defense, the million reservists—in the aggregate no slight fraction of the adult population. In close association are the weapons firms, the engineers and scientists and the serving lobbyists and trade associations, not excluding the army of Washington acolytes now, in a seemly way, called consultants. This huge structure is not a monolith; in particular, there is sharp, even relentless, competition between the services. But for nearly all, by the nature of the military culture, discipline is a high virtue. The good soldier is a good soldier because he accepts without question the purposes of the organization—accepts these purposes in the most admired (i.e., highly conditioned) case as superior to his own life itself. The singularity and notoriety of the Pentagon whistle-blower—the civilian who reveals error or extravagance—celebrate not the values of individual expression but its exceptional, even astonishing, character. Dissenting or critical comment on military procurement or policy has not recently been heard from the weapons firms—or from the engineers or scientists who serve them.

In all organization there is surrender of individual thought, voice or action to the purposes of the larger group. This is very great in the higher reaches of the modern corporation. There executives conform speech and action all but automatically to the purposes of the firm. It is why so much executive expression is so rarely memorable. But the military establishment taken as a whole is our most disciplined organization. Together with its property—its disposable income—it has in incomparable magnitude and effect two of the three great sources of power.

It has also, as I have said, formidable and even unique recourse to all three instruments for the enforcement of power.

Of the right of recourse to punishment one need say little. In a permissive age the military service, more than any organization, retains this power as regards its members; it is taken for granted that discipline will be so enforced. Civilians in the military establishment are not subject to courts martial; the threat of lie detectors and dispatch into some remote post signifying bureaucratic oblivion serves much the same end, as does the danger of the charge that one has threatened national security.

Elsewhere in the world, it may be noted, the recourse that the military power has to punishment goes far to account for the prevalence, one may say the blight, of military dictatorships, the control by the military of some forty of the total of 134 independent governments. These dictatorships, it has been urged, are more benign than the governments of the Communist countries—the latter are totalitarian, the military dictatorships only authoritarian. It is not a distinction that is evident to those who are subject to the physical punishments by which military rule is extensively enforced; it was not to those whose bodies have been disinterred in the Argentine cemeteries.

The second instrument for the enforcement of power is compensation; this for the military establishment is the natural counterpart of the vast financial resources it commands. It is essential, needless to say, for winning and maintaining the submission to its purposes of the armed services; unpaid soldiers over the centuries have been notably unreliable. And, as a similar commonplace, it wins the compliance of the civilian bureaucracy—the Pentagon. This pecuniary influence extends out to the weapons firms—to the large sector of the economy that has a strong financial stake in defense expenditure and manifests this in devout submission to the military purpose. The compensatory power then reaches beyond the military–industrial complex, as it was so durably characterized by Dwight D. Eisenhower, to politicians. There are few American congressmen and senators who do not subdue their convictions as regards military spending when a Pentagon project in their own district or state is involved. Reflecting an intelligent concern for the threat of nuclear devastation, legislators from New England and along the East Coast have been generally critical of the more promiscuous aspects of the arms build-up of the last few years. They have strongly supported the nuclear weapons freeze movement. Nearly all voted against the MX. But these convictions were extensively set aside a year ago in the competition to win the basing of an ancient and now missile-armed battleship with the accompanying and exceedingly modest prospects of jobs and revenue. It was a uniquely visible, even slightly bizarre, example of the compelling character of the compensatory power of the military establishment.

Finally among the three instruments for the exercise of the military power—along with the threat or reality of punishment of its members and compensatory power or the promise or reality of pay—there is conditioned power. This, as I have said, is the submission that comes because it is deemed to be normal, essential or right, the submission that reflects belief. As compensatory power is the natural counterpart of disposable income, so conditioned power is the natural counterpart of organization—the conditioning or persuasion that serves the purposes of business enterprises, government, unions and other groups and that is won by the education, indoctrination or persuasion that are a primary function of all organization.

Conditioned power is the most important and, without doubt, the least understood instrument of the military power. It has many forms. One is the everyday ascription of virtue by the military culture to the individual who substitutes the goals of the organization for his own. This anciently has been the purpose of military training and related instruction. The soldier, as Tolstoy observed, learns to surrender thought to the regiment. In ordinary civilian education there is merit in thinking for one's self—always provided that it is not carried to socially inconvenient extremes. Military instruction, including that of the related civilians, emphasizes the superior virtue of the aims and ends of the organization. It is for serving these, not for the vigor or percipience of individual expression, that medals are awarded and both military and civilian promotions are accorded.

The military power also gains greatly from its association with patriotism. This, the subordination of individual will or preference to the higher purposes of the state, is, even more than religious obedience, the most taught and least challenged of human values. And it is, indeed, an important element of a workable social order; the alternative to acceptance of the higher purposes of the state is ungovernability, disorder and perhaps chaos. From this comes the instinct that everywhere requires instruction of the young and the not-so-young in the principles of patriotism, as they are called, and the rebuke of those who are resistant, negligent or, God forbid, subversive.

What is less to be approved is the way in which the military establishment, including the weapons industry, turns patriotism to its bureaucratic and corporate goals and makes opposition seem unpatriotic. This is seen with the greatest clarity in the authorization of new weapons—in recent times, the cruise missile, the MX and binary poison gas. Those in opposition to these weapons have risked and even invited the charge of being unduly casual about national security and the national interest or, perish the terrible thought, soft on the Russians—in a word, unpatriotic. But this use (or misuse) of patriotism and the prior social conditioning are not confined to the question of weapons procurement. They protect the military budget as a whole; as noted, even the most committed critic of our military expenditure must explain that basically he (or she) is in favor of a strong national defense. Patriotism, needless to say, was evoked vigorously in support of the Vietnam War; that of those opposing was held to be very much in doubt. Similarly as regards recent operations in Central America and the Caribbean. The President and Secretary of State Schultz came close to saying last autumn that it was because of its questionable commitment to patriotic goals that the press was kept out of the Grenada operation. Not all of this use or misuse of patriotism has been serviceable to the military power, a point to which I will return.

To be effective, the social conditioning of the military power has two further requirements. It must have a credible enemy. And it must have effective control of the information that affects public belief—that serves the social conditioning on which the power depends. In the years since World War II, North Korea, North Vietnam, Cuba, Qaddafi in Libya, the Sandinistas in Nicaragua and the guerrilla forces in El Salvador have rendered service as enemies. And notably, also, Communist China. But in greater or less measure all these states have depended for their credibility on their presumed position as instruments of the USSR. When division between Russia and China became inescapably evident, China was transmuted into an honorary bastion of freedom and free enterprise. To make the guerrilla forces in El Salvador or the Sandinista government in Nicaragua a plausible threat to the United States the

Kissinger Commission was required to make them agencies of the Soviet Union. Coincidentally with the arms build-up of recent years went a similar intensification of emphasis on the military threat from Moscow. The second was in all respects essential for the first and for the strength of the military power in general.

Associated with this need for an enemy is the control of information, including that on the weaponry and the intentions of the required enemy. This protects the social conditioning against the intrusion of information adverse to the needed belief. In practice, such control has two aspects; these are classification and complexity.

The official purpose of classification—protection of public secrets—is to prevent information on weaponry, underlying technology, strategic designs and other such matters from falling into unfriendly hands. The second, now-all-but-explicit purpose is to prevent information in conflict with the military (or other public) purpose from reaching and influencing the American public. This, in turn, is the source of the major pressure for extending classification and for punishing violation. The pressure here is both subtle and very great; as a sometime Washington hand, I speak from some experience. Rarely was I responsible for, or associated with, an error or aberration in public policy when I did not wonder if it might legitimately be kept a secret. From this impulse comes the continuing tension between the military power and the press. Considering the importance for the military power of social conditioning and the supporting control of information, it is a tension that is both wholly predictable and much to be welcomed.

The second and somewhat less appreciated instrument for the control of information lies in the technical and political complexity of modern weaponry and military policy in general. The weapons are technically very complex. So is the process of design, development or more distant contemplation and planning. So are parallel matters in the Soviet Union and so is the assessment of Soviet intention. All of this has the effect of confining policy on weaponry—as also associated cost and budget requirements—to a narrow group of specialists or presumed specialists. Potential critics, politicians and the public are either excluded or they choose to exclude themselves on the grounds of ignorance, technical incompetence or the compelling appeal of less alarming subjects.

This monopoly of policy is nearly complete where arms control is involved. For decades policy and negotiation have been the private domain of a small number of individuals, the nuclear arms control theologians, who have laid claim to special, indeed nearly exclusive, competence on the subject. Intervention by outsiders brings an indignant and, on some occasions, a contemptuous response. What can those so uninformed contribute? One of the several virtues of the nuclear arms freeze movement was in taking policy away or partly away from the arms control theologians and putting it clearly in the public domain. It is the reason, also, that this movement has been viewed with such discontent by those who have made arms control policy their exclusive preserve. It rudely challenged their monopoly of esoteric knowledge and bypassed the complexity that gave them power.

Not only does the technical and political complexity of weaponry decisions and arms control policy remove the subject from the people at large; it also nullifies the efforts of technically informed critics. They are drawn into the deeply complicated debate; in the process they are drawn away from the larger constituency of public concern. This has been the fate of university and other scholarly critics. In seeking to meet the arms control theologians on their own terms, they have often become, in effect, their allies. An example of this is to be found in otherwise well-intentioned recent work at my own university. As everywhere else, there is deep concern at Harvard over the threat of nuclear confrontation and conflict. A year or two ago President Derek Bok asked scholars to address the subject seriously. One result was the book *Living with Nuclear Weapons* by the Harvard Nuclear Study Group. This volume serves primarily to emphasize the complexity of the subject, the arcane nature of the resulting disagreements, the bizarre character of the compromises then required and the general inaccessibility of the subject to the larger public.

Finally there is the matter of civilian control. The oldest restraint on the military power, one that for long was deep in our national consciousness and law, is the ultimate assertion of civilian authority in military matters. This, another sadly unnoticed point in our time, has wholly disappeared. For long there has been a tendency for such authority to be exercised by civilians who, out of study or their own past wartime experience, were determined to show that they were as accomplished in the martial arts as any military man and could, on frequent occasion, be more aggressive as to military action or adventure than the serving officers with whom they were associated or over whom they presided. "I may be a college professor (a lawyer or a businessman), but in a crunch I can be bolder than any general." Such were the civilian attitudes that did much to put and keep us in Vietnam. To those professing such attitudes the present administration has added a cadre of high civilian officials in the Pentagon extensively drawn from the weapons firms themselves or their Washington lobbyists and consultants. That individuals so selected would serve as a civilian restraint on the military power has a level of absurdity that is difficult to characterize. It is control of the military–industrial complex by the military–industrial complex. Better, perhaps, the soldiers and certainly cheaper, for they would not be so intimately involved with contracts with, and procurement from, the firms they have served and to which they will return.

I summarize. The modern military power embraces in property and pecuniary resources and in massive and relatively disciplined organization two of the three primary sources of power, and it has all three of the instruments for the enforcement of power. Of these—punishment or the threat of punishment, compensation and social conditioning—the last is the least appreciated and the most important. It invokes the better instincts of patriotism and concern for national interest. It threatens the critic with the charge of being insufficiently committed to these values, somehow aligned with the enemy. By classification it limits access to information adverse to its purposes and enhances the image of a valid enemy. Who wants to be casual where the Russians are concerned? On weapons and arms control policy social conditioning is protected from criticism or even public intervention by the technical and political complexity of the issues involved. It is an awesome thing.

Yet it would be wrong to surrender hope. Great as the military power has become, it is not plenary. Nor is it beyond public and political reach. As it is necessary to understand the sources of the strength of the military power in our time, so also it is necessary to perceive—in a suitably apt phrase—its windows of vulnerability. To these I now turn.

There is, first, the dramatic conflict that the Reagan Administration has made so impressively visible between the modern military establishment and civilian welfare needs, primarily those of the poor. In the years after World War II, military expenditures were widely viewed as a generally passive complement to welfare expenditures. To some they appeared as a useful investment buttress to economic activity and growth. During the Vietnam years there was a change: military outlays came to be seen as a cause of inflation, the occasion for unwelcome increases in taxes. It remained, however, for the Reagan Administration to put them in a truly antisocial light. Beginning in 1981, the military budget was sharply increased; this, it was held, made necessary the highly publicized cuts or curtailments in civilian expenditures with special incidence on the urban poor. The military increase was seen as making necessary the civilian decrease; the military budget and the military power were thus placed in direct conflict with civilian well-being at the lower end of the income scale. Politicians, especially those with an urban and minority clientele, were for the first time given a clear choice as between the Pentagon and their own people. Few friends of the military, on reflection, could think it wise to place military spending so starkly in conflict with the needs of the least affluent of Americans. It might be noted that it is from the families most affected by this conflict between military and social expenditures that recruits for the services are extensively drawn.

The second assault on the military power has come from the political commitment to the wrong wars. The Vietnam War—the preoccupation with Indochina generally—was a disaster for the military establishment. This is now widely conceded; it is made evident in the recurrent statements of the hope that Vietnam has at long last been forgotten. But now has come the compulsion to remind. This arises from the aberrant fascination with El Salvador and Nicaragua and the unfathomable objectives in Lebanon. All are a superb design for retrieving the Vietnam memory and for stirring further concern as to the military power.

War, unless with Grenada, is a serious business. Only when, as in World War II, there is nearly universal support does the military power escape criticism; a simple majority does not serve. When as in Vietnam and in Central America or Lebanon there is strong and highly articulate opposition to war or military operations, this becomes indistinguishable from opposition to the military power itself. And this is understood by senior American military officers—some at least. They have been far from enthusiastic about our Central American intervention; not a few have seen it as irrelevant to the real problem, a source of damage to the reputation of the armed services. On leaving office a few months ago, General Edward C. Meyer, until then the Army Chief of Staff, noted that the conflict there is "based on the legitimate concerns of the people" and does not lend itself to military solutions. General Wallace H. Nutting, on completing a tour of duty in the area, offered a similar view: "The fundamental causes of dissatisfaction are the existing social, political, economic inequalities."

The third and most important source of vulnerability of the military power arises from the nature of modern weaponry. In past wars only a limited number even of the armed forces were at risk—the foot soldiers, the lower-ranking officers and the sailors. And not since the Civil War in the United States has any appreciable part of the civilian population been in danger. War and resulting death were the experience of the youngest and least articulate members of the national community. With nuclear weapons all has changed; death is now the prospective experience of all. Soldiers and civilians, the old and the young, the rich and the poor, are all at risk.

This sense of being endangered has been deepened by the educational efforts of a wide range of civilian groups—of scientists, physicians, the Quakers, the Catholic bishops, artists, writers and many more—that have come together to stress the terrors of nuclear war. It has also been abetted in remarkable measure by the civilian leadership of the Pentagon and the national security establishment. From these has come the talk of limited nuclear war, protracted nuclear war, prevailing in nuclear war, and of the levels of "acceptable" casualties in nuclear war. And from those charged with civilian defense has come a uniquely lunar set of recommendations for survival in nuclear war: plans for an orderly evacuation of the cities at 35 miles an hour, promises that "with enough shovels" all can make it, warnings that those evacuating the cities should take their credit cards with them. This impulse of the Administration to frighten the American people is something of a political puzzle. Death, especially when for one's self and one's family and not some distant foot-slogger, is not a politically attractive proposition.

However motivated, the result for the military power is strongly evident. The armed forces and the defense establishment generally, which were once associated with protection of the country, have now an inescapable association with its destruction. Where once people looked at its arms and equipment with a sense of reassurance, they now contemplate the thousands of nuclear warheads and the MIRVs, Pershing IIs, cruise missiles, the MX, with fear, even panic. Gone is the thought of protection by the military; in its place is the ever-present threat of obliteration.

Again the lesson has not been lost on the military itself. There is some and, one hopes, increasing recognition that modern weaponry is unrelated to any rational military use. And to a marked and rewarding degree the leadership in the pressure for arms control has been assumed by a dedicated group of former high officers of the armed services.

I have in this chapter considered the nature of the military power, its strengths and, as above, its points of vulnerability. But a word must be added on the more urgent lines of responding activity.

I do not urge as antidotes to the military power a greater military assault on the civilian social budget, more bad wars, a greater proliferation of weapons or talk of nuclear war, effective as these have been. The fact that modern weaponry no longer defends but obliterates must, however, be kept strongly in the public view. Not a few who objected to *The Day After* as obscene, horror-ridden or merely too frightening were affirming its effectiveness in winning appreciation of the dangers of modern military weapons, the importance of having an end to the arms race. All must be made to see that modern weaponry has made a complete break with all past military tradition.

There must, needless to say, be a solid and politically sustainable design for arms control. And this must be accessible to the general public; it cannot be at a level of complexity that supports the monopoly of the nuclear theologians within and outside the government. This was and remains the contribution of the movement for a freeze on the development, production and deployment of nuclear weapons, what has made this movement so serviceable in support of arms control: it allows the public full access to arms control policy for the first time. There is, in consequence, no doubt as to where the public stands.

As we in the United States must be alert to resist the monopoly of this issue by the arms control theologians, so we must resist the control of information by which they and the military power are so extensively sustained. The tension between those who would stamp everything secret and those whose business it is to inform the public must be strongly encouraged. Policies ostensibly for the purpose of keeping information from the Russians serve even more importantly to keep it from domestic critics and the American public. There must be no doubt as to the importance of secrecy as a support to the military power. The plea of national security must never be allowed either to avoid or to dull criticism.

The first responsibility of every politician, one to which each should be held, must be to bring a strong judgment to bear on the resources the Pentagon commands, the weaponry it seeks, the political and military purposes it supports. Let it not be supposed, as now, that the Pentagon is the only bureaucracy that should not be called a bureaucracy, that has no internal dynamic of bureaucratic expansion.

We must reassert *effective* civilian control of the Pentagon—the oldest of our constitutional concerns. The present control of the military–industrial complex *by* the military–industrial complex is a parody on the whole concept of civilian authority. So, going back to earlier administrations, has been the intrusion into positions of responsibility of the pseudo-soldiers, those civilians who feel they must outdo the military in martial ardor. Henceforth we must have civilians in the military establishment who are fully conscious of the importance of civilian responsibility.

Finally we must be aware of the critical role of an enemy for the military power. I am not especially enamored of the Russian political and economic system. Looking over its history and my own, I doubt that I would have survived there to my present mature years. But we must be consistently skeptical of those who urge the military power or ambitions of the Soviet Union in order to enhance their own. We must not suppose that the Soviets are more suicidal than we. Civil communications must be maintained, and there must be joint concern and continuing joint arrangements for preventing nuclear war by accident or in some moment of political or military confrontation. Those who speak in these days of nuclear superiority and inferiority must be reminded of the metaphor of a young Harvard colleague of mine, William Ury, who has been constructively concerned with these matters. It tells of two boys in a closed garage with several inches of gasoline on the floor. One has six large matches; the other has seven smaller ones. They debate as to who is strategically superior.

14 WHAT POLITICAL SIGNALS SHOULD OUR ARMED FORCES SEND?

Robert Neild

Professor Robert Neild is a Professor of Economics at the University of Cambridge and a Fellow of Trinity College. He worked in operational research in the Royal Air Force during World War II. From 1964 to 1967 he was Economic Adviser to the Treasury, and from 1967 to 1971 he was the first Director of the Stockholm International Peace Research Institute. He is the author of How to Make Up Your Mind About the Bomb.

It is easy to assume from the constant debate in the press about particular weapon systems or about the tactics of the armies in West Germany that NATO is an organization whose sole concerns are military. But such a view is too narrow. Whether consciously intended or not, any military formation sends out political as well as military signals.

Because of the fragile condition of international relations, it is important that the political signals emanating from the forces of the two major blocs in the 1980s should be right. They will only be right if hard thought is put to the matter, and if it is given an appropriately high priority in planning. We cannot affect the Warsaw Pact directly, but we can affect our side; and thus indirectly we can affect both. At present, the political signals emanating from both the Warsaw Pact and NATO are dangerous. Each reads the other's signals as aggressive. The military policies now being put forward look like reinforcing the negative aspect of those political signals.

I shall in this chapter consider what policy over political signals NATO should adopt. The arguments are general. They could be applied to any alliance or country.

Aims

It is necessary first to be clear about the political aims of NATO. While the broad purpose is defense, NATO's apparent aims have often been mixed and ambiguous. The governments of different member countries, and different departments and factions within those governments, have had different aims: they have varied in their degree of alarmism and aggressiveness, or conversely, in their degree of complacency and passivity. And there have been changes over time, when, for example, different political parties have come to power in NATO countries or when developments in the Soviet Union have increased or reduced fear in the West. The election of President Reagan in the United States and Mrs. Thatcher in Britain are recent examples. The death of Stalin and the rise of Krushchev are earlier examples. I shall assume that the aim of NATO is to defend present frontiers, not to roll back the Iron Curtain by military means, aware that there have been those who have hankered after the second objective.

I must then make an assumption about NATO policy over economic pressures. The assumption I shall make—because it is necessary to the development of the argument—is that the aim of NATO is to minimize the cost of defense. Again this is by no means an uncontroversial statement. An alternative assumption is that the aim of NATO is to raise its military expenditures in order to challenge and strain the Soviet politico-economic system. The latter sometimes seems to be the policy of the United States government under Mr. Reagan. In a confidential document entitled *Fiscal 1984–1988 Defense Guidance*, written by senior Pentagon officials and made public in the *New York Times* in May 1982 we read that now, in "peacetime," a threefold strategy should be adopted to carry a crusade against the USSR and to destroy it by economic and technical strain. First, trade policies should be designed to deny the USSR access to technology, and to increase pressure on the economy; second, arms procurement should favor weapons "that are difficult for the Soviets to counter, impose disproportionate costs, open up new areas of major military competition and render the accumulated Soviet equipment stocks obsolescent;" third, the West should redouble efforts to foment unrest in the satellite states of Eastern Europe. The *Defense Guidance* is not formal policy, but it emanates from the highest levels. It indicates a type of thinking that should, I believe, be rejected as naive and dangerous. I shall note some of its implications later.

Types of signal

Political signals about military policy can be conveyed by declarations of intentions or by visible changes in military capabilities. Once one nation or group of nations has adopted a peaceful or hostile view of another, they may be pretty unresponsive to signals of either kind that contradict the preconceptions they have formed. An example is the wishful thinking about Hitler in the 1930s. It persisted in the face of considerable evidence that his intentions were hostile and that his forces were being built up. In the confrontation between NATO and the Warsaw Pact now, there is so much suspicion that declarations of peaceful intentions—which are often made—are ineffective. Capabilities are the dominant signals. Experts and amateurs look at the available evidence as to the forces of the other side and make pronouncements about how great is "the threat" posed by those forces.

To convey that its aims are defensive, NATO might in theory make quantitative or qualitative changes in its forces. But the pursuit of a "balance" of forces is taken to be the means of ensuring peace. Quantitative strength is therefore judged by the criterion of balance. The question is asked, "What is the military balance?" or "Are their forces larger than ours?" or "Do they have more of this or that type of weapon?" And the answer can rarely be reassuring.

The reason for this is that precise measurement is made impossible by asymmetries in geography, population, economics, mobilization, training, weapons, leadership, the reliability of allies and many other things. Many assumptions have to be made. Subjective judgment becomes all-important. In an atmosphere of suspicion and fear, the instinct to over-insure becomes dominant. Out of concern to ensure that they are not "wrong" in a manner that endangers their nation, the military tend to focus on a maximum estimate of the enemy's strength and compare it with a cautious estimate of the strength of their own side. These assessments easily become part of an enshrined wisdom. Because they are presented in numbers or ratios, the assessments look "hard" and reliable. Yet that is not necessarily so. The assessment is no "harder" than the assumptions on which it is based.

Because they are biased by fear and worst-case analysis, the judgments of the military balance made by NATO and the Warsaw Pact are not the same. This is well illustrated by the rival glossy handbooks about the military balance put out by the United States and the Soviet Union in 1981 and 1982.[1]

In this setting it is scarcely feasible to signal that your aims are defensive by making *quantitative* changes in your forces. For if the pursuit of balance is held to be the means of achieving peace, to curtail your forces—or to curtail the rate of increase in them—relative to the forces of your opponent is to move away from balance and hence to jeopardize peace in the eyes of the watchdogs of balance. Added to which, if measurement is imprecise and judgment is biased by suspicion, the view is always likely to be taken, on one side or the other, that its forces are inferior, that it must expand so as to catch up.

The pursuit of balance—upwards in the acquisition of arms or downwards in arms control and disarmament negotiations—is a most futile and dangerous exercise, futile because asymmetries make balance impossible to define, and dangerous because asymmetrical and fearful perceptions mean that the pursuit of balance leads to an arms race. To say that you are pursuing balance in arms is not a declaration of moderate aims. It is a declaration that you are engaging in a competition in arms.

All the same, when the pursuit of balance is the general practice, it is not feasible just to renounce that practice without putting anything in its place. This brings us to the quality—as distinct from the quantity—of forces.

Qualitative changes

Qualitative changes may offer a feasible way of signaling peaceful intentions. Consider *non-nuclear* land forces in Europe, plus their air support. Consider what qualitative aspects of their capabilities could be used to signal peaceful aims.

First, the ability of the forces to attack could be minimized and their ability to defend maximized. A decision to move in this direction would mean a conscious rejection of the old military adage that "attack is the best form of defense." It would mean that the highest priority was given to the nature of the *political* signal generated. But such a decision cannot be made without regard to the military sciences. Only if it can be convincingly argued that "defense is the best form of defense" can one expect to carry the armed forces and public. The scope for doing this will depend partly on the technology of the era and how it is exploited. For example, early in this century the machine gun helped defense. Then, during and after World War I, the tank, against which the machine gun was ineffective, helped attack. In the era of electronics through which we are now passing, the precision-guided munition, with its high accuracy and high lethality against tanks and other mobile vehicles, looks as if it could be exploited to the advantage of defense. A force armed mainly with these weapons would look much more defensive than one armed principally with tanks. The trend in this direction already visible in NATO forces is to be welcomed.

But weapons are only one of many variables which will determine how defensive are your forces—and how defensive they are seen to be by your opponent. Other characteristics that matter are their mobility (in terms of such indicators as mechanized divisions, airborne forces and river crossing equipment), their doctrine and training, the extent and disposition of their stockpiles of military supplies. Logistics have a further, important implication for the political signal that is sent. A tank equipped and supported for a role in mobile, in-depth defensive operations in West Germany is different, especially in its logistic train, from a battle tank intended to drive to the Urals. The Soviets know that and can see that. Thus, it is not so much the *quantity* as the *potential reach* of the logistics operation that forms an important political signal. The cost to NATO of keeping stockpiles of military supplies has been high, but that has been a consequence of the huge appetite for fuel, ammunition and spare parts of the mechanized armies and the air forces on which NATO has relied until now. If reliance on precision-guided munitions increases, the required size of munition stockpiles may go down and greater dispersion may be possible: precision-guided munitions, being single-shot, expendable weapons, do not require refuelling or repair after use; nor do they need to be concentrated at runways or other expensive common facilities.

The second requirement of defensive forces is that they should not present rich concentrated targets, the vulnerability of which is such that they can easily be wiped out. Airfields are an example. Vulnerability means that your forces are not an effective defense; and it creates instability by tempting your opponent to attack. If two sides have forces that have an offensive capability and are deployed in a vulnerable manner, instability will be most acute: both sides will face a temptation to attack pre-emptively.

The third requirement is that the forces should not depend on mobilization and concentration (meaning movement of mobilized troops from a long distance to their fighting stations) since in those conditions there can be a race to mobilize and a temptation, on the part of the nation that wins that race, to attack in order to take advantage of its temporary superiority. That is another form of instability. It can be avoided by relying on a mixture of professional troops permanently on station, and of local reservists.

The implication of these three requirements is that to constitute an effective defense with limited offensive capability, the forces should be permanently *in situ*, dispersed, equipped and trained in a defensive mode. The forces should be capable of holding an enemy attack without resort to nuclear weapons, and should be so deployed that it would be clear to the nuclear-armed opponent that no decisive military advantage would accrue from nuclear bombardment: it would not stop resistance.

Present policy

NATO's present policy, the "flexible response," relies on first use of nuclear weapons to compensate for a perceived inferiority in non-nuclear forces.

This policy has been criticized within NATO on the grounds that it is suicidal to rely on first use of nuclear weapons to defend yourself. It has been argued that the member countries of NATO could today afford to strengthen their conventional forces and so raise the nuclear threshold.

The fashionable view as to the type of weapons and forces that should be acquired for this purpose has been forcefully set out in the ESECS Report, which was produced in 1983 by a distinguished group of recently retired NATO commanders, academics and others familiar with arms.[2] The main features of the policy proposed in that report are these:

a It relies on a new generation of "smart" non-nuclear weapons to be used as substitutes for tactical nuclear weapons. These smart weapons are accurate missiles with ranges up to several hundred miles, each of which will deliver many guided submunitions that will steer themselves accurately at, for example, tanks or aircraft on the ground. These weapons would be operated in conjunction with real-time target surveillance and target acquisition. They would be used to destroy Warsaw Pact air bases, forward concentrations of forces and second echelon forces coming up through Poland and East Germany.

b It envisages continued reliance on nuclear weapons to make the Warsaw Pact's forces operate in a "nuclear-scared mode."

c It rejects defense in depth, endorses forward defense and the possession of mobile forces that can counterattack and reconquer lost territory.

Few people would not endorse the idea that the nuclear threshold should be raised. But what about the policy proposed for this purpose, based on the acquisition of smart weapons. What signals will it send to the Warsaw Pact? How will it look from their side?

The prospect before Warsaw Pact analysts is that, on the assumption that the smart weapons will work, NATO will acquire the ability to knock out, with non-nuclear weapons, Warsaw Pact air bases, forward concentrations of forces and second echelon forces coming up to the combat area. At the same time, NATO will increase and give additional range to its mobile armored forces. Worst-case analysis will suggest that, by using its smart weapons, NATO might achieve a position where, having neutralized a large part of the forces opposing it, it could advance into Warsaw Pact territory: NATO's offensive capability will look greater than before. That is a consequence of the characteristics of the forces proposed for NATO.

If, instead, NATO were to adopt the smart weapons and at the same time were to redeploy its armor and restructure its forces in a defensive mode, following the criteria suggested above, the new policy would have, and would be seen to have, enhanced defensive potential and reduced offensive potential. The smart weapons would still be used to reduce Warsaw Pact concentrated forces. The effect of using them would be to reduce the weight of attack that the defensive forces had to stop: they would be complementary to the defensive forces and would ease their task.

In short, present proposals are sending the wrong political signals, judged by the definition of aims adopted here. The proposals seem likely to produce an accelerated non-nuclear arms race, in addition to whatever happens to the nuclear arms race. It is worth considering what possible explanations there are for this.

One possible explanation would be that the economic aim of the advocates of this new policy is not to minimize costs but to challenge and strain the Soviet politico-economic system. To achieve that aim it is necessary that the policies adopted should increase NATO's offensive potential and be threatening. Only then will NATO alarm the Warsaw Pact and force it to spend more.

Another possible explanation is that the advocates of this policy simply fail to take into account how the Warsaw Pact is likely to react. That sounds so naive as to be scarcely credible. But in fact it seems to be true. Take the ESECS report, mentioned above. So far as I can see, *no* consideration is given to the possible reactions of the Warsaw Pact to the policy for NATO proposed by the authors. The fact that there is an arms race is not mentioned, let alone the risk that the recommended policy might aggravate the non-nuclear arms race. Nor is this behavior unusual. It is the position taken at each round in the arms race by those who advocate the acquisition of a new generation of weapons. Professor Herbert York has called it "the fallacy of the last step," meaning that the proponent of a step in the arms race ignores the counter-step the opposing nation will take and the subsequent steps each nation will take in reaction to the other. That those involved in the acquisition of new weapons and the development of the new doctrines that go with them—in this case the new smart weapons—should behave in this way presumably owes something to the fact that if they did not do so, if instead they thought about the reactions of the other side and the subsequent steps in the arms race, they would feel that the acquisition of today's new weapons looked pretty futile. The argument for acquisition would be deflated. They close their eyes.

A third explanation is that the new policy is an exercise in the selling of a new, expensive and fancy set of weapons and that strategic analysis of alternative ways of solving NATO's problem has been a subordinate matter. Certainly the ESECS report relies on dogma and assertive judgment, not analysis of alternatives. It reads like an armorers' manifesto.

Probably all three explanations played their part. This does not mean that each author consciously considered, let alone accepted, all, or any, of them. Rather, these are the sorts of things that may have influenced the way in which the group reached agreement on the nature of NATO's problems and on a politically acceptable solution to them. The achievement of agreement in a group usually means making concessions to the person or persons who are dominant while refraining from articulating or even exploring too deeply the reservations and counter-arguments that might be made. All of us who have worked in committees know that. It is why it is important with a report of this kind to consider what people do not say, and why, as well as what they do say.

The moral that might be drawn is that it is dangerous not to think out precisely what are the objectives and consequences of alternative military policies or to fail to examine the full context within which military policy exists—a moral which is none the worse for being an approximate repetition of what Clausewitz said a long time ago. And as I have tried to show, moving forward to a more politically sophisticated and, above all, safer military policy is entirely possible—once the moral has been learnt.

15 CAN NATO AFFORD A NON-SUICIDAL STRATEGY? *Malcolm Chalmers*

Malcolm Chalmers is a defense economist researching British defense policy at the School of Peace Studies, University of Bradford. He has previously served as a government economist in Botswana. He is the author of The Cost of Britain's Defence.

For the last thirty years, it has been argued that Soviet conventional superiority is such that, without resort to nuclear weapons, Western Europe would be overrun within a few days; and that a credible conventional defense for NATO cannot be achieved without massive increases in defense spending. US Secretary of State Alexander Haig, for example, stated in 1982 that NATO would have to "triple the size of its armed forces and put its economy on a war footing" before Western Europe could be defended with conventional forces.[1] This line of reasoning has allowed NATO to oppose proposals for a European nuclear-weapon-free zone and for a "no first use" policy. Given Soviet conventional superiority, it is argued, such proposals are tantamount to capitulation to Soviet wishes. In the British government's view: "If we tried to achieve parity with the Russians in conventional weapons, the cost would be enormous."[2]

This economic argument was the main justification for the United States' policy of "massive retaliation" in the 1950s. Reflecting this policy, large numbers of battlefield nuclear weapons were deployed as an "economical" substitute for conventional firepower. In the early 1960s this policy began to be challenged by advocates of greater reliance on conventional forces. It was argued that the creation of an intercontinental Soviet nuclear force now made "massive retaliation" incredible. NATO planning began to place more emphasis on conventional forces in the hope of delaying the resort to nuclear weapons; and some improvements in conventional defense capability followed. Simultaneously, however, the recognition that massive retaliation would be suicidal prompted a search for "limited nuclear options" as well as conventional options. The sophisticated systems needed for these nuclear war-fighting scenarios then necessitated a further build-up, despite the widespread belief that nuclear war, once started, could not be controlled or limited in any meaningful sense.

NATO's new strategy was thus not without its contradictions. The rethink of the 1960s had led to the rejection of massive retaliation as suicidal and irrational. Yet "flexible response" provided no more than a short pause for reflection before the strategic arsenals were unleashed. Even today, after seventeen years in existence, NATO's Nuclear Planning Group cannot agree on any credible use of nuclear forces which does not escalate to a global holocaust.

The main justification for this irrational dependence on nuclear weapons continues to be the inability of conventional defenses to hold off a large-scale Soviet invasion. Yet, upon closer examination, this justification appears weak. For NATO has had the conventional capability to give it a good chance of defeating a Soviet conventional invasion since at least the mid 1950s.[3] While such a defeat could not be guaranteed in advance, nor could the Soviet Union be assured of victory. Conventional forces alone should thus be sufficient to deter all but the most foolhardy Soviet leaders.

If this conclusion did not contradict so clearly the official position of NATO governments over the last thirty years, it would not be a surprising one. After all, the Western countries have a collective GNP about three times that of the Warsaw Pact. According to the Stockholm International Peace Research Institute, their combined defense expenditure is $286 billion—almost twice the Pact's $148 billion total.[4] Their total armed forces number 5·8 million.[5] And, in any major war, the Soviet Union would have to deploy a large proportion of its forces in the Far East to counter China and to protect key military installations on its Pacific coast. An invasion of Western Europe would, in present circumstances, be certain to turn virtually every other significant military power in the world against the Soviet Union. Even if a nuclear holocaust were avoided, a collapse of its own empire and the loss of its East European satellites would be a more likely outcome than a successful domination of the European continent.

Nor does the Soviet Union have a marked local numerical superiority in Central Europe which it might be able to exploit in a short blitzkreig campaign to catch NATO unawares. In the British government's *Statement on the Defence Estimates, 1983*, the Soviets are given an advantage in both overall manpower in Central Europe and in "soldiers in fighting units" of only 1·2:1.[6] Indeed if the whole French army was included, and not only French forces in West Germany, NATO forces would outnumber the Warsaw Pact in both categories.

Claims are continually made by Western governments that the Pact has a large superiority in weaponry. However, such comparisons take little or no account of qualitative differences between the equipment of the two antagonists. If other factors—such as mobility, survivability and firepower—are also considered, a more meaningful index of military capability can be calculated. The US Defense Department has done just this, and concludes that the Pact has only a 1·2:1 equipment advantage on the Central Front—in line with manpower estimates.[7]

The importance of qualitative factors can be illustrated by looking at the example of tactical air power. The Pact has a 2·1:1 advantage in numbers of fixed-wing tactical aircraft in Europe.[8] Yet NATO has *triple* the aggregate payload of Pact aircraft at distances of 100 miles, and *seven times* their opponents' payload at 200 miles.[9] In this category, as in many others, NATO's superior equipment compensates for its numerical inferiority.

Moreover, recent trends do not suggest that the qualitative balance is altering to the West's disadvantage. Since 1977, NATO defense spending has been growing at about 3 percent per annum in real terms, with most of the increase devoted to new equipment. This growth does not appear to have been matched by the Soviet Union. The CIA, in a recent report to the US Congress, estimates that there has been *no* increase in Soviet spending on new weapons and equipment for the last seven years, and only a 2 percent per annum real increase in total defense spending.[10] If spending has any positive relation with military capability, therefore, one must conclude that there may have been a shift in the qualitative balance toward the West in the last few years.

Finally, some defense analysts concede that NATO could stop a "standing start" Pact attack, but argue that, within a few days of mobilization the Soviets could achieve an overwhelming numerical superiority, and thus proceed to break through NATO conventional defenses. This possibility must be taken very seriously. It should be noted, however, that the Pact would only achieve a dangerous numerical superiority (2:1 or more) if NATO delayed mobilization for seven days or more.[11] This appears implausible. At no time since World War II has the Soviet Union moved divisions to East Germany during a crisis. To do so on a significant scale would be such a clear signal of aggressive intent that NATO mobilization would be likely to follow within three to four days, rather than seven. Provided that this continues to be the case, the Soviets cannot achieve a decisive numerical advantage on the Central Front, with or without mobilization.

It is therefore a tragedy of immense proportions that the current integration of nuclear weapons in NATO Central Front forces would not even give conventional defense a chance to work. Battlefield weapons would be used without reference to political leaders. As one student of these issues has noted:

> "Political command and control . . . would be exceedingly difficult to maintain with anything like the current posture of thousands of nuclear weapons under the direct (i.e., physical) control of battlefield commanders . . . deep armoured penetrations, massive refugee movements, unremitting attrition, pressure applied day and night regardless of weather, and lack of a well-defined forward edge of the battle area would all produce such chaos and confusion that *decentralized decision-making would become a de facto reality*."[12]

The tragedy is compounded because, without extra expenditure and without recourse to first use of nuclear weapons, NATO could, in the event of war tomorrow, defend Western Europe with a good chance of success. The presence of thousands of nuclear weapons in Europe is now the main factor preventing such a defense being mounted. Their removal is a precondition for the creation of non-suicidal defense of the peoples of Western Europe.

A new strategy for NATO?

There has been a recent spate of proposals from leading figures in the military establishment which argue for greater emphasis on conventional components of NATO defenses. This interest is a result of several factors. Firstly, Western leaders hope, by a greater emphasis on conventional forces, to allay public concern that NATO defense is "mortgaged to the nuclear response." Secondly, new technologies appear to open up new possibilities for conventional forces—as they have done with nuclear forces—and thus create opportunities for new conventional roles. Thirdly, military leaders believe that the best way to obtain more resources from reluctant treasuries is to emphasize that higher defense spending can raise the nuclear threshold.

Two of the most important proposals are those developed at Allied Command Europe, under General Bernard Rogers, for attack of Warsaw Pact follow-on forces, and the recommendations of a detailed report of the European Security Study (ESECS) *Strengthening Conventional Deterrence in Europe*.[13] Both proposals identify a major threat to the NATO front line from the Soviets' considerable follow-on forces exploiting gaps created by the initial attack. Should these follow-on forces succeed in breaking through in large numbers, it is argued, NATO command, communication and supply networks would be rapidly destroyed, and the entire front would begin to crumble. The Alliance would be forced to choose between capitulation and the use of nuclear weapons.

The solution proposed for this potential dilemma is to prevent, or retard, the reinforcement by follow-on forces of the Soviet front-line troops. To do this, it is believed, a greatly increased conventional capability for destroying fixed and mobile targets deep inside Eastern Europe should be acquired. The only weapons now available which are capable of the required degree of destructiveness are nuclear weapons—carried by NATO's tactical air force and now being complemented by cruise and Pershing II missiles. However, by employing emerging technologies for intelligence, command and control, and accurate weapon delivery, it may soon be possible to destroy targets deep behind Soviet lines using non-nuclear munitions. At first, this "deep strike" mission will need to rely on manned aircraft, armed with munitions capable of dispersing bomblets over a wide area in order to destroy an armed formation or airfield. In the long term, the mission can increasingly be filled by conventionally armed missiles.

General Rogers argues that a 4 percent annual real increase in defense budgets would enable him to acquire an effective conventional capability for deep strike, and would increase the prospect for avoiding nuclear first use. The ESECS report also recommends acquisition of advanced weapons for attacking follow-on forces. It estimates their cost (including support personnel) over a ten-year period at $20 billion plus or minus 50 percent, and argues that this can be funded by a defense budget "about 1 percent higher than the present NATO commitments, if such commitments are extended beyond 1986."[14]

These proposals have received widespread support within NATO and indeed the Rogers recommendations are already being incorporated in NATO plans. Yet they are quite inadequate for the problems that confront NATO today, and in crucial respects actually increase the dangers that we face. They do not reduce NATO's reliance on nuclear weapons, they threaten to obscure the clear firebreak between nuclear and conventional war, and they could lead to a destabilizing conventional arms race in Europe.

Under the Rogers proposals, the threat of nuclear first use is retained, and both short-range battlefield and medium-range theater nuclear weapons continue to be modernized. The deployment of cruise missiles at sea, on land and in the air, and the stationing of Pershing II missiles in West Germany, represent the latest stages of this development. Particularly suitable for "war-fighting" roles, their deployment demonstrates the continued search for limited nuclear options. Moreover, despite the considerable improvements in conventional forces planned for the 1980s, NATO intends to dismantle only the most obsolete of its short-range weapons. The recent decision to withdraw 2,000 warheads over six years has clearly been timed to divert attention from cruise and Pershing II deployment; yet its scope was so limited that it cannot be seen as more than a token gesture. There has been no attempt to remove a significant proportion of the 2,000 short-range nuclear artillery shells held by ground forces—weapons that are militarily obsolete, and are under the physical control of units likely to be engulfed in the first battles of a war. Yet without serious consideration of how to reduce reliance on nuclear weapons, planned improvements in conventional forces will be without purpose.

Given the large numbers of nuclear weapons still in NATO arsenals, the new conventional systems are also likely to blur the nuclear firebreak in a very dangerous way. It will be impossible to distinguish conventionally armed cruise missiles from nuclear ones while in flight, and if a large-scale attack is launched, the Soviets may assume the worst. Moreover, the use of submunitions will enable non-nuclear weapons to destroy targets on the ground with the effectiveness of small tactical nuclear weapons,[15] further increasing the scope for misunderstanding.

Finally, concepts of deep strike against follow-on forces can easily evolve into a policy for counter-offensive. Indeed Professor Huntingdon follows just this logic. He proposes the creation of a capability for conventional retaliation, arguing that:

> "A conventional retaliatory strategy is based on the assumption that the West Germans . . . will put up a more unified, comprehensive, and determined resistance to occupation by Soviet arms than the East German, Polish, Czech, and Hungarian armies and peoples will to liberation from Soviet armies . . .
>
> "Surely it is ethically more desirable to deter by threatening to liberate Eastern Europeans than by threatening to incinerate Russians."[16]

This emphasis on counter-offensive is potentially destabilizing, and sends the wrong signals to the Soviet Union. The existence of a NATO offensive capability would fuel tension during an East European crisis. Moreover it would encourage those who advocate "horizontal escalation"—

responding to a perceived Soviet offensive in one theater by a counter-offensive in another theater. This concept enjoys some support in the U S, though it is unappealing to European governments. It would add further to inter-bloc tension and could precipitate a conventional arms race.

Current NATO plans, and the closely related ESECS report, provide no comfort for those hoping to reduce the risk of nuclear conflict. The combination of continuing growth in defense spending, an attempt to acquire a greatly enhanced conventional offensive capability, and a U S leadership devoted to militant anticommunist rhetoric, is a volatile and dangerous brew.

A safer defense

A safer defense policy must start from the premise that a reduction in reliance on nuclear weapons is absolutely essential. Useful first steps in this direction could include the removal of all battlefield nuclear weapons, the adoption of a "no first use" policy, and a unilateral or mutual nuclear freeze. While taking these steps of nuclear de-escalation, Western political leaders would need a defense policy that meets important and deeply felt concerns both of their own peoples and of the Soviet leadership. The demonstration that Western Europe can be adequately defended without nuclear weapons will help convince its people that "either red or dead" is a bogus choice, and add new weight to the forces for nuclear disarmament. And, by continuing to forgo the capacity for major conventional thrusts into Eastern Europe, NATO would reduce the potential for Soviet mistrust of Western intentions. This would help to build confidence between the two blocs, and would reduce the impetus given to the conventional arms race by mutual misperception.

The development of a new policy which meets both these criteria will not be an easy task. Three decades of official propaganda have succeeded in substantially discrediting NATO's conventional defense forces. The public image of overwhelming Warsaw Pact superiority will take time and considerable effort to dispel. This effort will be helped by visible evidence that improvements in conventional defense are being made.

Furthermore, while current conventional capabilities may now provide a credible deterrent to conventional invasion, the Warsaw Pact continues, like NATO, to improve its forces. As long as no constraints are placed on this conventional arms race, NATO will need to plan ahead: forces that can defend Western Europe in 1984 may be quite inadequate in 1994. How, we must ask, can NATO structure its defense in such a way as to simultaneously reassure both its own peoples—by the provision of a visibly adequate deterrent to invasion—and the Soviet leadership, by refusing to acquire a major offensive capability?

Proposals for a new direction in NATO policy which base themselves on a concept of non-provocative defense start with the same problem as General Rogers has identified—the possibility of a "breakthrough" by Soviet follow-on forces. However, they respond in ways that are unambiguously defensive. Firstly, we need a strengthening of existing border defenses with new anti-armor munition, and the construction of fortifications and obstacles. Secondly, there must be a deepening of the area of forward defense with improved reinforcement capabilities, which would require Pact troops to fight through successive layers of highly trained formations, and allow NATO more time to counter Pact force concentration. Finally, there will be an increased role for territorial defense through the entire area of West Germany: Improvements in each of these capabilities would be clearly defensive, since they would not add significantly to NATO's ability to attack Pact territory.

The costs

Proposals for an alternative defense policy based on these concepts are growing in number.[17] The recent report by the Union of Concerned Scientists, for example, argues that a "no first use" policy is possible with only modest improvements in conventional forces.[18] And a recent study by Professor William Kaufman of MIT concludes that NATO could conduct a successful forward defense for at least thirty days, with a 90 percent plus chance of success, for only 3 percent annual real growth in spending.[19]

The most cost-effective of the measures proposed by both the UCS and Kaufman would be the construction of an obstacles-and-fortifications network along the Central Front, at an estimated cost of less than $1 ½ billion. Such a barrier, it has been estimated, could decrease the effectiveness of an invasion force by as much as 40 percent, and greatly reduce the need to use all NATO ground forces in manning the front. This would enable more units to be assigned to mobile reserves and, in Kaufman's view, "reduce to essentially zero the probability that an enemy could achieve even a temporary advance with a smash and grab attack."[20]

A series of further measures could also increase the credibility of NATO's conventional defenses. An increase in war stocks for existing NATO divisions to enable them to fight for an additional thirty days would need roughly $40 billion. Improvements in prepositioning of equipment and the capability to ferry supplies by sea from the US would cost approximately $7 billion.[21] Finally, eight additional reserve divisions would cost $43 billion, assuming that training and war reserve stocks were included. In total, all these improvements would cost less than $100 billion—a 1·5 percent annual real increase in NATO defense spending over six years.[22]

A further possibility for improvement of conventional defense—mentioned but not costed in the UCS report—would be the creation of light infantry forces capable of rapid mobilization and armed with modern antitank weapons. These forces would provide a wide area defense network able to wear down an attacker in multiple minor engagements. This concept is discussed in some detail by the West German General Jochen Löser, who argues that, within the Bundeswehr, "the forces required for wide area defense can be doubled by employing the available reserve potential in combat."[23]

A similar proposal is made by Steven Canby, who argues that an effective use of reserve forces could yield additional mobilizable combat units, equal in quality to active units, at only 20 percent of the cost.[24] This would enable the German, French, Dutch and Belgian armies to triple their division count for a 15 percent increase in their total defense budgets. For NATO as a whole, this would represent only a 3 percent increase in defense spending—½ percent per annum if spread over six years. In Canby's view, an increase of this magnitude, combined with restructuring of active forces, would give NATO the probability of success in a prolonged conventional war.

Even if these estimates are unduly optimistic, NATO could implement substantial improvements in conventional defense for an annual 2 percent increase in defense budgets over six years (a total of $120 billion). The measures outlined here would strengthen conventional deterrence, avoid the difficulties involved in the current emphasis on deep strike, and reassure public opinion that a non-nuclear defense of Western Europe is a feasible, and affordable, alternative.

The savings

Moreover, an alternative defense policy could allow savings in three areas—nuclear forces, out-of-area capabilities, and oversophisticated technology. These would more than offset the extra costs involved in a conventional Central Front defense.

Nuclear weapons procurement and development would be substantially reduced, or ended, were NATO to adopt "no first use" or a nuclear freeze. "No first use" would allow the scrapping of battlefield nuclear weapons and deep cuts in other nuclear forces. As Lord Carver has pointed out:

"Genuine acceptance of a policy of 'no first use' by both sides could be an important first step in reducing the grossly inflated nuclear arsenals of the USA and USSR. Two categories of nuclear weapons are linked to first use: battlefield systems and counterforce ones. They account for the vast majority of warheads on both sides."[25]

Funds currently allocated to new counterforce weapons—MX, Trident (US, UK), cruise, Pershing II, etc.—could be redirected elsewhere. Nuclear weapons' recurrent costs—security, maintenance and manning of NATO's 6,000 warheads—could also be cut. Dual-capable systems could be redeployed in a conventional role, and in some cases retired. These savings could be further increased were the superpowers to agree to "deep cuts" in their nuclear arsenals—as proposed by the American Committee on East–West Accord and outlined by Admiral Gayler in the concluding chapter of this book.

The United States plans to spend over $222 billion on more modern nuclear forces over the next six years,[26] almost twice the $121 billion required for the improvements in NATO conventional defenses already outlined. A nuclear freeze, even without deep cuts, could thus provide the funds for NATO to implement conventional force improvements and, simultaneously, reduce planned levels of total defense spending.

A non-provocative defense policy should also involve a reduction of out-of-area capabilities for European states, particularly Britain and France. The global intervention forces and commitments which these powers retain are a legacy of their colonial past, and should have no place in a defense and foreign policy designed to be non-provocative. Such reasoning may also apply to the USA: the current build-up in the Rapid Deployment Force and offensive naval forces could be cut back, and the US commitment to policing the process of domestic political changes in less developed countries curtailed. Given the US's current superiority in interventionary forces, substantial cuts could be made without creating a power "vacuum" that the Soviet Union might be tempted to exploit.[27] An alternative defense concept that excluded French and British out-of-area intervention, and reduced similar US commitments, would release resources for European defense.

Thirdly, an alternative defense might hope to make savings by reducing spending on oversophisticated weapon systems. This would involve a lower priority for items such as aircraft carriers, strike aircraft and battle tanks. The extent of such savings would depend on how far policy was defensive as well as non-nuclear. Aircraft carriers, for example, are principally relevant for "power projection" in out-of-area and offensive operations. A conventional air–land battle strategy based on counter-offensive is likely to prove more expensive than an emphasis on barrier defense and/or defense in depth.

The potential savings from reducing expenditure on "gold-plated" weapons are considerable. The main obstacle to change is likely to be military conservatism—the understandable commitment of officers and men to the maintenance of force structures and types of equipment on which their training and careers are based. Since weapon systems are rarely tested in action—unlike civilian products—the tendency to rely heavily on the last major war is strong. That war took place forty years ago, and it was followed by a period of rapid and continued technological change, so such a tendency is likely to be profoundly misleading. Yet it plays a large part in explaining the remarkable stability in the basic structures of Western armed forces.[28]

Finally, and more problematically, a large increase in the reserve forces of European powers, together with prepositioning of US Army equipment, may in future allow less emphasis to be placed on maintaining sealift capability for the convoy of military supplies across the Atlantic.[29] There is no fundamental reason, given Western European levels of production and population, why defense in a protracted conflict cannot be sustained without large-scale seaborne reinforcement. And, in the more likely event of a short-duration conflict, such reinforcement would be of little consequence.

A note on burden-sharing

The savings from alternative defense would not be evenly distributed within NATO. They would be greatest for those nations who spend more on nuclear and global capabilities and with an emphasis on high technology in their European conventional forces. These include the US, the UK and France. Nations, such as West Germany and Italy, with no significant independent global or nuclear capability, and an emphasis on ground forces plus air support, would find few, if any, net savings. Since the states which would save most are also those with the greatest defense burdens at present, existing burden-sharing tensions could be relieved by an alternative policy.

However, it must also be recognized that this relative redistribution of defense effort could create tensions of its own. It will be particularly important that any additional German ground forces proposed should be deployed in an unambiguously defensive role. The Soviet insistence in the Mutual and Balanced Force Reduction Talks on a subceiling for the Bundeswehr in NATO's forces, and its willingness to reciprocate with a similar ceiling on Soviet forces, indicates their continuing fear of a revival of German militarism. NATO itself originated as much as a solution to the German problem as from fear of Soviet invasion. An alternative defense must take into account these important political factors, and not place too great a burden on the German armed forces.

A case study: the United Kingdom

We conclude by examining the implications of an alternative policy for one member state—the United Kingdom. Since World War II, the UK has consistently spent a greater proportion of its national income on defense than any of its main allies (and economic competitors), with the exception of the United States. This disparity is a result of the failure of successive governments to revise commitments and attitudes inherited from the imperial past. The retention of independent nuclear, naval, and extra-European capabilities, together with the simultaneous commitment of land and air forces to continental defenses, has ensured that Britain's military burden remains higher than that of other European NATO members.

There is considerable evidence to suggest that this high level of military spending has diverted scarce resources from investment, civilian research and development and exports, has impeded economic growth and has thus contributed to Britain's relative economic decline.[30] This decline has been so precipitate since 1950 that, if past trends were to continue for a further twenty-five years, Britain could be the poorest country in Europe (East or West), with the possible exception of Albania.[31] Yet the gap in economic performance has not been noticeably closed either by the onset of world slump since 1973 or by the recent windfall from North Sea oil discoveries.

Despite economic stagnation, Britain has increased defense spending by 21 percent in real terms since 1978/9, further widening the gap between itself and its European partners. The defense budget for 1983/4 was £15·7 billion ($24 billion)—5·4 percent of estimated Gross Domestic Product. The government is committed to implement the NATO 3 percent target and *in addition* pay Falklands-related costs until 1985/6.[32]

So far, this spending growth has been financed without equivalent increases in taxes and/or borrowing, by utilizing the rapid growth in government revenues from the North Sea. From the mid 1980s, however, this income will peak, and then start to fall by at least £1,000 million per year. As a direct consequence, after 1985/6 there is likely to be a reduction, and perhaps a halt, in defense spending growth, unless there is a dramatic worsening of international tension. The recent Treasury insistence on formally abandoning the NATO 3 percent target after 1985/6 is only the first move in efforts to prevent a major fiscal crisis in the late 1980s. If real spending is frozen for the rest of the decade, as the Treasury clearly wishes, it is questionable whether all present military commitments can be maintained untouched.

Moreover, if military spending is not to help destroy the economy it is supposed to defend, it is clear that a freeze in the real level of defense spending will be insufficient. Burden-sharing considerations suggest that a substantial narrowing of the gap between British and other European defense spending levels will be both a necessary, and a reasonable, component of an alternative NATO defense policy.

An alternative policy will need to find savings in one or more of the UK's five main defense roles:

defense of the UK itself: coastal defense, air defense, ground defense of military installations, etc.

the independent nuclear force

the capability for intervention outside the NATO area (including the Falklands)

antisubmarine warfare commitments to NATO in the Northeast Atlantic

an army and tactical air force for the defense of West Germany.

There will be little room for economies in defense of the UK itself. Indeed, non-provocative defense might require greater emphasis to be given to some of the forces devoted to this role—coastal patrol, defensive mine-laying, air defense. The degree of emphasis would partly reflect British concern for a "fallback" option were forward defense in Germany to fail or NATO to break up.

There will be a strong case for abandoning the program to build a force of four Trident missile submarines. Trident has been widely criticized within Britain for the contribution it will make to the escalation of the nuclear arms race. Many influential commentators, including Field Marshal Lord Carver, former Chief of Defence Staff, are agreed that an independent nuclear force serves no military purpose.[33] Indeed the attachment to such a force appears to reflect more a yearning for past British imperial grandeur than a consideration of defense priorities within NATO.

Trident will cost 6–8 percent of the total defense budget in the late 1980s and early 1990s.[34] This would thus be an immediate, and substantial, source of savings. Further economies could be made by ending all other nuclear weapons spending—Polaris running costs, research and development, production of military fissile material, etc. A non-nuclear defense would also permit cuts in the numbers of dual-capable systems. And, even where cuts were not possible, improvements in effectiveness would result. At a minimum, abandonment of a nuclear capability would save 10–15 percent of the defense budget in the late 1980s.

In 1983–4, Falklands defense spending will reach £900 million—35 percent more than that spent on air defense (£579 million).[35] After equipment lost in the conflict is replaced, and major capital projects are completed, the garrison will cost £400–450 million annually (including basic costs of forces while deployed in the South Atlantic). This figure, however, may underestimate the potential distortion of priorities. The Royal Navy now deploys, on average, over a quarter of its entire frigate and destroyer fleet, and up to half of its most modern ships, in support of Fortress Falklands.[36] To match Argentine rearmament this deployment may need to be increased in future—at the expense of NATO deployments.

If spending on nuclear forces and Fortress Falklands were ended, together with related support costs, 13–18 percent of the defense budget in the late 1980s would be saved. This saving could be used to relieve pressure on other defense roles, in addition to releasing scarce resources for non-military purposes.

If a Falklands settlement were reached, money could be saved in other ways too. In addition to ending the strains already mentioned, a settlement would allow the government to renew and extend former Defence Secretary John Nott's plans, outlined in June 1981,[37] for streamlining the UK's maritime forces. Aircraft carriers could be retired and the construction of oversophisticated frigates and destroyers (such as types 22 and 42) discontinued. The surface fleet and general out-of-area capability could be reduced further and a more cost-effective antisubmarine capability for the North Atlantic provided principally by a combination of mine barriers, hunter-killer submarines and land-based air power.

Some further savings might be possible by a move away from expensive weapon platforms for air and land forces. The scope for economies here is likely to be less than at sea—at least in the 1980s. The Tornado strike aircraft program is now almost complete, yet it would lose most of its rationale were NATO to abandon the nuclear role and de-prioritize deep strike. Certainly the programs to add new weapons systems in the mid and late 1980s—including conventionally armed cruise missiles—would be potential sources of savings. The air defense version of Tornado—the F2—is at a rather earlier stage of production and the possibility of savings here may, in theory, be greater.[38] The emphasis on defensive forces, however, is likely to mean that halting this program would involve additional expenditure on alternative means of air defense. In the search for economies, attention might then focus on the Jaguar/Harrier replacement and other programs for the 1990s.

The Army's shift of emphasis from tanks toward "smart" antitank weapons should be encouraged. However, a credible conventional defense on the Central Front may also involve an increase in the proportion of the budget devoted to the British Army on the Rhine (BAOR) in its role as a rear-based mobile force supporting wide-area defense forces. Such an increase may involve an increase in the number of reserve (Territorial Army) units available for rapid reinforcement of the active divisions in Germany. Major reductions in BAOR costs would require a successful agreement with the Warsaw Pact on mutual force reductions.

In total, therefore, an alternative policy could hope to save up to 20 percent of Britain's planned defense budget by the late 1980s—more if accompanied by negotiated force reductions. On reasonable assumptions, this would reduce the proportion of national income devoted to defense from 5·4 percent (1983/4) to 4·4 percent (1989/90).

Conclusion

Western leaders often use Soviet conventional superiority in Europe to justify NATO's refusal to adopt a "no first use" policy. This justification appears weak. Even with existing forces, the Soviets could not be confident of victory in a non-nuclear war.

The credibility of NATO conventional defense could be further increased by a combination of modest improvements in conventional forces and major cuts in planned nuclear forces. Conventional force improvements could be funded in their entirety by ending current programs for new "war-fighting" nuclear weapons. Indeed, were such cuts to be combined with reductions in out-of-area and offensive capabilities and a reassessment of oversophisticated weapons systems, a net decrease in NATO defense spending would be possible.

16 THE WAY OUT: A GENERAL NUCLEAR SETTLEMENT *Admiral Noel Gayler*

I have earlier spoken to the sensible military use of nuclear weapons, and have found that there is none. We and the Soviets are in an extraordinarily dangerous place. We have between us 50,000 nuclear weapons; the Soviet tank armies stand poised on the borders of Europe; NATO is in return deploying first-strike weapons—in a game of "chicken." In thirteen years of negotiations about cuts, weapons on both sides have tripled. Communications of every sort are turned off, deliberately. Arms control negotiations are at a standstill, while nuclear arms build-up on both sides is accelerating. Distrust, hostility and invective characterize the relations between our two countries. The political and ideological struggle between the US and the USSR has a potential outcome that, while still unlikely, is intolerable—nuclear war.

America and Russia must both bear grave responsibility for this sorry and dangerous state of affairs. We are in fact like two men struggling on the edge of a cliff, oblivious of the abyss into which we both may fall.

The nuclear war we are both risking has consequences out of all proportion to any conceivable objective we or they might have. We must therefore also ask why our preoccupation with nuclear weapons continues. Sometimes nuclear weapons programs are justified as expressions of "will" or "determination." Apart from the absurd cost in security and in resources which these nuclear programs demonstrate to an adversary, they make lousy signals because they are invariably misread. Not incidentally, they make lousy programs, being generally divorced from any military or technical rationale.

A successful joint strategy will have to take account of the legitimate security requirements of both great powers, and of their allies. These are not always in conflict. It is therefore of first importance that nuclear issues be sorted out from all others. They have transcendent importance and present no real conflict of interest.

President Reagan recently called for a renewed dialogue on arms control and reducing the risk of nuclear war. The signals he gave were mixed, however, since he again took the occasion to accuse the Soviets of treaty violations and other misdeeds.

Earlier, Chairman Andropov talked of restoring confidence and renouncing hatred. Other senior Soviets have said that we cannot discuss single elements of nuclear issues in isolation. Finally Andropov said that the Soviets are ready for radical solutions. All of this argues that the time has come for a major and comprehensive settlement of the nuclear weapons issues between us.

The US Administration now has a major opportunity to sustain and even revive nuclear arms control. Nothing could better serve the security of the United States and the West, and better allay the well-founded concerns of the entire world about nuclear war. It is first of all vital to resist the space hawks and the nuclear Mafia, within and outside the Administration, who urge the President to portray alleged Soviet treaty violations in a light that would discredit all arms control agreements, on the ground that the Soviets cannot be trusted. Those agreements can and should be crafted so that trust, while always desirable, is not essential to our security. This is possible because no conceivable Soviet violation big enough to tip the nuclear balance could escape our intelligence.

What are these "violations," and what is their significance? Some are not violations of treaties at all, but simply things we wish the Soviets would not do. Some are old questions, long since satisfactorily settled, dug up again to pad out an indictment. And some are matters of genuine but technical concern, which should be resolved privately in the only proper forum—the Soviet–American Standing Consultative Commission established to do just that.

None of the claimed Soviet actions, and none of the alleged American actions which might be considered technical violations, have any real military significance. Populations in the Soviet Union cannot be defended against ballistic missile attack, no matter where the Soviets place high-powered radars. Whether ICMBs are new or old, fixed or mobile, in compliance or out, they can still destroy cities. So with the rest of the allegations. The point is, nuclear compliance issues may or may not have political and legal significance, but they do not and cannot change the security of either side.

Other issues—chemical and biological warfare—may have military importance, but they do not enter into the nuclear stand-off. If we attempt to handle all issues between us and the Soviets before we achieve nuclear arms control we will have a long wait indeed. And nuclear war—the one thing which could destroy us all—cannot be allowed to threaten us forever. So we need solutions, usable ideas.

Some of the ideas that follow are in fact novel, and some old. But their time has come. We and the Soviets are not helpless to stop and reverse the drift toward nuclear war.

The negotiations on nuclear arms reduction, as they existed before they stopped completely, were mostly a continuation of the same tired old process. They were adversarial. They did not recognize that, in the context of nuclear weapons, the enemy is not the Soviet Union, and it is not the United States. It is the nuclear weapons themselves. Our common interest is to get rid of them, not to seek some unilateral "advantage."

The negotiations have always had concealed objectives. They have been characterized by a lot of posturing, by arbitrary classification into theater, tactical and strategic weapons, by haggling over the numbers and the technology, and by inflexibility on both sides. There have been a few new ideas: that we should count warheads rather than "delivery systems," that we should combine negotiations so we can have room for flexible trading. Some have been adopted; most have not.

A major problem in arms control is the devotion to gradualism, to small steps, to little increments here and there, each one to be carefully haggled over. The problem is that we are trying to go up a down escalator, and the escalator is going down faster than we are going up. So we and the Soviets have got to do something big, something new, something now.

That something can only be a general nuclear settlement. First with the USSR, then joined by other nuclear powers, and finally combined efforts to prevent the spread of nuclear weapons around the world.

Let us turn now to the elements of a general nuclear settlement with the USSR.

The first part may be the most important of all—to make an end to the intemperate, childish and threatening rhetoric between us.

One must ask, what would be the frame of mind of a president or a premier (or a commander) who could actually start a nuclear war? To give the signal to kill other human beings in the tens and hundreds of millions, and to invite a like fate for his own people? It would seem there would have to be three things dominant in his mind:

> He would have to regard the people he was about to incinerate as somehow less than human. They would have to be demonized, stripped of their human attributes.
>
> He would have to be mortally afraid.
>
> He would have to see no alternative to the terrible deed he was about to do.

To get into this frame of mind requires long-term attitude building. We are engaged, we and the Soviets, in building such attitudes right now. We must both reverse this process, at our peril.

Second, we must both give up nuclear war-fighting doctrines. The three most dangerous doctrines are:

> The doctrine of first use against conventional force, whether called "limited" or "tactical" or anything else. This is an indirect way of saying, "Start a nuclear war."
>
> Counterforce, sometimes called "prompt hard target kill." This doctrine creates the dangerously destabilizing premium on shooting first. To threaten to destroy missiles in their silos or (even worse) the leadership will surely lead them to pre-empt.
>
> Protracted or "winnable" nuclear war. There can be no winners, and very probably no bystanders. All will lose—adversaries, neutrals, innocents and belligerents alike.

The third mutual effort necessary is to improve communications of every kind. Good communication is far more needed in time of trouble than in easier times.

There should be secure video conferencing with simultaneous interpretation available to senior policy officials at all times—especially the heads of state. Military control centers should be in practiced and continuous communication so that unusual events which could be interpreted as threatening can be quickly and effectively explained. We might indeed have prevented the Korean airliner tragedy of September 1983: "What in the world are you flying over us here?" "We're not flying over you!" "Well, what is?" After a pause and search: "Hey, that Korean left Anchorage a while ago—where is he?" That sort of situation could be clarified with modern communication and with staffs accustomed to dealing with each other.

Other military measures to increase confidence include continued advance notice and explanation of military maneuvers and redeployment of threatening forces, both conventional and nuclear.

Trade is itself a powerful form of communication, establishing confidence as well as mutual economic advantage. The day-to-day fulfillment of commercial obligations sets powerful precedents of reliability and mutual interest. Scientific, cultural and people exchanges are also effective in countering mutual distrust.

A fourth necessary element of a global nuclear settlement is a mutual moratorium on the further development, testing and deployment of new nuclear weapons. The commonsense idea that we and the Soviets should not build up further while we are trying to negotiate reductions has obvious validity. The difficulties have lain in major problems of verification, definition and negotiation which have led many to characterize a negotiated freeze as impractical. These difficulties can be avoided by a mutual informal moratorium by the heads of government on those many elements of a freeze that we can define and verify. An immediate possibility is a comprehensive test ban.

Fifth, we must together avoid the extension of nuclear war capability into new areas, whether technical or spatial. At first glance, it may seem attractive to export war to space, rather than to conduct it on earth. But if space has military consequence, as it has in full measure, the linkage to earth becomes inescapable. Attack on communications, navigation, reconnaissance and intelligence satellites is dangerously threatening and destabilizing. Our eyes and ears would no longer be available.

Finally, we and the Soviets need to make deep, fast and continuing cuts in the numbers of nuclear weapons of all kinds. Stockpiles at the present level are ridiculously excessive to any reasonable need for deterrence; even more excessive are the plans of each country to build many thousands of new weapons in the next few years. The sheer numbers carry obvious danger: the risk of accident is at least proportional to the numbers of weapons; so is the risk of unauthorized firing and the vulnerability to hijacking.

More important, the enormous numbers give credibility to first-strike, counterforce and nuclear war-fighting scenarios. Both directly and indirectly they increase the probability as well as the consequences of nuclear war.

More important still, these numbers lie an order of magnitude above the threshold of total yield which, if used, would create the "nuclear winter," resulting in the probable destruction of all human life in the Northern Hemisphere, and perhaps earth.

Analysis and commonsense alike mandate the imperative necessity for drastic cuts.

The classic and unsuccessful negotiations to date have attempted agreement on a mix of weapons and weapons systems to be cut back to agreed levels. These negotiations have suffered from three continuing obstacles:

> Verification, an obsessive concern of the Americans, has been impeded by an equally overwrought Soviet concern with espionage and sovereign pride.
>
> Equity has been difficult to agree on as between major differences in weapons systems and strategic circumstances. It is further bedeviled by the nuclear wild cards of Britain, France and China.
>
> Arbitrary division of negotiations into strategic, theater and tactical classifications has little operational reality but has created major obstacles both to mutually acceptable definition and to horse-trading.

These and similar problems can be comprehensively handled by emphasizing the process of reduction rather than end goals to be negotiated in advance.

One such process is "build-down." In its original form, it provided that for every new warhead built there would be two destroyed. Even though new weapons were built, there would be an automatic net reduction. Unfortunately, this simple and workable idea has been corrupted, first by the deal for MX and second by suggested weaseling on the two-for-one ratio, so that it is now suggested that some variable ratio be employed.

A better proposal has its basis in the straightforward notion that the way to get rid of nuclear weapons is to get rid of nuclear weapons. Our proposal is:

> US and USSR turn in nuclear warheads containing fissionable material, and convert that material to nuclear fuel for burning in power plants.
>
> US and USSR cease production of weapons-grade material.
>
> US and USSR agree to full-scope safeguards on nuclear grade plants.

Weapons conversion

Nuclear warheads have a number of components. We propose that both sides turn in warheads but hand over only the core of the warhead—the explosive nuclear fission device—whose fissionable material would then be converted to power-plant fuel. The other components of the warhead would be mechanically destroyed.

The scheme for weapons conversion can be summarized as follows:

> Each country hands over progressively larger numbers of explosive nuclear fission devices to a single conversion facility, built explicitly for this purpose, at a neutral site.
>
> Under supervision, the devices are dismantled and their fissionable material converted to power-plant fuel for generation of electricity.
>
> At any given time, each side chooses the devices it hands over. Any device qualifies, without regard to the type of warhead or nuclear weapon from which it is taken. Results are measured by the weight of fissionable material contained in the devices. (We avoid endless debates over classification and equity.)
>
> Soviet and American teams, with perhaps a third party as referee, identify and count each device, and weigh the fissionable material turned in. All are positively identifiable by scientific means. (That's verification, without intrusive inspection in either country.)

The proposal is equitable, practicable and verifiable.

Production halt

The proposal must be accompanied by a negotiated full stop to production of weapons-grade material. (A halt in production is much easier to verify than reduced production.) The production plants in use are well known, and clandestine production of significant amounts would present a number of observables. New production plants would also be difficult to conceal.

Newer methods of producing fissionable material, for example by centrifuges or laser-isotope separation, promise smaller physical plant requirements, but there is reason to believe that useful observables will exist in the event of significant clandestine production.

Safeguards

This proposal should also be accompanied by full-scope safeguards against diversion to weapons use of commercial power fuel. It is true that for the US and USSR, already possessing thousands of weapons, safeguards are less critical than they are for the non-nuclear powers who might, through diversion, acquire their first nuclear weapons. Nevertheless it is politically important that both superpowers accept international safeguards against diversion, or agree to joint inspections of commercial power facilities, or both.

Applicability

The proposal has several uniquely attractive features, aside from avoiding many of the problems of equity, verification and classification that have plagued earlier negotiations:

> It can stand alone, or it can provide a means to carry out reductions achieved through alternative formulas. This approach can fit into the framework of SALT, START or any other approach.
>
> As a stand-alone proposal, it is the only one that assures a real weapons reduction.
>
> It builds in clear visibility that inventory reductions are taking place.
>
> It promotes dramatic, immediate and continuing reductions in nuclear weapons.
>
> It is simple enough to be understood and sophisticated enough to work.

The process is practically risk-free, because each country makes its own selection of what to turn in, and that selection can be made, if necessary, on a day-to-day basis. No long-term commitment conceivably threatening the security of either country need be made. Equity is built in, since each country continuously determines its own optimum strategy. Verification of destruction is assured, without intrusive measures.

The actual destruction of weapons would be accompanied by a complete ban on the further production of weapons-grade nuclear material. Fortunately in both countries this production takes place in special, well-known plants. A total stop to production is, of course, easier to verify than partial or limited production.

Finally, electric power plants in both countries are subjected to international standard safeguards to inhibit diversion of plutonium from spent fuel. Credit is given to each country for the mass of fissile material from the weapons they have turned in.

Given the achievement of deep cuts by the superpowers, there remain two major requirements:

> Adherence of the other existing nuclear powers.
>
> Prevention of nuclear weapons development or possession by further states, or even political or terrorist groups.

Cooperation in policy and proportionate reductions by the United States and the Soviet Union is assumed to be well underway. Prevention of proliferation is a far more intractable problem. What can be said about it is that visible and continuing action by the superpowers is a prerequisite to political credibility in advocating no further nuclear development. The superpowers must lead the way if there is to be any chance of limiting the spread of weapons worldwide. US–Soviet cooperation is a necessary, if not sufficient, requirement.

We must see clearly that the risk of nuclear death can be averted only by the US and the USSR working together. Prevention is at least a two-handed game to be effective. The adversaries must understand each other better, must each adopt a coherent and productive strategy, and must each perceive safeguards insuring against undue risk. These requirements can be realized.

Understanding is not necessarily a matter of either trust or liking. Averell Harriman has said, "You can trust the Russians—to act in the Russian interest." When we see that the Russian interest parallels our own, as it does in the prevention of nuclear war, there is certainly a presumption that some trust is possible, though it is not necessary. Nor is it necessary that we like the Soviets, only that we recognize the humanity of the Soviet peoples and their right to exist and to be secure.

Many actions of the Soviet government toward their own citizens and the unfortunates along their borders are repugnant to us. But our common interest in survival mandates that we understand each other. There are cultural factors on both sides, a very different history, and almost theological preconceptions that make mutual understanding difficult, but it is none the less imperative.

There can be no question that Soviets at every level are aware of the nature of the dangers of nuclear war. They see accurately, as we do, that there can be no winners. They are preoccupied with the security of Mother Russia, so that they have no interest in risking its destruction. Since Khrushchev, the Soviets have not threatened the use of nuclear weapons, and they have subsequently specifically renounced first use.

Both the Soviets and the U S have from time to time made conciliatory statements at the highest level. Andropov talked of "restoring confidence and renouncing hatred." Senior Soviets have suggested that "there are hardly any problems in arms control if the political will for it exists." Presidents, Secretaries of State and Congressional leaders have given the prevention of nuclear war pride of place.

Both explicitly and implicitly each side has attempted single-handed strategies to prevent nuclear war through overwhelming superiority. These strategies involve such things as attempting to gain a technical or numerical advantage in nuclear weapons, economic pressures, threats, political and propaganda moves and attempts to keep the other side divided, uncertain and off balance. These are all attempts to coerce rather than appeal to mutual interest. All are self-defeating. Neither of the great powers is or will be in a position to coerce the other.

We and the Soviets need the vision to see that continuing to struggle for advantage in nuclear arms is futile and increasingly dangerous. We need also the vision to see that the way out of our common peril is straightforward and practical. Neither we nor the Soviets are helpless. We need only develop the political will to make a general nuclear settlement a reality.

REFERENCES

CHAPTER 1. NUCLEAR WEAPONS AND DETERRENCE

1 Eugene V. Rostow, address before the World Affairs Council, Los Angeles, California, September 10, 1982.

2 "A world at war—1983," *The Defense Monitor,* Vol. 12, No. 1 (Center for Defense Information, Washington, DC, 1983); M. Kidron and D. Smith, *The War Atlas: Armed Conflict, Armed Peace* (London, 1983), Part I.

3 Lord Mountbatten, address on the occasion of the award of the Louise Weiss Foundation Prize to SIPRI, Strasbourg, France, May 11, 1979.

4 President Jimmy Carter, State of the Union address, Washington, DC, January 23, 1980.

5 Vice-President Richard Nixon, address on national security, quoted in *New York Times,* March 14, 1954.

6 Secretary of Defense James Schlesinger, *Annual Report* (FY-1985, March 1974).

7 Secretary of Defense Harold Brown, testimony to the Senate Foreign Relations Committee: *Congressional Record,* September 19, 1980.

8 D. A. Rosenberg, "A smoking, radiating ruin at the end of two hours: Documents on American war plans for nuclear war with the Soviet Union 1954–5," *International Security,* Vol. 6, No. 3 (Winter 1981/2); Curtis LeMay (with M. Kantor), *Mission with LeMay: My Story* (New York, 1965); P. Pringle and W. Arkin, *SIOP: The Secret US Plan for Nuclear War* (New York, 1983), Chapter 2.

9 Budget of the United States Government, Fiscal Year 1983.

10 R. Halloran, "Pentagon draws up first strategy for fighting a long nuclear war," *New York Times,* May 30, 1982; Secretary of Defense Caspar Weinburger, testimony to House Appropriations Committee, September 24, 1981 (emphasis in original). For discussion of the *Defense Guidance,* see also T. Draper, "Dear Mr. Weinburger—an open reply to an open letter," *New York Review of Books,* November 4, 1982, pp. 26–31, and "On nuclear war: an exchange with the Secretary of Defense," *New York Review of Books,* August 18, 1983, pp. 27–33 (both articles reproduced in T. Draper, *Present History,* New York, 1983).

11 "Preparing for nuclear war: President Reagan's program," *The Defense Monitor,* Vol. 12, No. 8.

12 Principal Deputy Under Secretary of Defense Research and Engineering James Wade, testimony to the House Appropriations Committee, September 15, 1981.

13 For extensive discussion of the problem of horizontal proliferation, see G. Prins (ed.), *Defended to Death: A Study of the Nuclear Arms Race* (London, 1983), pp. 214–18; and G. H. Quester (ed.), *Nuclear Proliferation: Breaking the Chain* (Madison, Wis., 1981).

14 President Ronald Reagan, address to Parliament, London, England, June 8, 1982.

15 Lord Mountbatten, loc. cit.

16 Henry Kissinger, *Years of Upheaval* (New York, 1982), p. 1175.

CHAPTER 3. CURRENT NATO STRATEGY: A RECIPE FOR DISASTER

1 *Hiroshima and Nagasaki: The Physical, Medical, and Social Effects of the Atomic Bombings*, translated by Eisei Ishikawa and D. L. Swain (New York, 1981), pp. 337–9.
2 *Department of the Army Field Manual* 100–30 (Test) Tactical Nuclear Operations (HQDA, August 1971), par. 2–7.
3 ibid., par. 2–7e.
4 ibid., par. 2–9c.
5 See *The Soviet Theater Nuclear Offensive* by Joseph D. Douglas, Jr. (US Government Printing Office), p. 6. See also Jeffrey Record, *US Nuclear Weapons in Europe* (Washington, DC, 1974), pp. 41–3.
6 Jeffrey Record, *US Nuclear Weapons in Europe*, p. 21. See also *The Soviet Theater Nuclear Offensive*, pp. 9–14.
7 Michael E. Howard, "The forgotten dimensions of strategy," *Foreign Affairs* (Summer 1979), pp. 975–86.
8 Richard Pipes, "Why the Soviet Union thinks it could fight and win a nuclear war," *Commentary* (July 1977), p. 22. Pipes criticizes the lack of a US strategic doctrine and the failure to recognize that Soviet nuclear doctrine is superior to that of the United States. This is a valid criticism and a point well made. See *The Soviet Theater Nuclear Offensive* for why Soviet nuclear doctrine is superior. See also Dimitri K. Simes, "Moscow and war," *New York Times*, November 8, 1981.
9 See Arms Control and Disarmament Agency, *An Analysis of Civil Defense in Nuclear War* (Washington, December 1978), and Central Intelligence Agency, *Soviet Civil Defense* (NI-78-1000 3, July 1978). These studies refute many of the capabilities ascribed enthusiastically to Soviet civil defense.
10 Michael E. Howard, "Fighting a nuclear war," *International Security* (Spring 1981), pp. 3–48. In this article Howard criticizes US emphasis on nuclear strategy and the view of Soviet intentions as depicted by the Committee on the Present Danger. He credits the Russians with a better appreciation of the relationship of war to policy than is found in US scenarios and strategic journals. I am fully in accord with Howard's observations in this article.
11 Steven Canby, "European mobilization: US and NATO reserves," *Armed Forces and Society* (Winter 1978), pp. 227–41. Canby notes that with revised precepts, "continental Europe could triple its divisions at a cost of roughly 25 percent of current Army expenditures" (p. 241).
12 Clausewitz, *On War*, VIII-6B, p. 605.

CHAPTER 4. THE UNIMPRESSIVE RECORD OF ATOMIC DIPLOMACY

1 McGeorge Bundy, "The bishops and the bomb," *New York Review of Books*, June 16, 1983.
2 The case for the prosecution was presented by Gar Alperowitz in *Atomic Diplomacy: Hiroshima and Potsdam* (New York, 1956). His thesis has not fared well under analysis by more careful historians, many themselves revisionists—see, e.g., Barton J. Bernstein (ed.), *The Atomic Bomb: The Critical Issues* (Boston, 1976), pp. 69–71.
3 Truman's press conference is in the *Public Papers of the Presidents* (1952), at pages 290–96. His 1957 remarks appeared in the *New York Times*, August 25, 1957, and are quoted in Stephen S. Kaplan, *Diplomacy of Power* (Washington, DC, 1981), pp. 70–71.

4 Truman's message of March 6 is printed in part in his own *Memoirs, Vol. II, Years of Trial and Hope* (Garden City, New York, 1956), pp. 94–5, and is available also now in *Foreign Relations of the United States* (1946), Vol. 7, pp. 340–43. The whole episode is covered with great clarity in Bruce R. Kuniholm, *The Origins of the Cold War in the Near East: Great Power Conflict and Diplomacy in Iran, Turkey and Greece* (Princeton, New Jersey, 1980), pp. 304–37. Kennan's later remark and the one quoted below are in a letter to Kuniholm printed at p. 321.

5 Eisenhower to Nixon is in Richard Nixon, *The Real War* (New York, 1980), p. 255.

6 Nixon's recognition that he could not use nuclear weapons in Vietnam is described in his *Memoirs* at p. 347.

7 *Public Papers of the Presidents, 1963–4,* Vol. 2, p. 1051.

8 See "The lessons of the Cuban Missile Crisis," *Time,* September 27, 1982, p. 85.

9 For a good example of this sort of thing, see Adam Ulam, *Expansion and Coexistence* (2nd ed., New York, 1974), p. 612.

CHAPTER 7. WORST-CASE ASSUMPTIONS: USES, ABUSES AND CONSEQUENCES

1 For recalling these 1914 and 1938 examples, I am indebted to Frank J. Stech, "Self-deception: the other side of the coin," *The Washington Quarterly,* Vol. 3, No. 3 (Summer 1980), p. 137.

2 See Raymond L. Garthoff, "The Soviet SS-20 decision," *Survival,* Vol. XXV, No. 3 (May–June 1983), pp. 110–19.

CHAPTER 8. SOVIET POLICY AND THE ARMS RACE

1 *Pravda,* January 15, 1960.

2 See, for example, the comment made by Secretary of Defense McNamara in April 1965: "the Soviets have decided that they have lost the quantitative race, and they are not seeking to engage us in that contest . . . there is no indication that the Soviets are seeking to develop a strategic nuclear force as large as ours." *US News and World Report,* April 12, 1965, p. 52.

3 Major General N. Talensky, "Anti-missile systems and disarmament," *International Affairs,* No. 10 (1964), p. 18.

4 On this debate see Raymond Garthoff, "BMD and East–West relations," in Ashton B. Carter and David N. Schwartz (eds.), *Ballistic Missile Defense* (Washington, DC, 1983), pp. 286–313.

5 *Krasnaya Zvezda,* September 23, 1983.

6 See, for example, Brezhnev's speech in Tula in January 1977, *Pravda,* January 19, 1977; and his speech to the 26th Party Congress, *Pravda,* February 24, 1981.

7 *New York Times,* October 2, 1981, p. A26.

8 Christopher Donnelly, "The Soviet Operational Maneuver Group—a new challenge for NATO," *International Defense Review,* No. 9 (1982), pp. 1177–86.

9 The Soviet commitment not to be the first to use nuclear weapons was made in a statement by Brezhnev to the United Nations. See *Pravda,* June 16, 1982.

10 *New York Times,* March 24, 1983, p. 20.

11 *Pravda,* March 27, 1983.

12 Quoted by John Newhouse, *Cold Dawn. The Story of SALT* (New York, 1973), p. 90.

13 N. S. Khrushchev, *Report of the Central Committee to the 20th Congress of the CPSU* (London, 1956), p. 28.

14 N. V. Ogarkov, "V interesakh povysheniya boevoi gotovnosti," *Kommunist Vooruzhennykh Sil*, No. 14 (July 1980), p. 26.
15 *Pravda*, February 24, 1981.
16 *Pravda*, July 2, 1982.
17 *Pravda*, October 28, 1982.
18 *Pravda*, September 29, 1983.
19 Joint Economic Committee, US Congress, *USSR: Measures of Economic Growth and Development, 1950–80* (Washington, DC, 1982), p. 123.
20 See Holloway, op. cit., pp. 116–17; and also Richard F. Kaufman, *Soviet Defense Trends*: A staff study prepared for the use of the Subcommittee on International Trade, Finance, and Security Economics of the Joint Economic Committee, US Congress (Washington, DC, September 1983), pp. 4–6.
21 Kaufman, op cit., p. 6.
22 Philip Hanson, *Trade and Technology in Soviet–American Relations* (New York, 1981), p. 32; and Abram Bergson, "Soviet economic slowdown and the 1981–85 Plan," in *Problems of Communism* (May–June 1981), p. 26.
23 On the relationship between Grechko and Kulikov, and between Kulikov and Ogarkov, see Andrew Cockburn, *The Threat: Inside the Soviet Military Machine* (New York, 1983), pp. 65–9.
24 Brezhnev's speech is in *Pravda*, January 19, 1977; Ogarkov's comment may be found in *Pravda*, August 2, 1979.
25 See N. Ogarkov, "Na strazhe mirnogo truda," *Kommunist*, No. 10 (1981), and N. V. Ogarkov, *Vsegda v gotovnosti k zashchite otechestya* (Moscow, 1982), pp. 15–17.

CHAPTER 10. THE MORALITY OF NUCLEAR DETERRENCE

1 B. Brodie (ed.), *The Absolute Weapon* (New York, 1946), p. 76.
2 C. S. Gray, "Dangerous to your health: the debate over nuclear strategy and war," *Orbis*, Vol. 26, No. 2 (Summer 1982), p. 349.
3 Quoted in H. Summers, Jr., *On Strategy: The Vietnam War in Context* (Carlisle Barracks, 1981), p. 3.
4 Quoted in *National Observer*, March 13, 1976, p. 4.
5 A. Speer, *Spandau: The Secret Diaries* (New York, 1976), p. 192.
6 P. Bracken and M. Shubik, "Strategic war: what are the questions and who should ask them?" *Technology in Society*, Vol. 4, No. 3 (1982), p. 161.
7 R. Reagan, address at United States Military Academy, May 27, 1981, quoted in *Army Times*, 8 June, 1981.
8 "On nuclear war: an exchange with the Secretary of Defense," *The New York Review of Books*, Vol. 30, No. 13 (August 18, 1983), p. 27.
9 L. Freedman, *The Evolution of Nuclear Strategy* (London, 1982), p. 399.
10 *Report of the President's Commission on Strategic Forces* (Washington, DC, April 1983), p. 3.
11 H. Kissinger, "NATO: the next thirty years," *Survival*, Vol. 21, No. 6, pp. 266–7.
12 Quoted in *New York Times*, May 25, 1946, p. 13.
13 See B. Paskins and M. Dockrill, *The Ethics of War* (London, 1979), pp. 48–57, for a summary of the evidence and argument on this point.
14 T. Merton, *The Nonviolent Alternative* (New York, 1980), p. 161.
15 Quoted in G. Herken, *The Winning Weapon* (New York, 1980), p. 201.

16 W. Churchill, "Speech on the defence estimates," March 1, 1955, *Hansard*, No. 537, col. 1898–9.
17 *US Military Posture Statement for Fiscal Year 1983* (Washington, DC, 1983), p. 19.
18 H. Kissinger, *The Necessity for Choice* (New York, 1961), p. 56.
19 Quoted in *The Challenge of Peace: God's Promise and Our Response* (Washington, DC, 1983), p. 54.
20 ibid, p. 61.
21 Quoted in A. Wohlstetter, "Bishops, statesmen, and other strategies on the bombing of innocents," *Commentary*, Vol. 75, No. 6 (June 1983), p. 16.
22 ibid, p. 17.
23 E. Abrams, "Nuclear weapons: what is the moral response?" *Department of State Bulletin* (December 1982), pp. 38 and 41.
24 John Paul II, "Address to scientists and scholars," *Origins*, Vol. 10, No. 4 (1981), p. 621.
25 C. Krucoff, "Minding his profession," *The Washington Post*, July 25, 1983.
26 J. Kennedy, commencement address at the American University in Washington, DC, June 10, 1963, *Public Papers of the Presidents of the United States, J. F. Kennedy, 1963* (Washington, DC, 1964), p. 461. Information related to this speech supplied by Professor McGeorge Bundy.
27 ibid., p. 464.

CHAPTER II. NUCLEAR WEAPONS AND INTERNATIONAL LAW

1 Judge Tanaka in the South West Africa cases (ICJ Reports, 1966), at p. 291, quoted in Rosalyn Higgins, "The identity of international law," in *International Law: Teaching and Practice* (1982), p. 29, to which chapter I am much indebted.
2 See Higgins, op.cit., p. 29.
3 D. Schindler and J. Toman, *The Laws of Armed Conflicts* (2nd ed., The Hague, 1981).
4 Adam Roberts and Richard Guelff, *Documents on the Laws of War* (Oxford, 1982), pp. 271–2, to which I am much indebted. And see Geneva Conventions Act 1957.
5 This was reinforced by Resolution 2675 (XXV) in 1970.
6 Roberts and Guelff, op. cit., p. 377.
7 See the Congressional Research Service paper "International law on the use of nuclear weapons and the United States position" (Washington, DC, 1979), by Ellen C. Collier; and Roberts and Guelff, op. cit.
8 Collier, op. cit., p. CRS–29.
9 For this point and for other comments I am indebted to my colleague Dr. F. Weiss.
10 Collier, op. cit., p. CRS–32.
11 "Nuclear weapons versus international law: a contextual reassessment," *McGill Law Journal* (July 1983), pp. 564–6.
12 op. cit., pp. 137–9.
13 Roberts and Guelff, op. cit., p. 139.
14 Paras. 642–9.
15 For this point I am indebted to my colleague Dr. F. Weiss. I am also generally indebted to my colleague Mr. P. Windsor.

CHAPTER 12. THE MILITARY AND POLITICAL BACKGROUND OF THE NUCLEAR AGE

1 Montesquieu, *De l'esprit des lois*, 1.3; my italics.
2 For a full and accessible account, see W. H. McNeill, *The Pursuit of Power: Technology, Armed Force and Society since 1000* AD (Chicago, 1982), especially Chapters 7 and 8.
3 A further account of Kant's position can be found in Chapter 2 of my *Philosophers of Peace and War* (Cambridge, 1978).
4 See *Mémoires de guerre: l'appel*, p. 31, para. 2. The translation is my own.

CHAPTER 14. WHAT POLITICAL SIGNALS SHOULD OUR ARMED FORCES SEND?

1 US Department of Defense, *Soviet Military Power* (Washington, DC, 1981), and USSR Ministry of Defense, *Whence the Threat to Peace?* (Moscow, 1982).
2 *Strengthening Conventional Deterrence in Europe: Proposals for the 1980s*, Report of the European Security Study (London, 1983).

CHAPTER 15. CAN NATO AFFORD A NON-SUICIDAL STRATEGY?

1 *New York Times*, April 7, 1982.
2 Oral answer, Blaker, May 3, 1983, *Hansard*, Col. 7.
3 A. C. Enthoven and K. Smith, *How Much is Enough*? (New York, 1971). A detailed assessment of the current conventional balance in sea, land and air forces is contained in William W. Kaufman, "Nonnuclear deterrence," in John D. Steinbruner and Leon V. Segal (eds.) *Alliance Security: NATO and the No-First-Use Question* (Washington, DC, 1983). Kaufman concludes that NATO already has the ground, air and sea forces to make a Soviet offensive a highly risky undertaking. Only after making a series of implausible "worst-case" assumptions, he argues, is the conventional wisdom of an overwhelming Pact superiority credible.
4 Stockholm International Peace Research Institute, *SIPRA Yearbook 1983* (Stockholm, 1983). Official Western sources suggest a much narrower margin. The US government gives NATO expenditure as $215 billion to the Pact's $211 billion. (US Arms Control and Disarmament Agency, *World Military Expenditures and Arms Transfers, 1970–79*, 1982.)
5 International Institute of Strategic Studies, *The Military Balance 1982–83* (London, 1982), p. 132.
6 *Statement on the Defence Estimates, 1983*, Vol. 1 (London, 1983), p. 22.
7 J. J. Mearsheimer, "Why the Soviets can't win quickly in Central Europe," *International Security*, Vol. 7, No. 1 (1982), p. 8.
8 *Statement on the Defence Estimates, 1983*, p. 22.
9 Carnegie Endowment for International Peace, *Challenge for US National Security: Assessing the Balance: Defense Spending and Conventional Forces*, Part II (Washington, DC, 1981), p. 71. See also B. R. Posen and S. Van Evera, "Defense policy and the Reagan Administration," *International Security* (Summer 1983), pp. 15–19.
10 *Economist*, November 26, 1983, pp. 62–3.
11 Mearsheimer, op. cit., p. 8.
12 P. Bracken, "The NATO defense problem," *Orbis*, Vol. 27, No. 1 (1983), pp. 90–91.
13 B. W. Rogers, "Sword and shield—ACE attack of Warsaw Pact follow-on forces," *NATO's Sixteen Nations* (February–March 1983). European Security Study, *Strengthening Conventional Deterrence in Europe* (London, 1983).

14 European Security Study, op. cit., p. 13. Note, however, that several participants in the study were extremely skeptical of the emphasis on high technology. Kenneth Hunt, a member of the working group on advanced technologies, said that "There was a good deal of cynicism about whether it will work when it is said that does not come out in the study." See *National Journal* (October 22, 1983), pp. 2152–7.
15 D. R. Cotter, *Potential Future Roles for Conventional and Nuclear Forces in the Defense of Western Europe,* in European Security Study, ibid., pp. 230–33.
16 S. P. Huntingdon, "Conventional deterrence and conventional retaliation in Europe," unpublished manuscript prepared for US Army War College Strategic Studies Institute Conference on "Defense and deterrence in the 1980s: new realities—new strategies," July 28–30, 1983.
17 The most comprehensive discussion so far of non-nuclear defense options is the Report of the Alternative Defence Commission, *Defence Without the Bomb* (London, 1983).
18 Union of Concerned Scientists, *No First Use* (Cambridge, Mass., 1983).
19 Kaufman, op. cit., pp. 88–9.
20 ibid., p. 65.
21 For a discussion of the economics of prepositioning and convoys, see Paul H. Nitze and Leonard Sullivan, *Securing the Seas—the Soviet Naval Challenge and Western Alliance Options* (Boulder, Colorado, 1979).
22 Union of Concerned Scientists, op. cit., pp. 34–5.
23 J. Löser, "The security policy options for non-Communist Europe," *Armada International,* No. 2 (1982), p. 73.
24 S. L. Canby, "Military reform and the art of war," *Survival,* Vol. XXV, No. 3 (1983), pp. 122–3.
25 Lord Carver, "No first use—a crucial controversy," *Council for Arms Control Bulletin* (May 1983).
26 Center for Defense Information, "Preparing for nuclear war: President Reagan's program," *The Defense Monitor,* Vol. X, No. 8 (1982).
27 B. Posen and S. Van Evera, op. cit., pp. 30–34, provides a useful critique of the Reagan Administration's build-up of interventionary forces.
28 M. Kaldor, *The Baroque Arsenal* (London, 1982).
29 S. L. Canby, op. cit., p. 123.
30 A survey of the evidence on the links between military spending and British economic decline is contained in M. Chalmers, *The Cost of Britain's Defence* (London, 1983).
31 S. Pollard, *The Wasting of the British Economy* (London, 1982), p. 6.
32 *Statement on the Defence Estimates, 1983,* op. cit., p. 26.
33 Field-Marshal Lord Carver, *A Policy for Peace* (London, 1982).
34 M. Chalmers, op. cit., pp. 63–5.
35 House of Commons Defence Committee, Third Report, *The Future Defence of the Falkland Islands* (London, 1983), and *Statement on the Defence Estimates, 1983,* Vol. II (London, 1983).
36 P. Rogers, *A Note on UK Naval Deployment in the Falklands* (Bradford, 1983).
37 *The Way Forward,* Cmnd 8288 (London, 1981).
38 For the UK component of the total Tornado program, the total estimated cost is £11,300 million at 1981 prices. 75 percent of this total will have been spent by April 1985.